Wine Is Our Bread

Max Planck Studies in Anthropology and Economy
Series editors:
Stephen Gudeman, University of Minnesota
Chris Hann, Max Planck Institute for Social Anthropology

Definitions of economy and society, and their proper relationship to each other, have been the perennial concerns of social philosophers. In the early decades of the twenty-first century these became and remain matters of urgent political debate. At the forefront of this series are the approaches to these connections by anthropologists, whose explorations of the local ideas and institutions underpinning social and economic relations illuminate large fields ignored in other disciplines.

Volume 9
Wine Is Our Bread
Labour and Value in Moldovan Winemaking
Daniela Ana

Volume 8
Moral Economy at Work
Ethnographic Investigations in Eurasia
Edited by Lale Yalçın-Heckmann

Volume 7
Work, Society, and the Ethical Self
Chimeras of Freedom in the Neoliberal Era
Edited by Chris Hann

Volume 6
Financialization
Relational Approaches
Edited by Chris Hann and Don Kalb

Volume 5
Market Frictions
Trade and Urbanization at the Vietnam–China Border
Kirsten W. Endres

Volume 4
Industrial Labor on the Margins of Capitalism
Precarity, Class, and the Neoliberal Subject
Edited by Chris Hann and Jonathan Parry

Volume 3
When Things Become Property
Land Reform, Authority, and Value in Postsocialist Europe and Asia
Thomas Sikor, Stefan Dorondel, Johannes Stahl and Phuc Xuan To

Volume 2
Oikos and Market
Explorations in Self-Sufficiency after Socialism
Edited by Stephen Gudeman and Chris Hann

Volume 1
Economy and Ritual
Studies of Postsocialist Transformations
Edited by Stephen Gudeman and Chris Hann

Wine Is Our Bread

Labour and Value in Moldovan Winemaking

Daniela Ana

berghahn
NEW YORK • OXFORD
www.berghahnbooks.com

First published in 2022 by
Berghahn Books
www.berghahnbooks.com

© 2022, 2024 Daniela Ana
First paperback edition published 2024

All rights reserved. Except for the quotation of short passages for the purposes of criticism and review, no part of this book may be reproduced in any form or by any means, electronic or mechanical, including photocopying, recording, or any information storage and retrieval system now known or to be invented, without written permission of the publisher.

Library of Congress Cataloging-in-Publication Data

Names: Ana, Daniela, author.
Title: Wine is our bread : labour and value in Moldovan winemaking / Daniela Ana.
Description: New York : Berghahn Books, 2022. | Series: Max Planck studies in anthropology and economy ; volume 9 | Includes bibliographical references and index.
Identifiers: LCCN 2021040509 (print) | LCCN 2021040510 (ebook) | ISBN 9781800733411 (hardback) | ISBN 9781800733428 (ebook)
Subjects: LCSH: Wine industry—Moldova. | Wine and wine making—Moldova. | Viticulture—Moldova.
Classification: LCC HD9385.M6292 A53 2022 (print) | LCC HD9385.M6292 (ebook) | DDC 338.4/7663209476—dc23
LC record available at https://lccn.loc.gov/2021040509
LC ebook record available at https://lccn.loc.gov/2021040510

British Library Cataloguing in Publication Data

A catalogue record for this book is available from the British Library

ISBN 978-1-80073-341-1 hardback
ISBN 978-1-80539-317-7 paperback
ISBN 978-1-80539-430-3 epub
ISBN 978-1-80073-342-8 web pdf

https://doi.org/10.3167/9781800733411

Contents

List of Illustrations	vi
Acknowledgements	vii
List of Abbreviations	ix
Introduction	1
Chapter 1. The Making of an Export Industry: Moldovan Winemaking under Different Sociopolitical Systems	29
Chapter 2. The Value of Homemade Wine: Debates on Heritage	58
Chapter 3. Labour Force Reproduction: Economic Strategies in a Post-Soviet Winemaking Village	83
Chapter 4. Sending Wine around the World: Globalization and Work Rhythms in the Bottling Section	105
Chapter 5. Nature, Value and Globalized Markets: Articulating the Purcari Terroir	131
Conclusion. Wine on the Periphery as an Illustration of the Transnational Dynamics of Value Creation	153
Glossary of Terms	165
References	168
Index	183

Illustrations

Figures

Figure 1.1.	The Purcari castle seen from the Dniester bank at sunset, June 2017.	46
Figure 1.2.	Organization chart of the production department at Purcari (2017).	53
Figure 4.1.	Diagram of the filling process. The parts in grey are active in the process, the ones in black are inactive.	110
Figure 4.2.	Diagram of the labelling process. The parts in grey are active in the process, the bottle filler (in black) is inactive.	111

Maps

Map 0.1.	The Republic of Moldova. Purcari, in the south-east.	4
Map 1.1.	Map of Purcari village.	44
Map 1.2.	The Purcari Winery perimeter.	50

Tables

Table 1.1.	Wine import structure in Russia, 2005–7.	31
Table 1.2.	Purcari (first attested in 1560), total population 1812–2014.	47
Table 4.1.	Employees in *smena* 1 at the bottling section, Purcari Winery.	112
Table 4.2.	Cost advantages at the Purcari Group level compared with other European wine-producing countries, reproduced from the public document 'Purcari Corporate Presentation 2018'.	120

Acknowledgements

Engaging ethnographically with wine and winemaking in Moldova was possible due to the openness of the winemakers and workers in Purcari, and my interlocutors in the fieldwork are the first people I want to thank. As I have anonymised all their names in the book, I will not name them in this section either; nevertheless, it is their kindness and readiness to share time and stories with me on which this book relies. Many thanks to Mr Petru Șarcov in Chișinău, who has offered me immense support during all the critical moments in my fieldwork, from the very first day to the last. He taught me what it means to help someone in the most efficient and disinterested manner. Father Viorel Cojocaru and a few other friends in Chișinău have offered important assistance, helping me get access to and navigate bureaucratic matters during fieldwork. I also want to thank the management of Purcari Group for allowing me to take part in the activities of the Purcari Winery and vineyards, and for access to the dormitory; workers' cafeteria; Mr Ion's minibus for rides between Purcari and Chișinău; and, in general, for their trust.

This project has been funded by the Max Planck Institute for Social Anthropology, as part of the International Max Planck Research School for the Anthropology, Archaeology and History of Eurasia (IMPRS ANARCHIE). Professor Chris Hann has encouraged me during this time, and I want to express my appreciation for his close mentorship and patience. I am also highly indebted to Professor Michael Müller for his enthusiastic and constructive guidance. I am thankful to Professor Marion Demossier for her supportive critique of an earlier draft of the manuscript, and for very stimulating discussions on all things wine-anthropological.

Writing the book was also a learning journey through the rich exchange with anthropologist friends and colleagues. Ștefan Voicu has been my constant companion throughout this project and I want to thank him for reading the whole manuscript and for sharing great ideas with me, and for being an entertaining and encouraging friend. At different stages, several chapters in the book have also benefited from comments by generous and insightful friends: Alina Apostu, Louise Bechtold, Natalia Buier, Jennifer Cash, Ana Chirițoiu, Deborah Jones, Christof Lammer, Sergiu Novac and André Thiemann. Discussions and exchanges with my colleagues in the weekly seminar at the Max Planck Institute for Social Anthropology between 2015 and 2019 helped me to better shape my ideas.

Moreover, I thank Dr Robert Parkin for his immense help with improving the language in the first draft of the monograph. Three anonymous reviewers have read the final draft of the manuscript, and I want to thank them for their perceptive critiques and encouraging comments. Part of the materials in chapters 1 and 5 were published in 2021 in an article entitled 'Politics, Markets and Wine: Indexing Post-Cold War Tensions in the Republic of Moldova' in *Ethnologie française* 2021(3): 535–47.

Either during fieldwork in Moldova or while in Halle preparing the monograph, Camelia Badea, Marek Mikuš, Lilia Nenescu, Niko Olma, Diana Popa, Victoria Priscu, Vitalie Sprînceană, Sylvia Terpe and Duygu Topçu had an important influence on various levels – from archival help and fieldwork assistance to other types of aid and inspiration. Breaks from writing have been as important as the writing itself, and I want to thank Stanciu and Diana in Cluj, Çiçek in Berlin, and Roxana and Gurgu in Bucharest for opening their homes for me throughout periods of intense work.

Undertaking a large portion of the monograph revisions during the COVID-19 pandemic period meant further stress while focusing on the project in the midst of worldwide insecurities and a series of lockdowns. Deep thanks to my parents and sister in Romania for bearing with the distancing throughout this time, and for offering me support and trust over the years during which this project has unfolded. In Germany, Clemens' encouragement and kindness made, in any case, the last couple of years of writing more beautiful; therefore, my final heartfelt thanks here go to him.

Abbreviations

AOC	Appellation d'Origine Contrôlée
BNS Moldova	National Bureau of Statistics Moldova
CAP	Common Agricultural Policy
CEO	Chief Executive Officer
CIS	Community of Independent States
Comecon	Council for Mutual Economic Assistance
EU	European Union
GDP	Gross Domestic Product
INAO	Institut national de l'origine et de la qualité
INVV	Institutul Național al Viei și Vinului (National Institute for Vine and Wine)
MDL	Moldovan leu
MSSR	Moldovan Soviet Socialist Republic
NGO	Non-Governmental Organization
OIV	International Organisation of Vine and Wine
ONVV	Oficiul Național al Viei și Vinului (National Office for Vine and Wine)
PDO	Protected Designation of Origin
PGI	Protected Geographical Indication
PHC 2014	Population and Housing Census in the Republic of Moldova in 2014
SRT	Social Reproduction Theory
UNESCO	United Nations Educational, Scientific and Cultural Organization
USAID	United States Agency for International Development

Introduction

In late September 2017, the Moldovan national agency in charge of wine promotion organized an event in Prague called the 'Wine Vernissage by Wine of Moldova'. This was part of a series of events outside the Republic of Moldova that were intended to increase the popularity of its wine abroad. It was hosted in one of Prague's mediaeval buildings, the New Town Hall, and the event was invitation-based, targeting wine importers, distributors and journalists in the Czech Republic. The Prague vernissage happened shortly after the end of my one-year ethnographic fieldwork in Moldova researching winemaking, and I headed there at the invitation of one of my Moldovan interlocutors. Attended by a few hundred invitees, the event started with a brief timeline of Moldovan wine history presented by a diplomat from the Moldovan Embassy in Prague. Behind the speaker were the Moldovan flag and a large banner bearing the country's brand logo, 'Wine of Moldova'. As Czech wine drinkers and sellers were lured with the promise of ancient Moldovan vineyards and cellars, they were also reminded that the reason they now had quality wines coming from this region was 'the Russian embargo, which proved to be a chance for us', as the diplomat admitted. The intention was to use the wine bottles in the vernissage hall for a 'walk-around tasting', while a Moldovan folklore ensemble was preparing to come on to the stage after the speech had ended. After a final thanks to the assembled Czech public for giving Moldovans 'an occasion to sell [their] wines', and the announcement that a few of the wines on show at the event were already available in the local branch of Tesco, the musical ensemble, dressed in 'traditional' attire, took the stage to entertain the crowd with folk music, the standard cultural offering at Moldovan celebration events.

Some of the wines mentioned as being available in the supermarket were produced in one of the most prestigious wineries in Moldova, Purcari. Located in the eponymous village in the south-east of the country, Purcari is one of the Moldovan wineries that have managed to increase sales of bottled wine in Western markets considerably in the last decade. This village was the main site of my ethnographic fieldwork, which I carried out between August 2016 and August 2017. The acknowledgement of the winery in the Czech Republic pointed to the successful circulation and consumption of its wine: the fact that high-quality Moldovan wine could be found on the shelves in a Central European country was an achievement, because Moldova had long been almost absent from markets outside the former Soviet space.

Until 2006, the republic had sold most of its wine production to the Soviet and, after 1991, Russian markets. However, in the spring of 2006, Russia imposed a ban on Moldovan wines claiming that they contained heavy metals and pesticides over the allowed limits. The impact of the ban was significant: in 2005, wine revenues comprised 9% of the country's gross domestic product (GDP), but by 2007 that figure had plunged to 2.3%. The trade gradually recovered, reaching 4.8% of GDP by 2014. Key to this recovery was a reform in the wine sector that helped Moldovan wineries to access new markets outside Russia or to broaden existing ones. The reform consisted of changes to wine legislation, new production technologies and marketing strategies, and the promotion of indigenous grape varieties as unique products of Moldova. Also, quality-tracing devices such as Protected Geographical Indications, recognized at the European Union level, were put in place and the country-wine brand, 'Wine of Moldova', was created in 2014. Some of the sector-wide strategies for market renewal yielded good results, with sales of bottled wine from some Moldovan wineries growing considerably. In this context, Purcari arguably became the most successful Moldovan winery – and Purcari wines became increasingly popular in neighbouring countries to the west.

How does a Moldovan winery reinvent itself to become competitive in a saturated, globalized wine market? What socio-economic relations are mobilized in this process of value creation, and how is intense transnational competition in a crisis-ridden sector affecting the local winemaking community? This book follows the changes in the production of value in Moldovan winemaking from the late socialist period until the present day, as new socio-economic processes were put into motion by the entry of Moldovan wineries into the globalized wine market. Through its main focus on the production of value at different stages in the winemaking process and on wine workers' livelihoods, the book challenges the established theoretical focus on consumption and market differentiation in anthropological studies of wine while also contributing to a better understanding of the challenges that exist in a winemaking region in the former Soviet space.

Value is relational and is produced through the exploitation of human labour – that is, the undervaluation of human labour in order to create the surplus value necessary for the survival and reproduction of a capitalist producer (Turner 2008; Moore 2015). However, I also extend the notion of surplus value by acknowledging that it can be enhanced beyond the production level: through marketing and through consumers' 'labour' of ascribing meaning to a commodity, a product can be branded and more value extracted from it through this affective relationship (Foster 2005). Drawing on this understanding of value, I follow the actions and relationships that produce value in the Moldovan wine world at a critical moment in time and from a contested sociocultural space. The themes of the chapters in the book reflect the areas of productive activities that enhance the value of Moldovan wine in domestic or transnational markets. A crisis of both the economy and prestige; the 'creative destruction' of homemade wine; the exploitation of labour; and, again, the creative differentiation of work through the classification of environmental features of a winemaking location are the critical points of surplus-value creation that I identify and analyse. These aspects are deeply embedded in a society that construes winemaking and wine consumption as part of its collective identity. Despite the complex nexus of meanings that surrounds Moldovan wine, social anthropologists have rarely researched the social relations of this winemaking country (Map 0.1).

Wine, Postsocialism and Globalization

Why has this been the case, given the long history and, more importantly, the high degree of sociocultural and economic importance attached to winemaking by Moldovans? My answer comes from three main directions that relate to the type of research foci in the history of the discipline, a reduced interest from outside in ethnographic research in Moldova and the position of Moldova and its wine industry in processes of globalization. First, wine production became a topic of research for Anglo-Saxon sociocultural anthropologists rather late in the history of the discipline (Pratt 1994; Ulin 1996; Lem 1999; Demossier 2010; Black and Ulin 2013). Due to the initial focus of anthropology on societies outside the West, winemaking did not fit its agenda, being an activity too closely associated with white Europeans. Secondly, the 'anthropology of postsocialism' has shown less interest in researching the independent Republic of Moldova than other states belonging to the former Eastern Bloc. Finally, although studies focusing on either globalization in 'postsocialist states' (Berdahl 1999; Creed 2011; Gille 2016; Aistara 2018) or in the world of wine (Black and Ulin 2013; Jung 2016; Demossier 2018; Inglis and Almila 2019) have increased in anthropology in recent years, Moldova has not been present as an example in this literature except in Cash (2015a, 2015b), who focused on household winemaking and its relation to the ritual and subsistence economy, because Moldovan commercial wine was almost absent from

4   Wine Is Our Bread

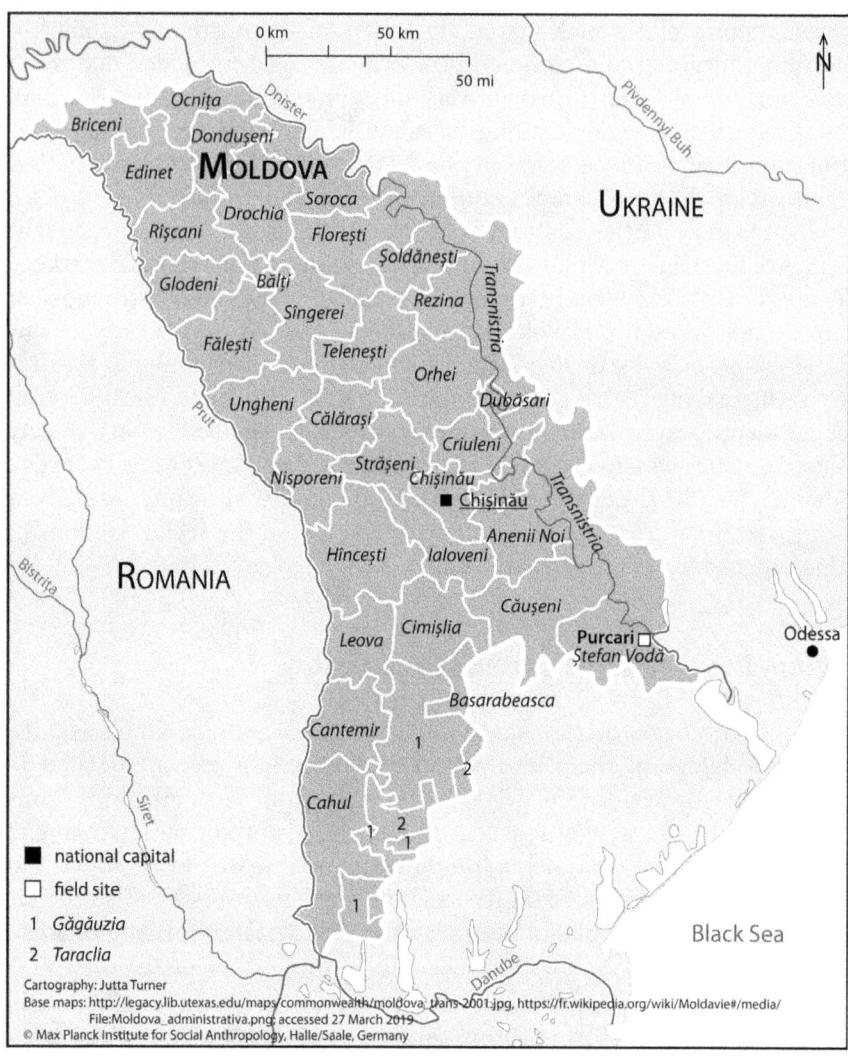

Map 0.1. The Republic of Moldova. Purcari, in the south-east. © Max Planck Institute for Social Anthropology, Halle/Saale, Germany.

international wine markets until the late 2000s. Until then, the stable trade relationship with Russia that had started in Tsarist times continued in different forms in different political regimes, but one aspect remained constant: up to 90% of the commercial wine production in the Soviet period and by independent Moldova was sold to Russia. The shock of the wine embargoes pushed many Moldovan wineries to seek access to trade partners outside this traditional market, and this moment of the insertion of Moldovan wine into the global market is the central event that has prompted the present study.

The ethnographic analysis in this book aims to address these three dimensions and to show that anthropological research on wine provides rich insights into how global hierarchies of value (Jung 2016) influence winemaking communities, pertaining to the prioritization (or the marginalization) of local cultural and economic models. Research on the wine-industry reforms in Moldova yields new insights on the globalization of wine in general and on changes to local communities in particular – and, at this stage of access to the new markets, the power relations that structure the discourse on quality are more discernible. This is noticeable from the manner in which discourses on quality change, from the certification systems that are adopted, or from marketing strategies that emulate or try to distinguish producers from more established players on the global wine market in order to create value. As has been the case over the three decades since the fall of the Soviet Union, the countries belonging to the former Eastern Bloc have struggled with inequality while seeking integration into European capitalism (see Creed 2011: 7). The Republic of Moldova has been drastically marked by poverty, and the story of its search for new markets for wine and for more widespread 'cultural' recognition as a quality wine-producing country in Europe is one of the dimensions through which one can understand its decades-long hardship.

Before going into further detail about the present dynamics of Moldovan winemaking, a few historical reflections on the globalization of wine will help in delineating and understanding current relations pertaining to the wine trade and wine consumption. Wine started to travel across the world's oceans in the sixteenth and seventeenth centuries, when the first steps were made in the globalization of the wine trade (Inglis 2019). This circulation of wine was led by technological developments and colonial interests that lasted throughout the eighteenth and nineteenth centuries. Starting in the mid-1900s, the phylloxera blight hit most wine regions around the world – with hindsight, becoming a transnational phenomenon that led to fundamental changes in the way in which viticulture and winemaking have been pursued right up until the present. Most importantly, cultivated grape varieties were homogenized to a great extent because many local varieties across Europe had been lost through phylloxera. This was a decisive event that compelled from producers an intensified global exchange of vine stocks, viticultural practices and wine. In parallel, the circulation of wine and reproductive materials was increased by the advent of the railways in the nineteenth century (Simpson 2011). In 1914, three quarters of global wine production came from France, Italy and Spain (Simpson

2011: xxxii), countries that dominated the global wine market throughout most of the twentieth century up until the present.

However, since the 1970s, wine-producing countries from the so-called 'New World' have become increasingly popular. The principal New World winemaking countries, which have been depicted as the opposite of the conservatism of the Old World, are the US, Chile, Argentina, South Africa, Australia and New Zealand. The 'Old World' of wine refers to European and Asian winemaking countries, in which wines are associated with long histories of production based around small-scale, artisanal producers, their quality explained and marketed as being connected to their place of origin (Banks and Overton 2010: 59). While the Old and New Worlds of wine are analytical categories adopted by various wine scholars using the perspectives of geography, sociology or history (Banks and Overton 2010; Inglis and Almila 2019; Campbell and Guibert 2007), in understanding the globalization of practices and trade from the late twentieth century onwards, I employ them only to only a limited extent in this book as they do not capture the complexity of wine styles, history or power differentials. For Moldova, as for other postsocialist wine-producing countries, being part of the 'Old World' geographically does not have the same implications as for West-European producing countries because while it does indeed have a millennia-long tradition of wine production, Moldova does not share a place of the same rank as the pre-eminent Old World wine-producing countries such as France, Spain or Italy. Yet it does not belong to the pattern of the New World wines either. Consequently, a new conceptualization of the complex global wine industry is necessary, using 'an approach which foregrounds the multiple "worlds of wine" as crosscutting, contingent and contextual' (Banks and Overton 2010: 58). Does calling Moldovan wine 'postsocialist wine', for example, make sense?

This question has arisen because the so-called 'anthropology of postsocialism' has been exposed under critical scrutiny from both Eastern and Western scholars for almost two decades: already in the late 1990s, several anthropologists started to ask when the term 'postsocialism' would stop making sense – that is, when the socialist past would stop affecting this space (Hann 2002; Thelen 2011, 2012; Buchowski 2012; Kalb 2014; Petrovici 2015; Ringel 2016). Hann (2002: 8) criticized the use of a concept of 'postsocialist culture' as a 'black box' in which differences are underlined at the expense of similarities between societies or groups. This view ties in with another line of criticism – namely, how the ideological mobilization of the ghost of socialism 'has managed to function as an enabler of policies maintaining low wages, reduced social spending, and diminished state involvement' (Chelcea and Druță 2016: 537) in different domains. Chelcea and Druță (2016: 522) also inquire as to how the evocation of state socialism influences class dynamics and political economies in Eastern Europe. They argue that keeping the discourse on the socialist legacy alive helps neoliberal ideology, while 'zombie socialism' aids the anti-communist (predominantly elite) discourse that has prevailed in the Central–Eastern European space in every decade since 1989. In this view, the continued relevance of the concept lies only in its reproduction of neoliberal ideology.

Implicitly, the validity of postsocialism as a spatio-temporal container has also been contested. Postsocialism firstly signified a spatial entity that referred to the region covering the former Soviet republics and East-European countries, where the socialist governments were dissolved between 1989 and 1991, and secondly a temporal one, referring to the decades following the fall of these socialist governments. It is difficult to lump together eastern and south-eastern Europe, Central Asia, the Caucasus and Russia (Tlostanova 2015) as postsocialist, as the countries in this space took different paths economically (Creed 2011; Chelcea and Druță 2016). Moreover, if we are to accept the 'transition' discourse, the Central- and East-European countries that in the early postsocialist years were aided to become functioning market economies are now all recognized as such. In this way, 'postsocialism' as a temporal signifier also expired.

Taking into consideration all the above critique, I contend that in order to understand the present dynamics within the Moldovan wine sector and its relations to external parties (such as wine critics, traders or consumers) when it sets out to compete with other wine regions around the world, a conceptual framework that incorporates the legacy of Soviet socialism is crucial. Moreover, as the ethnographic analysis that follows will show, memories of the socialist organization of society fuel the present alternative political imaginaries of Moldovan workers, who are central to understanding the current struggles of the Moldovan wine industry and the nature of contemporary capitalism in the former Eastern Bloc, where neoliberal processes of further industrial dismantling in favour of regimes of flexible accumulation are ongoing (Makovicky 2014a). The past specialization of each Soviet republic in specific types of products had the strategic aim of bringing the republics into relations of interdependence (Caldwell 2009: 8) – and this cultivated interdependence continued in various sectors after the fall of the Soviet Union, and strongly influenced these countries' socio-economic dynamics. My interlocutors often used idioms like 'Soviet mentality', 'Soviet type of people' or 'doing things like when we were with the Russians' to refer to values and meaning of their actions or those of others. Although most frequently they had negative connotations in the sense of rigid, authoritarian or rough ways of acting, they also pointed to the perceived steadiness, security and equality of this period.

In the Moldovan wine industry specifically, the marked influence of the relationship with the Russian powers across the last two centuries became straightforward to me over my year-long fieldwork. First, the development of winemaking schools started while Bessarabia was part of the Russian Empire (1812–1918), with the first school specializing in viticulture being founded in Chișinău in 1842. The steady increase in the vineyard surface area on this territory – the largest registered, 193,000 hectares, was in 1983 (Rusu 2011: 42) – was closely tied to Soviet and, later, post-Soviet Russian market demand, as I detail in the next chapter. Furthermore, in the Soviet years and the first two post-Soviet decades, socio-economic relations in the wine industry evolved around the presence of Russia's large-scale export market, in which Moldovan wine occupied the lower-quality segment.

Earlier ethnographies of winemaking in former Eastern Bloc regions have also traced the importance of the legacy of socialism in determining the value of wine. Yuson Jung's (2011; 2014; 2016) research on the wine industry in Bulgaria looks at the shift from an economy of quantity in winemaking to an economy of quality, the former being often considered an attribute of socialist winemaking (Jung 2016) among wine critics and consumers; a similar shift in values has also been examined by Walker and Manning (2013) in Georgia. These studies show that postsocialist decollectivization had an important influence on the way in which winemaking came to be organized, and they also stress the image of (post)socialist wine in the world of wine: quantity over quality, and little regard for detail such as terroir and place of origin. Although exaggerated in placing former socialist states in the category of 'quantity'-oriented winemaking, this perception still affects the circulation of wine in the global market (Walker and Manning 2013). Furthermore, Hann (2004) traced continuity and change in rural Hungary after socialism through the lens of winemaking in the marginalized winemaking region of the Tisza–Danube interfluve and described three cases showing variation in developments in winemaking under socialism. It is shown that, as in the case of Moldova, the phylloxera blight and industrial winemaking led to the loss of local grape varieties. After 1989, Hungarian wine had to struggle against similar imaginaries as its Moldovan counterpart does today – the assumption that former socialist countries produce unsophisticated, mass-produced wines as opposed to the quality, or terroir, wines dominating in Western Europe.

There are temporal considerations too in looking at wine production and circulation through the lens of the socialist legacy. Wine has a slow return rate and a slower pace in building reputation and prestige, essential in selling the commodity. This means that changes to the political system will not produce quick changes in a sector such as winemaking – all the more so when the region in question is dependent on exporting. This is not to say that other social and institutional changes are rapid, but that in the case of wine there is a nexus that yields a slow rhythm of transformation: not only do production practices need to change locally but for an export-oriented wine industry such as the Moldovan one, its prestige needs to be recognized by the critics and consumers of its importing countries as well. In practice, this means disposing of past practices and immersing oneself in the hegemonic value system of the global market.

I am not denying the partial agency of my Moldovan interlocutors in the reorganization of the wine industry, but after the loss of the traditional Russian export market and with the efforts of USAID and other Western partners, the project of reforming Moldovan wine meant aligning it with Western hegemonic standards of taste, quality, terroir discourses and imaginaries – similarly to other parts of the world (Jung 2014; Itçaina, Roger and Smith 2016; Swinburn 2013). After trade relationships with Russia went awry, Moldovan winemakers experienced the 'postsocialist global condition' (Gille 2010: 9; see also Creed 2011: 5) since access to transnational policy tools and belonging to cultures of commodification quickly became the condition for participation in globalized modernity. Gille (2010: 29) argued that 1989 was a missed opportunity for 'developing "indigenous" public spheres, the sprouts of which already appeared in the 1980s', because of a premature replacement of the national scale of representation with one at the transnational and supranational level. This view is useful in understanding and interpreting current changes in the sociocultural landscape of Moldovan winemaking, as the swiftness of the changes in this field and the direction in which winemaking practices and discourses are going leave little room for alternative local views on quality, taste or values in winemaking. There is, rather, a need and a willingness to show what I call cultural and institutional allegiance to recognized transnational players in the wine field. Notwithstanding, the socialist legacy in winemaking in Moldova is just one part of the factors influencing the transformations of this commodity. If, for example, the main portrait of Soviet-Moldovan wine was mass-produced wine, affordable for everyone, this has also been the image of Chilean or New Zealand wines until very recently. This way of producing and trading wine is not intrinsic to socialism: it has been part of the tendency towards mass production all over the industrialized world. Thus, when Moldovan winemakers and foreign critics are explaining the shift from 'quantity to quality' as the shift from 'socialism to capitalism' they are to a certain extent fighting the 'zombie socialism' coined by Chelcea and Druță (2016), this time referring to wine.

Given the implications of the critique addressed in this section, throughout the book I make critical use of the concept of 'postsocialism' and also use it interchangeably with the term 'post-Soviet'. I favour the latter term, given the teleological implications of 'postsocialism': in 1989, a particular form of socialism was ending – the Soviet kind – and in the near future socialist political regimes could come to power again, as the political yearnings of many of my interlocutors suggest (see chapters 1, 3 and 4 especially).

The Value of Terroir

While Purcari Winery is located at the margins of the European Union and the global wine industry, in Moldova and neighbouring Romania it is one of the best-regarded quality wine producers. This tension yields a prominent comparative dimension throughout the book, which serves to understand Moldova's winemaking sector not only locally but also in relation to its better-known competitors, especially those in France and Italy. Comparison centres on the 'terroir' discourse – still the strongest criterion of differentiation among wine regions around the world, albeit a contested one (Itçaina, Roger and Smith 2016). Thus, the book engages with the practices and discourses that surround terroir in Moldova and elsewhere, and develops a critical political-economy perspective on this concept. Further, it interweaves a materialist focus on terroir and wine with globalization theories that emphasize the tensions between local materialities and practices, and international regulations.

The definition of terroir varies among both winemakers and researchers, but it is commonly defined as the aggregate characteristics of the physical environment (soil, climate, slope inclination) and human factors (knowledge, technology, the 'soul' of the winemaker) that endow a wine with individual character (see Barham 2003; Kjellgren 2004; Trubek 2008; Certomà 2011; Demossier 2011; Unwin 2012; Monterescu 2017). Terroir is also related to distinct production practices outside winemaking (Besky 2014; Weiss 2016), and winemakers may also see it as a partner in the wine-production process (Teil 2017).

The history of terroir is closely linked to the emergence of the 'Appellation d'Origine Contrôlée' (AOC) system, starting in nineteenth-century France (Demossier 2011). As wines began to travel between increasing numbers of places in this period, accompanying anxieties arose related to places of origin because imitations of wine styles made in recognized regions became common (Inglis 2019). The Law of the Appellations d'Origine Contrôlées – the basis for today's AOC and for the European Union's quality regimes – was put in place in France in 1919, and the institute that regulates it ('Institut national de l'origine et de la qualité' or INAO) in 1935 (Meloni and Swinnen 2013). The AOC has been the main point of reference for other countries that adopted systems of classification of wine quality based on terroir like Italy; Spain; or, partially, Germany – and Moldova has followed similar steps in recent years. The discourse on terroir is today the hegemonic standard by which unknown wines are judged (Jung 2014), and analysing it closely reveals not only matters of taste and tradition in the winemaking region but also relations of power both local and global. Wine tastings, ratings and descriptions act as tools for establishing the place of certain wines in the 'global hierarchy of value' (Jung 2014: 26).

The adoption of the terroir discourse by the Moldovan wine sector after the mid-2000s has been part of a larger identity-seeking process among winemakers who have lost a traditional market and a response to the pressures of competitive wine markets in late capitalism. Thus, while drawing on the past terroir can also be seen as a technique of 'the social construction of the present' (Demossier 2011: 687), forging an identity for a place, a region or a country. Moldova has been no exception; virtually all winemaking regions around the world have 'reinvented' parts of their traditions and stories in the last three decades, driven by the need for differentiation in saturated markets. One iconic wine region, for example – Burgundy – felt the increased market competition particularly strongly, and its centuries-old terroir story has been destabilized. The story of Burgundy wine has been reshaped in the face of global changes, resulting in a combination of imbricated scales 'in which [the] local and global overlap harmoniously and in a composite fashion, while readjusting under the pressure of change' (Demossier 2018: 55). The reorganization of vineyards into smaller plots called *climats*, paralleled by the region's inclusion in the UNESCO patrimony, were processes accelerated by the success of new wine regions in markets around the world.

Yet, while Burgundians and other western-European wine producers reformulated a concept present in their discourses for centuries, Moldovan winemakers found developing a Moldovan terroir rather new. However, the new sets of quality standards based on geographical indication and terroir recognized at the European Union level were not painted on a blank slate (see also Gille 2016: 16), as at the basis of the exportable terroir are local soils, yeasts, grape varieties and winemaking knowledge. Thus, the praxis and discourse of terroir has been in fact dependent on the local context, so the Moldovan/Purcari terroir is a result of material and discursive frictions between local and global, unique and generic. 'Local materialities' are necessary for globalization or Europeanization to work (Gille 2016: 113). Articulating a Moldovan terroir was one of the changes needed in order to be able to speak the language of the global wine market. I emphasize the relative novelty of this concept in Moldovan winemaking because it did not have much relevance in the socialist years either. Indeed, although there were programmes for the delimitation of microzones of production in the Soviet Union in the 1930s,[1] similar to the French AOC (Walker and Manning 2013), they were not really followed up – so in the socialist states, the widespread practice was to manage grapes and their vinification centrally, by the state, and grapes from different regions were commonly mixed in the production process. The entry onto Western markets was paralleled at Purcari by renewed soil mappings and meteorological data recording or local yeast selection. The local history and these scientific data have been 'curated' into a new marketing discourse. Mapped soils are agricultural resources (King and Granjou 2020), and they create a scientific basis for differentiation in wine marketing, as I detail in chapter 5.

Homemade Wine

Although the focus of the ethnographic analysis in this book is on industrial-wine production and circulation, in order to grasp the dynamics of the Moldovan wine sector a close look at the significance of homemade wine is necessary. More than half of Moldovans live in the countryside and virtually every household in the south and the centre produces wine at home every year, mostly for its own consumption but also as a product for petty trade. This type of wine has been preferred by Moldovan consumers for decades while commercial, industrial wine has been produced predominantly for export. A 2016 survey showed that more than 70% of Moldovans find homemade wine better than commercial wine. Later in the book I will analyse in detail the implications that this divide has for the Moldovan wine market, but a central point is that commercial winemakers have difficulties in reducing their dependence on export markets in this context. Wine is, however, considered to embody the national spirit of Moldova, just like in other countries where it is a major product (cf. Guy 2003) – but is homemade wine the national drink, or is it the commercial wine made by professionals? In this book I show how these two broad categories of Moldovan wine exist in tension but also have important commonalities, borrowing knowledge and meaning from one another. At this point, I will only offer clarifications on the terminology and engage with the literature on organic foods and wine based on studies carried out elsewhere.

The term 'house wine' is frequently used among my interlocutors, yet in English the translation leads to some confusion as it more frequently refers to the bulk-wine option in restaurants. For this reason, I have settled on using 'homemade wine' throughout the book. It might be simpler to refer to homemade wine as 'natural wine', because in Anglophone anthropology it would create the least confusion: wine anthropologists writing about this type of wine refer to it as 'natural wine' (Ulin 1996; Black 2013; Kopczyńska 2013; Cohen 2013; Demossier 2018), but in the present case it would not be accurate enough ethnographically. Here, the 'house' component is primary; it signifies the web of production relations within the household, while the 'nature' or natural side comes after. But the way in which peasant winemakers in Moldova technically define homemade wine is nevertheless similar to definitions of 'natural wine' elsewhere, as in the Western countries epitomized by Jules Chauvet's approach.[2] This includes minimal chemical intervention, which means a healthier product; an emphasis on hygiene as a prime factor in reducing the need for preservatives; and the employment of very diverse ways of grape cultivation and vinification that require minimum or no pesticide input. While biodynamic and ecological wines have a system of certification in most wine-producing countries,[3] natural wine is the least-regulated category among the 'anti-establishment' wines. Natural wine has a loose and non-legislated definition. It does not have clear parameters, it can be made from organic or biodynamic agriculture, it rejects synthetic yeasts; no sugar is added, fining agents of animal origin are not used, it is not filtered, no SO_2 is used and no oak aging is involved (Cohen 2013: 261–62). Nevertheless, the underlying principle of natural wine is one of minimum intervention, chemically and technologically. The 'social' definition is that this natural wine is produced with one's own hands and is only rarely intended for the market.

While homemade wine is bound to the discourse of terroir, alternative production processes linked to the industrial, de-territorialized wine act as the true voice of terroir in some circles. One of the disputes boils down to control of the process of production, but the two sides follow different types of control with different aims. In the homemade wine-production process, the winemaker can trace the entire process of winemaking, from the operations over one year in the vineyard that culminate with the harvest to processing and storing the grapes. This ensures that the viticulture is ecological and winemaking 'natural'. On the other hand, at the factory a more detailed type of control is sought after: quality standards in the vineyard, the processing section, the cellar and on the bottling line.

In this book, homemade wine is also analysed as a signifier of Moldovan resistance to the industrialization of wine and food in general. My interlocutors very often called homemade wine 'wine without anhydride', the main substance used for its stabilization and preservation. As one of the basic changes that made possible the industrialization of food was the development in preservation methods (Goody 2012 [1982]: 72), rejecting industrial wine on the basis of a virtually harmless substance, but one which makes possible an 'unnaturally' long shelf life, seems only consistent. As in the case of food, the world of wine is nowadays sensitive to matters of production, composition or the philosophy behind the product (Gouez and Pétric 2007). In Western European and North American countries especially there are movements against industrial wine, and natural wines are a growing trend. Yet the concerns of Moldovan consumers coincide only partially with those of the supporters of the natural-wine movement in advanced industrialized countries (see Black 2013). As with organic foods and seeds, peripheral countries do not always have the same drives in their support for 'natural' organic products (Visser et al. 2015). If in advanced capitalist societies the organic market is a niche market targeting well-off consumers, in the former socialist countries of Europe economic constraints are frequently the primary reasons for consuming 'homemade' wine – thus making it more of a necessity than a choice, though matters of social status and local tradition are of comparable importance.

Labour and Its Reproduction

Robert Ulin's 1996 monograph on the Bordeaux wine cooperative movement, *Vintages and Traditions*, focuses on the historical constitution of quality in the region of Bordeaux and on relations of production and work as a cultural activity in winemaking. An encounter with a family of vintners in a Dordogne cooperative in the early 1980s made him reflect on Marx's theory of commodity fetishism, which led him to the insight that we often focus on a product and elide the topic of the producer. As an anthropologist of wine, he was frequently asked about the consumption aspects of wine and almost never about relations of production. His fieldwork started in 1984 and was spread out intermittently over eleven years, since which time the subject of the conditions of food production came closer to the light and sometimes even entered the spotlight, as in the case of commodities included in fair-trade schemes. In the case of wine, however, apart from the vintner, the production process – including the whole 'assembly line' – has not been subject to much scrutiny in anthropology. More than two decades after the publication of Ulin's book, Anglophone ethnographies of the relations of wine production still remain rather scarce (exceptions are Pratt 1994; Lem 1999; Crenn 2016; and Demossier 2018), despite wine being a commodity of great sociocultural complexity and economic importance in the present. When it comes particularly to work in winemaking, the dislocation of social relations in production and circulation has been prevalent. Food commodities such as chocolate and wine, which can be associated with distinction, have seen their social and economic production processes left on the margins. Winemaking workers, who carry out hard labour, are frequently dropped in favour of the artistry of the winemaker due to a 'strong emphasis on the wine grower as the only active worker of the land' (Demossier 2018: 40). Wine as a commodity has been represented in romanticized terms, as an instrument of social distinction, relaxation and idealized tradition (Bourdieu 1984). To give an important example, migrant labour in the vineyards has been neglected in anthropological literature despite its widespread existence in Mediterranean countries (Crenn 2016). Wine is associated with whiteness and European nations (Crenn 2016: 42), while migrant vineyard workers are seen as transient actors despite their prominent role in its manufacture. Focusing on Bordeaux field-sites, Crenn shows how racism regulates social and labour relations in winemaking regions in south-east France, where, besides the white French countryside, the category of the 'Arab' worker coexists in a precarious corner: the unacknowledged aspect of winemaking is its Muslim, Arab or Maghrebi workforce. With a complex history in the region, and with diverse countries of origin, large numbers of them are undocumented workers – but these realities rarely made the focus of anthropologists. In this way, the 'concrete images of labour' (Black and Ulin 2013: 6) are glossed over, the hierarchy of quality is naturalized through the hegemonic discourse of terroir (Jung 2014; Ulin 2007) and a historically rather immobile geography of wine quality is the result.

The title of this book – 'Wine is our bread' – paraphrases a statement by Katia, a 52-year-old manual worker in the Purcari Winery, who, when talking about her lifetime of work in the village of Purcari, said to me on a winter day: 'Wine is our bread. I'm afraid that's the only thing we can make money from here. What matters here in Purcari in the first place is the area; good wine is made in this microzone, with the slopes facing the sun.' 'Bread' (Romanian, *pâine*) is also used here with the same secondary meaning that this word has in English – that is, 'means of subsistence', 'work' or 'livelihood'. The present work addresses the scarcity of anthropological research on industrial-wine production in an East-European location, including the reshuffling of values and practices forced by globalization. I pursue this end by analysing how workers in the wine sector in Purcari experience the country's recent entry into the globalized wine market, and how their productive activities at home and in the winery contribute to the value of Purcari terroir wines.

An explanation of the historical distinction between 'labour' and 'work' is, from the outset, relevant as it provides an important place of reflection on what humans' transformative activity can mean in relation to different economic systems. The distinction between the two concepts appears in literature but it is by no means consistent (recent examples – Kim 2019;

Narotzky 2018; Kasmir and Carbonella 2014; Spittler 2003, 2008, 2009; Ulin 2002). In his book *Founders of the Anthropology of Work* (2008: 28), Gerd Spittler mentions how particularly difficult it is to maintain this distinction when one reads German writings, where the only word designating work or labour is *Arbeit*. He uses both the terms interchangeably, but explains an older preference to use 'work' rather than 'labour' – work is more suitable in his writing as it is referring more to non-capitalist societies and designates the mere transformative or interactive activity that leads to the creation of a product (Spittler 2009). Ulin (2002) chooses 'work' over 'labour' drawing on Hannah Arendt's criticism of Marx's failure to distinguish between the two. He justifies his choice as serving his thesis on refiguring work as cultural production: for Arendt, work is the social process through which humanity creates durable objects and relations while labour simply involves the human metabolic exchange with nature (Ulin 2002: 693). Labour is a more politically charged term, and it usually refers to wage work in capitalism. Indeed, other authors like Carbonella and Kasmir (2014) settle on using 'labour', defined as a political entity whose social protests and quietue, formal and informal organizations, and political cultures reflect its multiple engagements with capital and state as well as relationships with other workers – locally, regionally, and globally (Kasmir and Carbonella 2014: 6). Thus, in their understanding, labour is different from work, which is a social activity that does not include the 'livelihood' dimension. As the ethnographic analysis in the present book focuses specifically on livelihoods and relations of production in a winemaking village, I use the term 'labour' more often than 'work' to refer to the transformative and interactive activity in the commercial-winery context. However, I also use the two terms interchangeably in the book on a methodological ground: in a capitalist production system 'work' cannot be studied outside this context and, as the ethnographical chapters show, different productive activities in the household and in the firm overlap in the production of market value.

Temporally, the main focus is on the decades following 1989, when the new economic regimes in the former Eastern Bloc countries either brought flexibility to production regimes, labour recruitment and organization or else deepened it where it was already present. These changes in economic practice entailed changes in sociocultural practice as well. Flexibility in capitalism is nothing new, but it is expressed differently in different times and places (Narotzky 2015: 173). In Western countries, flexibilization followed the early 1970s and marked a break with 'Fordist' or industrial capitalism. In the former Eastern Bloc, flexible capitalist regimes took shape from the 1990s onwards. Commonly encountered changes were related to more irregular work schedules, product design was adapted to respond to greater market competition, and access to the labour market took new forms like subcontracting and temporary contracts (Kjaerulff 2015). Participant observation in the bottling section of Purcari Winery particularly shows how these tendencies played out in the livelihoods of wine workers.

Anthropologists undertaking research in former socialist countries came to study a wide range of socio-economic transformations and continuities that took place under the new political regimes, some specifically related to labour (e.g. Burawoy and Verdery 1999; Kideckel 2002; Dunn 2004; Kesküla 2016; Kofti 2016, 2018; Rajković 2018) and the work ethic (Heintz 2005, 2006),[4] with the proviso that until recently the topic of work and labour has been rather rarely a focus in Anglophone anthropology (Hann and Hart 2009). Some studies showed how the so-called 'transition' affected the working classes in the former socialist bloc and that dispossession and inequalities increased tremendously, with great material and emotional costs (Kideckel 2002). The worker became an increasingly less-valued social category, and a focus on entrepreneurs and management came to populate the public discourse (Grdešić 2015; Dunn 2004). This meant that recognition of the proletariat in terms of remuneration also decreased dramatically while a new factory-management discourse was built on criticism of the socialist system, which was dismissed as 'incompetent and inefficient' (Vodopivec 2010: 168) or associated with 'backwardness', 'stasis' and 'rigidity' (Dunn 2004: 64). Kofti (2016) showed that in Bulgaria, workers are depicted in the public discourse as lazy and inefficient, and as carrying with them an inefficient work ethic from the Communist years – a discourse similar to that researched by Müller (2007) in the former East Germany.

Nevertheless, here I focus particularly on a part of the proletariat that is difficult to define. The term 'proletariat' was developed in relation to urban, landless, industrial workers more than agricultural-estate labourers, and some social scientists use the term 'rural proletariat' for the latter type (Mintz 1974: 298). It represents wage-workers in rural areas working in capitalist agricultural enterprises, but the term has been defined in the so-called 'plantation societies', where landless workers in industrial agriculture predominate. Mintz's 'landless, wage-earning, store-buying and corporately-employed agricultural workers' (Mintz 1974: 300) are thus similar to industrial workers, but this typology rarely exists in this form. Rural workers often engage in secondary productive activities. Thus, I refer to Purcari workers as a 'rural proletariat' or 'rural workers', with the qualification that they are all owners of small plots of land that supplement their selling of their labour force. The income and products that come from these plots of land are central means of reproduction of the community, some of which is absorbed into the capitalist process of wine production in the Purcari Winery. Extracting surplus value from the workers thus relies to an important extent on the capacity of the rural workers to find additional sources of income besides their wages.[5] I explain this extraction of surplus value in the framework of social reproduction theory (SRT), which enables us to analyse how different areas of daily (working) life and reproduction are subordinated to capital. The peasant household functions simultaneously as a production unit, a consumption unit and a unit of biological reproduction, suitable for exploitation in different socio-economic contexts (Edholm, Harris and Young 1978: 124).

Within the category reproduction of labour in capitalism, Harris and Young (1981: 123–24) distinguish between three dimensions of the process: the reproduction of individuals within a class, i.e. of individuals in relation to the means of production; the reproduction of adequately socialized labour, i.e. within a specific ideological apparatus; and third, the category relevant to the present ethnographic analysis, the material reproduction of labour. This last-named category refers to the material dimension of how workers reproduce: 'the day-to-day maintenance of people adequately nourished, clothed, and "recreated" – in short, serviced – to work for capital' (Harris and Young 1981: 124). The costs can be taken on by a welfare state or by the so-called informal sector (Harris and Young 1981: 124). In Purcari, it is the household subsistence economy, or domestic labour, that takes on an important part of the material reproduction of the labour force in the absence of a welfare state.

The risk of domestic labour remaining unnoticed is not only driven by its usefulness to capital to stay in the shade, unproblematized. It has remained unproblematized in anthropology until recently too, given that it is

> directly attuned to the human organism and its physiological needs for food, cleanliness and protection, this ultimate derivation from the needs of the body gives the illusion that domestic work is a timeless activity, remaining substantially the same through all the major changes in the forces of production and across the entire ecological spectrum. (Harris and Young 1981: 131)

Although these reflections stem from feminist anthropology focusing on the gendered differences in the allocation of labour, I find them relevant to my focus on the class differentiation that the change from socialism to capitalism generated in Moldova.

Post-Soviet Moldovan Crises

A short journey through the recent history of the Republic of Moldova is necessary in order to have a better grasp of the transformations that are presently being analysed. Like other former members of the Eastern Bloc, Moldova's post-Soviet years have been marked by periods of crisis, which in the wine industry translated into periods of stagnation or regress. Anthropologists of East and Central Europe have explored the ways in which sociopolitical change has especially affected local agricultural communities (Creed 1998; Hann 2003a; Pine 2007; Aistara 2018). Two decades ago, there was 'widespread recognition that the replacement of socialist institutions by Western models of capitalist market economy, private property, and civil society has not brought the rapid beneficial changes' (Hann 2003a: 6) that many had expected. Almost three decades later, perceptions in parts of the postsocialist countryside have not become significantly more positive: possibly the disillusionment has become even deeper, as was the case with my interlocutors in the Republic of Moldova. For many, the capitalist market economy has meant deeper insecurities; private property has become a challenge to maintain; and, unofficially, 1 million Moldovans out of its total population of around 3 million live abroad. In this context, hopes and grievances were often compared unfavourably with the withered Soviet state (cf. Jung 2019: 20).

Starting in the early 1990s, conflicts emerged between the Moldovan government and groups wanting either independence from or unification with Russia. This led to Moldova's national territory being divided into three main administrative regions: Moldova; the 'Autonomous Territorial Unit of Găgăuzia'; and the 'Territorial administrative units from the left part of the Nistru river', or Transnistria. The last-named entity has functioned as an autonomous region since 1991, has a separate government from that in Chișinău and is considered the site of one of 'Eurasia's frozen conflicts' (Dunn and Bobick 2014: 406). Găgăuzia, although separatist, has functioned as an autonomous territorial unit within the Moldovan state since 1994. In these regions, the population is predominantly pro-Russian and maintains close ties to the Russian Federation both politically and economically. Wine is produced in all three territorial units, and the tensions that originated in the early 1990s are, to a certain extent, still felt in the way in which the wineries from the three regions are presently organized to promote Moldovan wine abroad.

However, the most drastic problems for the sector stemmed from the Russian embargo on wine in 2006, which lasted over a year, and, later, a new one imposed in 2013 and still partially in place.[6] These crises have led to a change of paradigm in wine production and marketing in order to focus on new markets – first, other (non-Russia) CIS states such as Belarus, Ukraine and Kazakhstan; and then, the European Union and China. The structures of political organizations have mirrored this division as the parties that made up the post-Soviet governments of Moldova took pro-European or pro-Russian positions, including in the public discourse. The country's media and intellectual and NGO environments often still orient their analyses in terms of 'external vectors' (Romanian, *vectorii externi*), with the 'pro-European vector' promising European integration (modernization, a free market, consumption) and the 'Russian vector' seeking to take Moldova under its protective arm (stability, a large market, familiarity). In 2001, the post-Soviet Communist Party won elections principally by promising closer ties with Russia. In 2005, it won by mobilizing the opposite vector, promising closer ties to the European Union. In 2009, the Communist government was ousted and was followed by two pro-European governments, which in fact transformed the country to an oligarchic regime that led the country into a new crisis, which culminated in the 'robbery of the century' (Romanian, *jaful secolului*) in 2014 with the theft of almost 1 billion dollars from local banks, or about 12% of the country's GDP. I carried out fieldwork between the autumn of 2016 and the summer of 2017, when discussions in the winery, in the villages, in Chișinău bars or in the media were punctuated by references to the leaks about the bank theft and by worries about what the transfer of the theft into the public debt meant for the 2 million Moldovans living in the country at that time.[7]

During the election campaign in autumn 2016, the candidates running for the presidency repeatedly said that they wanted to break away from geopolitical games and focus on the welfare of the Moldovan people. However, the two candidates running in the final round – Maia Sandu and Igor Dodon – formulated their electoral promises around the two opposite poles of Europe and Russia, while many Moldovan citizens continued in their turn to formulate their choices based on the same pole structure. One way of reading this readiness or perceived need to become part of a greater federation or state structure is that it constitutes continuity with the relations of dependence of the Soviet era, which – although paternalistic and hierarchical, and sometimes abusive – used to provide a redistributive framework that ensured dignified livelihoods for many. The void left by the dismantling of the Soviet Union and the subsequent straining of trade relationships could be filled by 'Europe' – the Western, modernizing entity in the view of many Moldovans. The ethnographic chapters in this book capture these aspects as they are experienced by workers in the winemaking village of Purcari.

Researching Moldovan Wine

In August 2016, I travelled to the Republic of Moldova to carry out ethnographic fieldwork in a winemaking community for one year. Isolating one site or following the multiple connections that de-centre single sites into multi-sites is a decision (Candea 2007: 172) grounded in methodological and political questions. My ethnographic fieldwork took place predominantly in one site, but I followed up on a few connections outside the village in order to grasp how consumption is staged and what kind of local story is re-enacted in the marketing discourses deployed at wine events in Chișinău and, for example, in Prague. Moreover, the political-economic focus of this book does bring the political dimensions of wine production and circulation to the forefront, and these connections are regional and global as much as they are local. However, I do not categorize my research as multi-sited; it involves a single, 'found-object' (Candea 2007: 179) type of site, providing a historicized snapshot of the relations of production in a winemaking village. Winemaking sites circulate through history and markets as bounded sites, and this particularity of the relationship between wine and place made the somewhat classical village field-site choice on my part the most methodologically sensible one.

Purcari – including the village, the winery and the wine region – has been an especially revealing site, given its relatively long production history in the region and the rapid rise in sales of its wine in different markets. While Purcari is one of the 'winegrowers at the margins' (Ulin 1996: 2) of the European Union and the global wine industry, in Moldova and neighbouring Romania it is one of the most popular quality-wine producers. Purcari boasts the only winery in Moldova where tourists are allowed in every production department, as they 'have nothing to hide', as the marketing director told me, except for the laboratory, where equipment is more fragile and space limited. This means that on a daily basis, groups of from two to thirty tourists are walked through all sections of the factory, the industrial cellars and the historical collection, which consists of 25,000 bottles of Purcari wine from vintages starting in 1948 and going up to the present.

I first arrived in the village in late September 2016, right after the company CEO had agreed to my presence at the winery. In Purcari, where my main field-site was located, I lived at the winery complex, in 'the dorm' (Romanian, *cămin*). This building contained rooms that were allocated to the winery's technical staff, none of whom were local, and to tour guides and the students carrying out university internships who usually came during harvest time. Contrary to the usual practice of ethnographers in rural areas of living with a host family, I chose to stay in the workers' building, because it kept me close to any activity that was happening in the winery also, it turned out to be handy for the winery administration in that they could easily call me in to lend a hand when there was sometimes a critical need for more staff. This was also valid for winery tours, as several times when the number of tourists exceeded expectations I helped with Romanian- and English-language tours.

I carried out participant observation in the factory and in the vineyards, being present for the main operations in viticulture and winemaking over the year. In the company vineyard, I worked almost exclusively with the Purcari workers' brigade throughout the year – made up of two to three teams containing only villagers from Purcari, from teenagers to retired people. There were four other brigades from four other villages there, but I had limited interaction with them. In the Purcari Winery, I worked in all departments except for the laboratory, and the forty-plus employees in the production department gradually became open to me from October. In autumn – during harvest, when the grapes were brought to the processing section – I could observe and participate in their selection, crushing and fermentation. Later on, I helped with the filtering, wine transfers, ageing, bottling, labelling and packaging of wine bottles, and also by cleaning equipment. In the winery, some of the workers received me reluctantly but most of them became glad to have a helper or a conversational partner around. Age and gender usually shapes the experience of ethnographic fieldwork, and this was also the case in my research – but not to the extent that I had expected. Wherever I could work at the same pace as the employees, workers of all ages and genders became open interlocutors and shared their knowledge about the work and the village.

My observations included attention to work and work rhythms in the vineyards and the factory, household work, winemaking and wine consumption, and at the same time I followed the comparative interpretations of Purcari villagers in order to grasp their understanding of the present and the recent past. In the village, I visited current and former workers of the winery; took part in religious celebrations, gardening and activities in the vineyards; or simply visited the cellars for a sample of homemade wine. Thus, my work in Purcari is partly an ethnography of a shop floor, partly an ethnography of the fields of the company or home plots in a 'found' fieldsite delimited as a wine region for centuries.

In the village of Purcari, workers are ethnically homogeneous – mostly Moldovans – and Romanian-language use is predominant, though switching between Russian and Romanian is also common. The main language of communication in the field for me was Romanian and, to a lesser extent, Russian and English. My ability in Russian was limited but this did not impact strongly on my exchanges with workers, all of whom were fluent in Romanian. My presence in the village as a single woman from Romania who had been educated at Western universities elicited diverse reactions that ranged from puzzlement to welcoming attitudes, to outright opposition. As I was not researching wine as a product alone, but moreover relations of production and the biographies of workers and other winemaking staff, my inquiries would sometimes lead to refusals from villagers who preferred not to voice criticisms or reveal knowledge about potentially sensitive topics such as privatization. I believe that the prolonged discussions and exchanges managed to bring more understanding to both sides, showing that a more horizontal exchange is possible. The implications of these tensions for the collection of the data on which this book relies were that they encouraged me to find a language in which to produce knowledge that minimizes hierarchical undertones. The main research topic – wine – is bound to reinforce and underline cultural hierarchies, both regionally and globally, that make the work of Moldovan winemakers and workers considerably harder. My aim throughout this book is to avoid teleological narratives of 'catching up' in writing about Moldovan wine, while I rely on my ethnographical data and a critical political-economy lens to explain how inequalities in this field have been constituted and maintained.

When researching industrial winemaking, I often interacted with technical staff in the winery and was at times considered unqualified to write about wine because I was a 'non-technical person' – yet most of the time, technologists and wine scholars were very helpful and open to speaking with a social scientist, finding my position as an ethnographer with an interest in how wine is produced and consumed to be perfectly legitimate. Vlad, the head of production at Purcari Winery, was one such person, and he had an important mediating role for my ethnographical study of the winery. He stressed that 'in Moldova it was not like in France', where workers of all kinds in wineries would talk cheerfully about their wine from the beginning: 'here people look at you with suspicion (mistrust) for a while, but it is just a matter of time for them to trust you and open up like no other'.

The largest body of the data on which this book relies comes from discussions, unrecorded interviews and participant observation. Some recorded narrative and biographical interviews were helpful in confirming or completing sequences of events in the lives of the employees and villagers. By the end of the fieldwork, I had conducted fifty-one formal interviews (narrative-biographical and semi-structured interviews) with workers at the factory, technical staff, older villagers in Purcari and academics in Chișinău. In the interviews, I mostly followed life stories and my questions explored personal experiences, values and systems of meaning, or descriptions of production processes related to winemaking or other products. In Purcari, I mainly interviewed workers I had met in the winery, but also other villagers (former winery workers, the more elderly villagers, winemakers). I contacted and was able to interview the latter group through ethnographic snowball sampling, as my winery interlocutors recommended individuals who could share their work experiences or details of local history with me.

I also gathered data in Chișinău, where I carried out archival research and interviews with experts in the wine sector, following the connections to and from Purcari. I spent time in the State Archive and the National Library Archive in Chișinău, where I gathered files pertaining to the history of Purcari village and the winery as well as to the Moldovan wine industry as a whole. Archival research gave me a clearer image of the history of the industry in today's Moldova, at present there being no published monograph that has gathered extensive data about it. Whenever possible, I attended wine-related events in Chișinău such as National Wine Day, the Wine Vernissage in winter and spring, and the 'Wine Friendly' sessions at which Moldovan wine was promoted by sommeliers and producers in order to popularize consumption of bottled wine.

Apart from the public figures that appear in the ethnographic analysis, all the names of the people featured in the book have been anonymised to protect the identities of workers and other interlocutors. However, the village and the eponymous company, Purcari, cannot be effectively anonymised as they are two very prominent actors in Moldovan winemaking, and any effort to keep the names private would soon fail. Moreover, villagers, the mayor and the winery management have never expressed any reluctance to my retaining the real name of the village and the company in the current work.

Structure of the Book

The five ethnographic chapters that follow are organized in such a manner as to address the way in which the value of Purcari wine has been historically constituted through relationships of export dependence on Russia, as well as through labour and advertising. In chapter 1, I trace the history of winemaking on the territory of today's Moldova up to the present-day in order to show how historically the growth of the vineyard surface in the region has been related to export markets on Russian territory for the past two centuries. It was in this historical context that dependence on the part of Moldova was created and maintained. I combine ethnographic data and archival research to show how winemaking has been depicted in historical publications and how supranational entities transformed Bessarabian or, later, Moldovan wine. The role of the Russian embargoes since the mid-2000s in recent reforms of the wine industry in Moldova is analysed in greater depth. The economic sanctions have acted as catalysts of the postsocialist transformations of wine production and marketing practices. I then analyse the institutional reform after 2006, and provide an overview of the legislation governing the reformed Moldovan wine sector as well as an analysis of the marketing organizations that have been created in recent years. I argue that in the case of wine, international regulations have led to contestation and a revised appreciation or re-evaluation of locality. The existing practices and discourses around Moldovan winemaking regarding wine styles, containers, labels, terroir, the marginality or exoticism of Moldova, and Soviet and post-Soviet tensions have been placed under scrutiny or rejected altogether as new regulations were adopted. These new developments are interpreted by interlocutors as a preferable form of dependence. In the last part of the chapter, I zoom in on my main research site, Purcari, to provide a history of the village and the winery as well as to consider how the organization of property and production at the national level starting in the 1990s affected the winemaking community there.

Household wine production is another revealing phenomenon for understanding the dynamics of the wine industry and the lives of the Purcari workers. In chapter 2, I describe how homemade-wine production is embedded in Moldovan society and analyse its role in the dynamics of the domestic wine market. The majority of Moldovans from both rural and urban milieus prefer to drink homemade wine rather than bottled wine. This preference is not only a matter of taste, and I show that it is primarily related to the embeddedness of homemade-wine production and consumption among Moldovans throughout the centuries. The dynamics of dependence analysed in the previous chapter are substantiated here through ethnographic data from the winemaking village of Purcari. In explaining how domestic wine production is partly responsible for the dependence of commercial wineries upon export, I focus on matters of hierarchization and differentiation in the field of winemaking as they are central to understanding the political economy of wine at large. To depict this, I rely not only on participant observation in the village but also on interviews with wine experts in the capital city of Chișinău. The latter group adds a new layer to the hierarchy between homemade wine and commercial wine.

Chapter 3 continues the focus on household activities in order to show how some socially reproductive activities are integrated into capital-accumulation processes. Drawing on Marxist scholarship arguing that capitalism relies in part on agricultural communities for the reproduction of labour power and that household work contributes to the reproduction of capitalism, I explore the social and economic processes that are necessary in reproducing labour power in the wine region of Purcari. Labour power as a commodity is fundamental to the whole system of capitalist production, although it involves non-capitalist processes of production, such as women's care work, subsistence gardening or resting; in this framework, they become 'naturalized' and taken for granted. The areas of social reproduction that contribute to the circulation of capital in Purcari are food provisioning, inhabitable and functional spaces, and rest options (holidays, free days, socialization outside the work space). I follow these areas in a comparative manner as my interlocutors framed them. Their socialist-era experiences still inform how the present is evaluated. I end the chapter by bringing together ethnographic data on local entrepreneurs, who, in comparison with the rural proletariat, have more income and more liberties; to a considerable extent they see themselves as the winners from the new regime, but even they notice that Moldovan capitalism has meant loss, decay and exclusion on both the pragmatic and symbolic levels.

Chapter 4 complements chapter 3 by further analysing production relations in winemaking. The observations used in this chapter come predominantly from the bottling section of the Purcari Winery, where orders need to be prepared and shipped all year round. Night and weekend shifts, and extended work hours in general, were introduced on a permanent basis in 2015, when the winery's sales started to grow again after the setting of the 2013 embargo and doubled by 2017. It shows how workers in this department experienced the flexibilization of time once the winery's sales rose rapidly. While the ethnographic data in this chapter show how daily life in both factory and home changed, it also depicts the ways in which the competition and brand ephemerality of late capitalism is forcing firms to reinvent themselves quickly. Wine is a more complex commodity than most, as it covers a wide range of cultural practices; therefore, wineries are constantly looking for criteria of differentiation in all these realms. The rapid transformations in the winery disturbed workers' rhythms and renegotiated what constitutes a competitive commodity or organization. I also show how the winery's entry into the global market led to contradictory transformations in the lives of the workers: while work times were increased and produced new forms of alienation and the degradation of certain aspects of life quality, an enrichment of industrial work time through rituals of commensality and socialization started to occur at the same time.

In the last ethnographic chapter, 5, I focus on the scientific and marketing work that was mobilized to articulate the Purcari terroir. Wineries around the world still need to show their adherence to terroir, as this is one of the values that the world market imposes on actors of this kind. It is the adoption of the terroir discourse by wineries around the globe that reproduces the present logic of the world wine market. Through participant observation in the Purcari Winery, interviews with scientists and marketing workers and discourse analysis of website and brochure content, I analyse the construction of the Purcari terroir and the reasons for emulating Western discourses. Marketing work in the competitive global wine field involves the selection of information in order to strike a balance between a location's generic and unique features. The main argument of the chapter is that, contrary to the positions of several authors in economic sociology and anthropology, there is no clear distinction or opposition between the uniqueness of commodities and their generic nature, and that the two categories constitute each other in the realm of commodities. Analysing the marketing discourse within this framework also serves as a foundation for discussion of the Soviet Union's legacy in the Moldovan wine industry. Like those of other wine regions outside the classical core of the so-called 'Old (Western) World', Purcari Winery negotiates its place in the new markets by emphasizing its localness and the uniqueness of its location as much as it seeks legitimation through positive comparisons with the produce of French wine regions. This chapter analyses what kinds of 'local materialities' are saved when the discourse of the winery changes in order to emphasize distinction and differentiation, as well as common points with the wines on European markets.

In the conclusion I show that there were two main drivers for change in Moldovan winemaking: Moldova's strained relationship with its main trading partner and the country's integration into a world wine market that has its own dynamics and contradictions, which a new actor needs to integrate. The overall aim of this book is to depict the local articulation of this nexus through an ethnographical study of workers and wine production, and of marketization. I follow industrial workers in winemaking in order to understand changes in the labour process as well as the experience of the everyday, both outside the winery and in the household. I track the ways in which the shift to new markets has led to changes in wine production, furthering both the flexibilization of labour in Moldova and the break with the Fordist industrial relations that characterized the Soviet years. The recurrent theme of the book is the materiality of changing wine politics seen through the narratives of labour and terroir.

Notes

1. A 'microzone' in the Soviet Union designated a restricted production zone for a branded wine, the closest concept to the French terroir in Soviet winemaking practices (Walker and Manning 2013: 205).
2. Jules Chauvet (1907–1989), considered 'the father of natural wine' in France, criticized the mainstream winemaking methods in the entire production process, from the vineyard to the factory. He was born into a family of *négociants* and throughout his life conducted experiments in winemaking (Cohen 2013). He strongly recommended the avoidance of chemical fertilizers and pesticides in the vineyard, and in the winery Chauvet came to condemn the use of additives such as SO_2 because the

presence of chemicals would attack beneficial indigenous yeasts. He considered its use avoidable if proper hygienic practices were followed.
3. Organic wines are wines made from organic agriculture, which typically excludes the use of synthetic fertilizers and pesticides in viticulture and the use of preservatives in the wine. Biodynamic wine is made from organic agriculture as well, but it includes Rudolf Steiner's methods for soil fertilization and all operations in the vineyard are done following certain astronomical configurations.
4. Other widely studied themes that bring insights as well on the value of labour and on working lives in the region have included changing property regimes (Hann 1993, 2002, 2003; Creed 1998; Verdery 1996, 2001, 2003), informal economies and domestic livelihoods (Pine 2007; Cash 2015a, 2015b), informal ties (Ledeneva 2009; Cash 2015c), urban change (Jansen 2015; Petrovici 2015, 2017; Ringel 2016), civil society (Gagyi and Ivancheva 2017; Mikuš 2018) peasant history (Cash 2014), language and ethnicity (Chamberlain-Creangă 2011; Heintz 2008), ecology (Dorondel 2016; Aistara 2018), migration (Demirdirek 2006, 2007; Keough 2016) and ritual (Cash 2011, 2013; Creed 2011; Gudeman and Hann 2015b).
5. This dynamic is a feature not only of capitalism: during the Soviet Socialist period, most households combined earnings from wage work and the private plot (Humphrey 1983: 269). Likewise, the local economy in Purcari and the surrounding villages relied not just on waged work in winemaking and the fruit and vegetable canneries but also on the supplementary household production of food by rural workers (see chapter 3).
6. At the end of 2020, only a limited number of Moldovan wineries exported wine to Russia and the export quotas remained low in comparison to the previous decades. In the first 2020 semester, the volume export quota for bottled wine to Russia was of 10.1 % and that of bulk wine was of 7.1% (Buletin informațional trimestrial, ediția 3/ august 2020, pp. 2).
7. At the latest census in 2014, Moldova's population comprised 2.9 million inhabitants. Its largest ethnic group is Moldovan (73.7%), followed by Romanians (6.9%), Ukrainians (6.5%), Găgăuz (4.5%), Russians (4%) and Bulgarians (1.8%). Over 80% of the population speaks Romanian or Moldovan (they are almost identical languages), followed by Russian and Găgăuz (PHC 2014). Yearly, the country receives around 1,2 million dollars in remittances from Moldovans working abroad – predominantly in Russia, the EU and Israel (IMF 2017). These remittances made up 15% of the country's GDP.

1

 The Making of an Export Industry

*Moldovan Winemaking under
Different Sociopolitical Systems*

> The best wine is sold wine.
> —Joke among Moldovan winemakers

On 20 March 2006, Russia's chief sanitary inspector, Gennady Onishchenko, signed a decree stopping wine imports from Moldova and Georgia. At that moment, 95% of Moldova's production of alcohol was for export, 75% of which was going to Russia. The wine sector was also responsible for 80.3% of food exports, and contributed 8% to the state budget and 9% to GDP in 2006.[1] At a press conference on 21 March, Mr Onishchenko claimed that Moldova and Georgia were exporting substandard wines to Russia containing pesticides and heavy metals over the legal limits. As of 27 March 2006, no Moldovan wine was allowed to cross the border into Russia, over two hundred railway wagons loaded with wine being stopped at the Ukraine–Russian border. On 31 March, the Moldovan Trade Union Federation in Food Industry and Agricultural Products, together with trade unions from other sectors, held a press conference at which they urged international trade union organizations 'to show solidarity with the workers of Moldova and to use all means to help unblock exports of Moldovan wines to Russia, to sensitize public opinion from all countries to the fact that the ban means the cessation of the activity of wineries, people becoming jobless, without incomes, and the rights of Russian consumers being infringed'.[2] The calls did not produce much support, and on 4 April, Russia banned sparkling wines and brandies as well in a process culminating on 9 April in a decision to ban all alcoholic products imported from Moldova. This series of decisions was followed by a written demand from the then prime minister of Moldova asking for the ban to be lifted, as it was 'harming both Moldovan producers and Russian investors'.[3]

During these troubled weeks, an expert delegation from Chișinău went to Moscow with a list of topics to negotiate, but they did not receive an immediate answer. At the same time, the chief sanitary inspector of

Moldova asked for a detailed report regarding the health issues that the Russians had brought up. The Russian officials finally refused to negotiate, while Moldova presented a report on the accusations: pesticides of class II toxicity, the problem that Russia had mentioned, had not been used on Moldovan soil since the 1970s. As Russia made no reply to this information, the Moldovan delegation called for an extraordinary meeting of the Economic Council of the Community of Independent States (CIS) to discuss Russia's ongoing discrimination against Moldovan producers – but, again, to no avail. A second, unsuccessful request was sent to the Russian prime minister by his Moldovan counterpart, and only in November 2007 was the embargo lifted. Table 1.1 shows shares of imported wine in Russia between 2005 and 2007.

This was the first ban that Russia had imposed on Moldovan wine imports in the post-Soviet period, and it was not going to be the last. The 2006 ban and three others that followed until 2013, the last of which was still partially in place in 2020, led to major changes to the Moldovan wine industry, which had to establish itself in other export markets, on which the wine sector therefore remained dependent to a great extent. This chapter looks firstly at the historical shaping and development of the Moldovan winemaking and asks how the export dependence dynamic developed: why did the wine industry grow to such an extent, and how did political regime changes transform it? In the second part of the chapter, I will focus on my main fieldwork site, Purcari, in order to introduce the village and the winery and explain how it was affected by its relationship with its export markets and also by property regime changes.

Moldova's Winemaking until the Nineteenth Century

Moldova emerged as a principality in the second half of the fourteenth century, and the territory of today's Republic of Moldova has been part of different political entities in the last few centuries. It came under Ottoman rule in 1538, but after to the Russo-Turkish war of 1806 to 1812, in which the Ottoman Empire was defeated, part of Moldova was incorporated into the Russian Empire in the latter year.[4] It was renamed 'Bessarabia' and became an imperial region (Russian *oblast*) and subsequently a Russian province (Russian *guberniya*) until 1918, when it came under Romanian rule. At the outbreak of the Second World War, Moldova was returned to Russian rule, becoming officially a part of the Soviet Union in 1944. Moldova has been an independent republic since August 1991, having been the Soviet Union's least urbanized republic (King 2000), and also among its least industrialized.

Table 1.1. Wine import structure in Russia, 2005–7.

Supplying countries	Share 2005	Share 2006	Share 2007 (1ˢᵗ trimester)
Moldova	50.7 %	16.9 %	0%
Bulgaria	16.5 %	27.7 %	31.4 %
Georgia	9 %	3.1 %	0 %
Ukraine	3.1 %	4.4 %	3.5 %
Hungary	0.9 %	2.1 %	2.9 %
Uzbekistan	0.09 %	0 %	0 %
Armenia	0.03 %	0 %	0.34 %
France	6.0 %	13 %	19.3 %
Spain	3.6 %	8.4 %	12.3 %
Germany	2.1 %	6.6 %	6.9 %
Italy	2.3 %	6.7 %	8.8 %
Cyprus	0.4 %	0 %	0.55 %
Portugal	0.07 %	0 %	0.2 %
Chile	1.82 %	3.4 %	6.7 %
Argentina	2.2 %	3.2 %	3.7 %
SUA	0.16 %	0.3 %	0.6 %
Australia	0.2 %	0.4 %	0.5 %
Hong Kong	0.3 %	0.7 %	1.1 %
Others	0.53 %	3.1 %	1.21 %
Total	100 %	100 %	100 %

Source: © *Viticultura și Vinificația in Moldova*, No. 4 (16)/200 pp. 31.

Winemaking on this territory has been supported externally since the beginning of the nineteenth century, when historical Bessarabia became part of the Tsarist Empire.[5] The province was incorporated into the Russian Empire in 1812 and since then Russia increasingly demanded Bessarabian wine. It progressively introduced high taxes on imported wine to protect domestic production (Schmidt 2012). Bessarabian vineyard surfaces and wine production grew due to the opening of the large Russian market, but unprecedented growth in production and number of markets came in the second half of the nineteenth century when Bessarabia was sending wine to all corners of Russia: in 1883, it accounted for almost 20% of the Russian Empire's wine production (Bittner 2015).[6]

An important influence to the development of Bessarabian winemaking in the 1800s was the Tsar's campaign to repopulate southern Bessarabia in the first half of the nineteenth century, when German colonists settled in the area, coming mainly from the Kingdom of Württemberg. Colonists also came from Switzerland, Poland, France and other Russian regions. They were required to be good agriculturists, winemakers or pomologists, so that the soils and climate would be harnessed for agriculture only by those who 'could be models in crafts and agrarian activities ... people with experience in cultivating grape vine, mulberry trees and other useful plants, or in cattle breeding...' (Schmidt 2012: 57). Many of the colonists kept vineyards and made wine in their new country. While the poorer families owned the land collectively in groups, other colonists were richer and could afford to rent land in addition to the 1.5 *desyatina* (given by the Russian Empire)[7] and to hire labour. The Purcari vineyards were among the winegrowing areas strongly influenced by this migration, as they came under the ownership of German and French colonists in the second half of the nineteenth century.

Later in that century, the blight that hit other European vineyards, *Phylloxera vastatrix*, affected Bessarabia as well. The first case was recorded in the north of the territory in 1883 (Bittner 2015). In the decades that followed, Bessarabian vineyard surfaces were reduced considerably as the 'radical method' against phylloxera – which meant uprooting and incinerating infected vines, followed by fumigation of the soil with chemical substances (Bittner 2015: 152–53) – used ineffectively across Europe failed in Bessarabia as well, leading to great losses in terms of incomes and grape varieties. The grafting technique that was used in France from 1869, still the most effective method against phylloxera to this day, was available to only a few cultivators in Bessarabia because it was very expensive. The local government of the Akkerman *uyezd* (administrative unit in the Tsarist Empire), the region to which Purcari belonged, ordered the plantation and grafting of grapevines locally at the viticultural schools in Akkerman and Tarutino at the beginning of the twentieth century. In 1907, only the school in Tarutino produced grafted seedlings – some 300,000 of them. At the same time, during winter, specialized viticultural workers trained peasants how to graft the seedlings themselves (Dölkers 1974: 105). But most of the peasant winegrowers resorted to planting hybrid vines,[8] obtained through the crossbreeding of American and European vines (Ciocanu 2015). Hybrids are resistant to phylloxera but yield grapes that, by oenologists' judgement, are of lower quality. Before the phylloxera outbreak, Bessarabian viticulture was almost entirely based on indigenous varieties, but after a couple of decades only very few indigenous grapes survived. Nevertheless, as the sector recovered by relying on hybrids and French varieties, it continued to export most of its production. A 1910 report (Pelivan 1920) stated that 30% of the total quantity of wine produced in Bessarabia was for domestic consumption, the remaining 70% being exported, but it is not clear if that included peasant wine. In the late nineteenth and early twentieth centuries, winemaking in this region was already in the process of modernization.[9]

The Early Twentieth Century: The Romanian Interlude

The incorporation of Bessarabia into Romania in 1918 brought a brief halt to the growing of Moldovan winemaking, as Romania was already struggling with overproduction. The whole country had to deal with this problem, and large quantities of wine were being left in cellars for years on end. In general, the interwar years proved discouraging for Moldovan winemakers: in 1921, 1924 and 1925, production was affected by major droughts, and after 1926 the Polish market for wines dried up (King 2000: 42). Moreover, grapevines could only be cultivated on land that was unsuitable for cereals (Schmidt 2012).

Through the 1921 agrarian reform in Romania, peasants were given land, using plots expropriated from the state, the church and large landowners (Romanian *boieri*). 'Casa noastră' was the state institution that implemented the agrarian reform, expropriating land and giving peasants property rights over it. Despite these changes, poverty soared among Bessarabian peasants during in the 1930s (Cash 2014: 167). Yet some reforms aimed at improving quality and traceability were implemented during Romanian rule, beginning with the reduction of direct-producing hybrid-vine-growing areas, which were seen as producing lower quality wine. The manner in which Dölkers (1974), the son of a Bessarabian German, writes about these wines is similar to the discourse present among professional winemakers today: peasants were used to drinking their own wine, so they resorted to make wine out of what was more affordable. But, he wrote, 'if a hybrid wine was made with enough care', one could not tell 'the difference from a noble grape wine' (Dölkers 1974: 106–7).[10] Another measure implemented during Romanian rule was favouring the plantation of the best-adapted grape varieties for each wine region and controlling the origin of wine through a regulation comparable to the French AOC but less elaborate, and punishments were introduced for those selling fake wine (Gusti et al. 1940). Overall, during the interwar period, vineyards larger than five hectares were rare in Bessarabia, and a vineyard would usually be added on to a vegetable garden. As each household made its own wine, subsistence-style production practices were not substantially altered. During this time, wine continued to be made on the left bank of Dniester (today's Transnistria) although not as a major economic sector.

Soviet Moldova: The Growth (and Stalling) of an Industry

On 28 June 1940, Soviet troops occupied most of Bessarabia and temporarily created the Moldovan Soviet Socialist Republic (MSSR). In 1941, Romania regained control over Moldova, a situation that lasted until 1944 when the Soviet Union finally established the MSSR. The country became independent on 27 August 1991. After the Second World War, we learn (depending on the source) either that viticulture suffered a great deal or that it experienced an unprecedented period of development. What is indisputable is that the Soviet period between 1944 and 1989 was that of the greatest expansion of winemaking in Moldova. These were also the years when land in the MSSR was collectivized. Public land and production facilities were reorganized, and the inequalities of the 1930s were levelled to a great extent through collectivization but also through deportations (Cash 2014: 166). Land and the means of production were organized either as *sovkhozy* (state-owned collective farms) or as *kolkhozy*, the collectively owned farms that were seen as an intermediate type of property ownership (Negură 2016). State winemaking was also organized in such collectives. From the 1950s until 1985, wine production grew constantly, with the largest producing area of 193,000 hectares of usable vineyards being registered in 1983 (Rusu 2011). Only a fraction of the quantity of wine produced during these decades could be consumed locally, so the larger share of it was intended for consumption all across the Soviet Union. The total volume of wine production grew 63-fold from 1940 to 1983, and in 1983 Moldovan winemakers produced one quarter of all the bulk wine produced in the Soviet Union – a total of 96.2 million decalitres.[11]

The manner in which economic activity was organized within the Soviet Union led to mutual dependence between Soviet republics, each region or republic having a designated place in the Soviet-wide division of labour (Kaneff and Heintz 2006: 10). The Soviet restrictions imposed on Comecon members in 1961 led to a barter-like system: the Comecon member states became specialized in producing only specific goods and became less capable of producing others, thus creating mutually dependent relationships. Wine was produced in the Soviet republics of Georgia, Moldova and Ukraine while satellite states like Bulgaria, Hungary, and, to a lesser extent, Romania also produced significant quantities (Romania produced wine but it exported only a small fraction, as is still the case today). Moldova maintained and increased its wine industry throughout almost the entire Soviet period.

In addition, as an agricultural region Moldova was responsible for producing fresh and processed vegetables and fruit for consumption in Soviet households. One unusual consequence of Moldova's agrarian specialization was the fact that secret departments operated on its territory producing food for the Soviet space programme. To this end, the Institute for Nutrition at the Soviet Academy of Science in Chișinău had a section for sublimated food for cosmonauts. Not only were dry fruit bars produced here, but also a wine for cosmonauts called *Sănătate* (English, 'Health') in a Transnistrian winery later called 'Buket Moldavii'. This wine was created in 1976 at the request of the Primary Design Bureau and the Experimental Machine-building Plant from Korolev, or 'Star City', by the then USSR Academy of Science's Institute for Nutrition in Chișinău.[12]

Everyday wines have also been enjoyed by cosmonauts, according to a widely circulated tale in publications and marketing texts in Moldova: it is the story of Yuri Gagarin, the Russian cosmonaut and first man in space, who in 1966 visited the underground cellars in Cricova, a winery close to Chișinău. He was known to periodically enjoy a good drinking session, and on this occasion he spent two days in the Cricova cellars – saying, after coming out, that it was 'easier to leave the Earth to fly into space than to leave the wine cellars in Cricova'. A photo of Gagarin during that visit hangs on the walls of the cellars to this day. The modernization of Moldovan winemaking thus came about not only through the industrialization of the country's plantations and wineries but also through this modernist project of space flight. Among my interlocutors, it was not only academics who brought up this connection between Moldovan wine and space technology but also two workers in Purcari who were old enough to remember, as children or adolescents, the successes of the USSR in space from the 1960s onwards. Unlike the case of the Serbian peasants who questioned the ideology of progress and the expenditure on space programmes while on the Earth poverty and economic hardship remained un-eradicated,[13] my Moldovan interlocutors felt part of the progress by being the ones who had made a small, liquid contribution to the cosmic life of the Soviet Union.

Back on Moldovan land, these export products varied in quality from high to less fine. 'Russia was big, and it was swallowing everything' is how a Chișinău university professor and oenologist, Veaceslav, put it; the all-accepting Russian market was often cited as the main reason why winemakers in Moldova or in other East-European countries were not very concerned about improving quality in the sense of how it was understood in Western winemaking countries. Much of the wine that Moldova was sending all over the USSR was the rather infamous *kriplionîi* (from the Russian Креплёное вино, meaning 'fortified wine'); these were fortified, sweet, white or red wines that emphasized strength rather than taste. Hungary was exporting a similar type of wine to the Soviet Union: wine that was considered the lowest quality that the country produced (Liddell 2003: 18). However, the question of the quality of wine in the former socialist countries is debated. First, producing large quantities of wine does not exclude quality, as Jung (2016) shows in her ethnography of Bulgarian winemaking. Second, although the command economy was demanding supplies for large markets – such that large quantities were produced – quality was not actually absent to the extent that Western consumerist discourses claimed when they dismissed socialist products as inferior (Walker and Manning 2013).

If the discourse that conceptualizes quantity and quality in wine as mutually exclusive properties has to a certain extent been deflated, there are other aspects of Soviet Moldovan winemaking that my interlocutors invoked as contributing to reducing the quality of wines. In these discussions with wine scholars and technical staff in the Purcari Winery who had been active during the Soviet years, there was ambivalence over how Soviet practices were usually addressed. On the one hand, they acknowledged the scientific and productive advances that viticulture and winemaking had made during these years with pride and satisfaction – referring to invention patents, technological advances and continuous striving to make a better product. On the other hand, they remarked that most of the wine produced was 'economic wine', as one interlocutor called it, intended to be affordable for everyone with a taste that did not vary too much, and that the speeding up of viticultural practices to keep production flowing had actually prevented the wines from reaching their full potential. In the latter case, this was because of the focus on fulfilling the Soviet five-year plans with their high production numbers, which led to workers striving to meet them regardless of the quality of the output. Because of this dynamic, young vineyards were favoured during the Soviet decades because they produced large quantities of grapes[14] – as opposed to the older vines, which produced fewer grapes but of better quality. Finally, the Soviet Moldovan wine industry made low profits as most of the wine produced from its vineyards was exported in bulk by train to other Soviet republics such as Ukraine, to Moscow or as far as Barnaul in the Altai region to be bottled –

with less than half being bottled in Moldova itself.[15] This structure of production, which favoured export and dependence on non-local technological facilities, made circulation of the commodity easier but at the same time created vulnerability. While most of the commercially produced wine was exported, Moldovans consumed wine made at home from vineyards planted on small private plots or from grapes stolen or otherwise obtained from collective farms. Yearly batches of 500–800 litres sufficed for a household. The consumption of alcohol became a problem in the Soviet Union under Gorbachev, creating one of the greatest challenges to industrial and household winemakers alike.

Gorbachev's 'dry law' – referred to most frequently by my interlocutors as the *ukaz*, from the Russian указ ('decree') – required 75,000 hectares of Moldovan vineyards to be grubbed up.[16] This was at a time when alcohol consumption in the USSR, mostly in Russia, had risen constantly from the 1950s to the 1980s. By the last decade of socialism, alcohol consumption was seen as 'a major cause of death, absenteeism, and low labour productivity in the Soviet Union' (Bhattacharya, Gathmann and Miller 2013: 237). The 'dry law' of 1985 was meant to reduce the state's production and sale of alcohol and eliminate the production of homemade alcohol ('moonshine' or Russian *samogon*), including wine (Nemtsov 1998: 1501). The campaign was successful to a certain extent, reducing the production of state alcohol and its consumption by more than half, but the attempt to control 'illegal' *samogon* production was not a success, reflected in the number prosecuted for its production doubling each year between 1985 and 1987. In October 1988, the law was officially repealed by the Central Committee of the Communist Party of the Soviet Union (Nemtsov 1998: 1502).

In Moldovan villages, groups of volunteers organized in brigades (popularly called *drujinas*) helped the police enforce the *ukaz*. This was more successful in some villages than in others. In the Suvorov *raion*, the administrative unit to which Purcari belonged under the Soviet Union, the Party's publications write that neighbouring villages to Purcari were quite successful in the 'fight against alcoholism' but other villages with wine factories such as Talmaza, to the north of Purcari, resisted the order to uproot their vines.[17]

A former food scientist at the Institute for Nutrition of the Soviet Academy of Science in Chișinău, Alecsandr (87 years old) recalled the years of Gorbachev's 'dry law' as a painful experience. Alecsandr was the father of one of my interlocutors, Masha, a tourism worker from Odessa. She introduced me to him on one of her trips from Odessa to Chișinău, where her father still lived (she had also been born there, but had moved to Ukraine with her husband). Masha knew that her father was involved in research relevant to the wine industry and that he also had direct experience as a food researcher during the years of the *ukaz*. He had worked at the Institute, which had two main departments, 'Winemaking' and 'Food Preservation', for thirty-five years. He was employed in the latter department. In 1985, in order to save some of the grapevines that were going to be grubbed up, Alecsandr, together with other researchers at the Institute for Nutrition, gathered a million tonnes of wine grapes from all over the country and put them to uses other than alcohol production. The head of department decided to process the fruit into 'grape puree', used as a sweetener. Alecsandr recounted that it was 'made from *Isabella*[18] and was beautiful, tasty and smelled nice'. He added: 'They put it in *zefir*,[19] marmalade, instead of sugar. Then we started to work with confectioneries producing sweets with this puree. ... And now it's all ruined.' The Institute for Nutrition has been reorganized in the post-Soviet period – its range of activities being reduced considerably, as in the case of other wine-related research institutions in the country.

'Talking about Money'

I heard my interlocutors in Purcari and Chișinău repeatedly use the expression 'people started talking about money' to refer to socio-economic relations after the fall of socialism. The dissolution of the USSR brought the wine industry in Moldova into temporary disarray. The wineries in the country either started working intermittently or closed down entirely. After independence, Moldovan agriculture suffered challenges from the weather, the depletion of winemaking equipment and disruptions to trade relations with CIS states (King 2000). After decollectivization was carried out in the early 2000s, the former collective-farm (*kolkhoz*) structure was reproduced under the name of 'association' (Heintz 2008: 7). The collapse of formal structures in Eastern Europe in the early 1990s led to an intensification of informal processes (see Creed 1998: 217).

At the Purcari Winery, the first few years after independence meant intermittent work, the processing and bottling sections having been leased temporarily to a Romanian wine producer. Most state wineries were privatized in the late 1990s or early 2000s – Purcari, for example, in 2003. It was the economic situation in the first decade of independence that led to this decrease in wine production. The early 1990s brought liberal economic reforms as in the rest of the former Eastern Bloc, the so-called 'transition policies' to a market economy, which were supported by the World Bank, the International Monetary Fund (IMF) and the European Bank for Reconstruction and Development. I draw on Moldovan sociologist Petru Negură's timeline of economic transformation in post-Soviet

Moldova, split into three phases. First, price liberalization was implemented in 1991–92, which led to rampant inflation of 1,670% in 1992 and 2,706% in 1993. During these years, poverty also grew as Moldovans' savings lost their value. In 1993, with help from the IMF, a national currency was created, the Moldovan leu (MDL). This was the second phase, that of monetary stabilization, between 1993 and 1997, when people started saving in MDL. During this period, Moldova's external debt grew considerably and the 1998 Russian financial crisis also deepened the Moldovan crisis.

The third phase, which took off only after 1997 (although it started slowly in 1994), was privatization. Until 1998, most arable land kept the structure of the old farms. Only after the adoption of the National Land Programme in 1998 did land reform accelerate. The slow pace of decollectivization was related to the opposition of the Agrarian Party, which was in power from 1992 until 1997, and there was also resistance from agricultural workers who did not want to dissolve the collective and state farms (Negură 2016). By the end of 2000, around a thousand state and collective farms had been redistributed to a million peasants, the sole recipients being former collective-farm workers because the *kolkhozy* had been collectively owned by the workers during the Soviet years (see Hann 2003b). The newly privatized land was split into three million plots of around half a hectare each, and each person received on average three of these fragmented plots (Spoor and Izman 2009: 104–5). Agricultural goods and land were slower to be privatized than other property, like houses. Once implemented, privatization was followed by a decrease in agricultural production – especially as the old *sovkhozy* and *kolkhozy* were frequently torn down and pillaged (Negură 2016).

Some of the redistributed land has been bought up by companies or entrepreneurs, initially at low prices. Spoor (2012) and Spoor and Izman (2009) showed that overall in the country it was not profitable for farmers to sell their land, because this turned them from former owners into workers in a country where rural poverty grew as a result of the post-Soviet land reform (Spoor 2009). In Purcari, present-day workers in the winery sold plots to the newly privatized winery at the beginning of the 2000s or to other associations. However, every household kept some land for its own subsistence agriculture and grapevines – resulting in a 'bi-modal or dual farm structure' (Spoor 2012: 185) after the land reform, with large farm enterprises and small peasant farms as the dominant types.

In the context of the socio-economic hardship of these years, the Moldovan Communist Party came to power in 2001, voted in by a majority of citizens profoundly disillusioned with the political structures at that time and wishing a return to the sense of stability they had enjoyed in the past when Moldova was in the USSR. Under post-Soviet communist rule, national identity was cultivated by evoking memories of a mythical time, and wine was entangled in this story that emphasized the long history of winemaking by Moldovans and implied an inextricable link between Moldovan identity and Moldovan wine. Rituals such as 'honouring the wine' (Romanian, *a cinsti vinul*) were evoked to support this revival (Bîrlădeanu 2013), and the wine industry was given the status of a protected industry. It was also at this time that a 'National Wine Day' was instituted, a festival in which virtually all wineries in Moldova present their wines to the wider public. On 19 April 2002, the Moldovan Parliament issued a decree stating that National Wine Day would be celebrated annually on the second Sunday in October in the Great National Assembly Square in Chișinău.[20] It has been celebrated in Moldova in October every year since 2003.

At the same time a national strategy was put together for the development of the wine sector in the following two decades: 2002 to 2020. The post-Soviet Communist government's strategy was to develop and maintain target markets as follows: 'the basic markets for wine product exports at the moment and in the near future will be the CIS countries, especially the Russian Federation, Ukraine, Belarus, Kazakhstan (70–80 percent), the countries of Europe and of America – 10–15 percent'.[21] Some of the directives of the strategy were carried out until 2006 by providing subsidies for the planting of specific grape varieties or the development of private wineries. After the 2006 Russian embargo, these actions were stopped and, for a couple of years, new grapevine plantations were mainly made of table grape varieties.

I opened this chapter with the events of March 2006, which were to bring about an important shift in the wine sector as a whole. Retrospectively, my interlocutors in the sector were somewhat hesitant when talking about this period and the 2006 ban: while the ban was politically motivated and the wines exported to Russia were not just poor-quality ones, people close to the sector admitted that some of them were either fake or of very low quality – and even that most of the wines produced for the Russian market were only of average quality at best. A professor at the Technical University in Chișinău said that it was a mystery to him why Russia chose to justify its ban without foundation, claiming that there were toxic substances in the wine. It would have been simpler and actually more truthful to have blamed the faulty organoleptic characteristic of the wines.[22] This person recalled that he had often travelled to Moscow on business trips and felt ashamed when, together with his students, he was testing the quality of wines coming from Moldova. Nevertheless, the trade in wine was thriving and winemakers were able to make 'quick money' – that is, enjoying substantial returns for periods of two to three years, whereas in the wine field investments normally have a much longer return time.

Until 2006, more than half of the wine produced countrywide was exported in bulk because of the lack of bottling lines (this was especially the case in the 1990s), but also because this entailed less risk and guaranteed large volume sales.[23] The country was exporting two to three times more wine than its vineyard area could produce according to the estimates of several interlocutors from the wine sector. Statistics on Moldova's vineyard area and the volume of harvested grapes were not available on the OIV website despite Moldova occupying the twelfth to sixteenth position in the world for the volume of wine it has produced in the last two decades. Avoiding publishing figures for the vineyard area until 2005–6 made the fake wine trade easier, as it then became more difficult to calculate the total quantity of wine produced.

My interlocutors in the sector framed these issues, first, as being abetted by the Russian owners of some Moldovan wineries, and second, as known to and tolerated by the Russian authorities. According to these interlocutors, these adulterated wines were less important in the decision to stop Moldovan wine sales in Russia than was President Voronin's refusal to sign the Kozak Memorandum regarding the federalization of Moldova that had been proposed by Russia. The memorandum advocated the de facto reunification of Moldova with Transnistria, together with Russian troops maintaining a presence on Moldovan territory until 2020. Although after this refusal Moldova lost most of its access to its main export market of Russia and was confronted with overproduction and a resulting decline in wine sales, interlocutors representing the industry usually interpreted the 2006 ban as a painful but necessary blow forcing a switch from 'the planned economy to the market economy', while the prospect of exporting to the EU market, which they saw as more trustworthy, seemed very attractive.

Despite the obvious hardship experienced by Moldovans, soon after the 2006 ban – in a personal discussion with Veaceslav, the researcher at the Moldovan Institute of Vine and Wine – Russia's chief sanitary inspector Onishchenko commented that 'Moldova should build me a monument at some point for stopping what you were producing; until Moldova publishes [figures for] vineyard areas [and] improve hygienic conditions in the wineries, until you prove the traceability of the products, you will not get back into the market'. However, a second large-scale round of economic sanctions in 2013 was also justified on quality grounds – the presence of phthalates in wine – although most voices in the media and the sector claim that it was linked to the signing of an Association Agreement between Moldova and the EU in June 2013. It therefore resembled to a certain extent the alleged cause of the 2006 ban, which was seen as being linked to the Moldovan president's rejection of Russia's federalization memorandum, and was therefore also political – albeit even more so because the problems with the fake or adulterated wine had almost been eliminated by 2013, as I detail in the next section.

Quality through Crises

I will now take a closer look at the changes within the wine sector that followed the 2006 ban – changes that sought to address some of the old problems. What did the post-2006 period mean for the way in which the Moldovan wine industry understood quality? A central aspect of the shift to diversify markets in postsocialist wine-producing countries has been the move from an economy of quantity to an economy of quality (Jung 2016; Walker and Manning 2013; Hann 2004) or to adopt more concepts from the EU wine regulation regimes rather than local ones (Smith and Grasseni 2020). Traditional markets had been lost, but before trying to access new markets the reputation of Moldovan winemaking had to be repaired.[24] Private and public actors active in the Moldovan wine sector joined forces with international institutions offering financial support in order to reorganize the sector. New institutions and new production practices were the focus of a reform that was implemented in the aftermath of the embargoes (Lazăr 2010). Winemakers continued to seek export markets, but unprecedented efforts were also made to increase the domestic market.

As some projects remained suspended after the 2006 shock, Moldova-Vin, the old state agency that had been steering the wine sector towards eastern markets, was closed in December 2009, its responsibilities being taken over by the Ministry of Agriculture in 2010. It was only with the founding of the National Office for Vine and Wine (ONVV) in September 2013 that a specialized institution to manage winemaking came again into existence. The ONVV has been a crucial actor in the reform of the wine industry, being responsible for implementing state policies; changing the previous strategy of the sector, which was focused on markets in Russia and other CIS states; and developing programmes for new target markets in the EU. The ONVV is an institution with public–private partnership, funded half by private wineries and half by the Moldovan Finance Ministry. The funds are administered through the Vine and Wine Fund, also created in 2013. This development fund has been added to the Moldovan Vine and Wine Law–60–70% of it to be used to promote wine on both the domestic and export markets, the rest of the funding to be allocated for other research projects in wineries. After the Fund was created, that part of the money that was supposed to come from the state was delayed for several years. There have been other financial support that the ONVV receives and they come from 'strategic partners' such as the US Agency for International Development (USAID) and other foreign organizations that support several industries in the country. For example, USAID has been working with the Moldovan wine industry since 2005. Within the USAID project, this industry category falls under the 'socioeconomic development' programme, which aims to 'help low income states to manage their resources better'. It offers technical and financial assistance, USAID money being non-refundable. The priorities of the programme have been viticulture and winemaking development through technology transfer and staff training, as well as 'certain lobby functions, [defending] the interests of the sector, in legal actions, with ... customs'[25] or the gradual introduction of new quality management systems.

Especially the introduction of the Protected Geographical Indication (PGI) scheme was a change of paradigm in relation to quality traceability. At the time of my fieldwork, there were four Moldovan Viticulture Geographical Regions recognized at the EU level and forty wines with PGI were being produced, making up 10% of the volume of production (ONVV 2017); one Protected Designation of Origin (PDO) was planned for the region of Purcari. Quality control in many winemaking regions is principally done through systems of origin traceability such as PGI, PDO or Appellation d'Origine Contrôlée (AOC). Under European legislation, PGI is a less strict control-of-origin system than PDO, as PGI requires the product to prove a historical link to a territory and for at least one phase of its production to take place in that region; for PDO, all the processing and manufacturing needs to be carried out in that specific region. The explanation that many of my interlocutors gave for not developing PGIs or PDOs in Moldova until recently was, again, the context of the export market because the demand in Russia was for cheap and lower-quality wines, which discouraged the development of quality wines. In this way, local producers became comfortable with a lower standard of quality and did not bother so much with designations of origin or spelling out the local characteristics of their wines.

For the four wine regions in Moldova, the specialists working with the ONVV developed a list of the grapes that are best adapted to each region. The lists are dominated by French and Georgian varieties, and local varieties occupy only a fraction of Moldova's entire Moldovan vineyard area (10% local grapes, 17% Caucasian, 73% international). This small proportion of indigenous varieties was seen as an issue by winemakers and marketeers

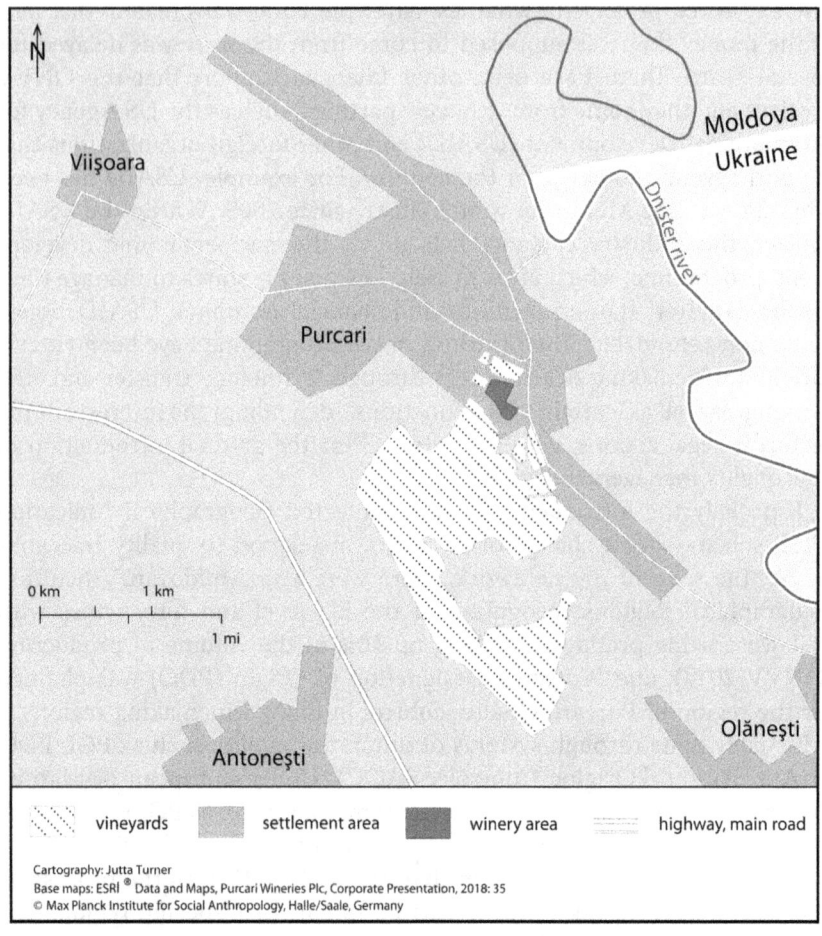

Map 1.1. Map of Purcari village. © Max Planck Institute for Social Anthropology, Halle/Saale, Germany.

alike, as indigenous grape varieties are the frontrunners of virtually every wine region in the so-called 'Old World' wine countries. The director of the ONVV, Gheorghe Arpentin, explained Moldova's position as of the present day:

> The export markets for wine have changed: the international varieties do not present a substantial interest as compared to indigenous varieties. The international market is convinced that the grapes that grew up in a region for a long time are the best ones. And Moldova, apart from having a low number of grapes of its own, also has a small surface of indigenous vines: from almost 100 000 hectares vineyards, 1% is planted with local grapes. (Chișinău, July 2017)

Local grape varieties are the so-called 'signature grapes' that have some uniqueness in the market (Karpik 2010). Moldovan winemakers cannot easily compete with the numbers of indigenous grape varieties used for wine in Italy (just under four hundred) or Georgia (over three hundred): in 2017, only six indigenous varieties could be presented as Moldovan[26] – all overlapping with grapes on Romania's list of indigenous varieties.

Interlocutors from different contexts repeatedly asked why Moldova should need to craft a 'new individuality' on the global market with its grapes. If it makes good wine, then that should be enough – and other artifices, such as the emphasis on the taste of wine made from local grapes, should be unnecessary. Although not completely counterintuitive, a hyper-detailed description of individual varieties and then of specific plots is, as Demossier (2018) argues, an invention of recent decades when winemakers have had to cope with the internationalization of the wine market. 'The definition of taste attached to specific grapes is the key to the globalisation of the wine market and to the positioning of wines in international settings of food consumption' (Demossier 2018: 116–17). While Moldova can claim the local expression of international grape varieties to be 'unique', the most intriguing category of 'local taste' comes from indigenous varieties. Globalization, in order to work, needs to hinge on 'local materialities' (Gille 2016: 113) and local sets of values.

Purcari Winery, my main research site, has been at the forefront of many of these recent changes in the wine sector, whether as a financial contributor or by adopting new production or marketing practices. I turn now to presenting its history and its relationship with external actors (markets, empires, rulers or grapes) – in order to show how the transformations of the last two centuries have been played out in the relations of production and the livelihoods of the winemakers and workers in this winemaking village.

Purcari, the Village and the Winery

As one leaves Chișinău and takes the national road south towards Anenii Noi, signs announcing the number of kilometres to Purcari Winery start to appear at the side of the road. The village of Purcari (Map 1.1) is situated 120 km from Chișinău. Seven kilometres before the winery, one takes a left turn off the national highway and drives along a smaller road with vineyards on one side and orchards on the other. This leads to Viișoara, the village neighbouring Purcari, the second (and last) village in the Purcari commune, with a population of approximately three hundred. The next village one arrives at is Purcari itself, with a population of around 2,300

Figure 1.1. The Purcari castle seen from the Dniester bank at sunset, June 2017. © Daniela Ana.

and spreading along the right bank of the Dniester valley on a south-facing slope. Nothing seems out of the ordinary for a Dniester-valley village – small, charming houses, some of them painted in a typical blue lime wash, with little vineyards, flower gardens, various fruit trees and stork nests on electricity pylons – until one arrives at the end of the village towards its other neighbour, Olănești. There, further into the valley, a castle appears in the background next to a large hill full of vineyards (Figure 1.1).

This is announced on a large banner as *Vinăria Purcari*, or 'Purcari Winery'. Here is 'the territory', as it is often called by its employees: a well-trimmed enclosure that contrasts with the rest of the village, where a factory, a number of cellars, a hotel with a restaurant, two ponds and a fruit-tree orchard make it clear that one has arrived at the destination depicted on billboards tens of kilometres away.

The winery is considered to be the oldest in the country – and part of its history, and that of the village over the last two centuries (Table 1.2), revolves around the presence of foreign colonists, mainly German, who settled in the region in the mid-nineteenth century.[27] These colonists are said to have been attracted to Purcari by the fact that the area was suitable

Table 1.2. Purcari (first attested in 1560), total population 1812–2014. © Daniela Ana.

Year	1812	1827	1897	1904	1930	1940	1950	1970**	1989**	1993	2004	2014
Population	380	860	1,519	1,690	2,597	3,708	1,631*	2,776	2,482	2,609	2,253	2,368

Sources: Leașco, Smolin and Smolina (2009), primarii.casata.md (accessed 22 June 2021) and the 2014 census of the Republic of Moldova.

Notes:
* This decrease was the result of Second World War deaths, and deportations in 1941 and 1949.
** Between 1965 and 1985, the hamlet of Gamza was merged with Purcari village; a dozen households comprising Gamza were located on the hill where the Purcari Winery vineyards are today.

for winemaking, as several documents from the nineteenth century maintain. In an entry on 'Bessarabian wines' in the Russian *Brockhaus and Efron Encyclopaedic Dictionary* (1891), details are given about winemaking in Bessarabia, describing the practices of peasant winemakers and the grapes they cultivate in a rather depreciative tone. The Dictionary states that wines from Bessarabia were rarely very good due to a lack of technology and knowledge among peasants,[28] but we also learn that 'the most convincing are Shaba [Shabo], Purcari and Răscăieți, which indeed should be considered the best wines in the whole of Bessarabia' (Brockhaus and Efron 1891: 614). Another document, a report published by the International Jury for the 1900 Exposition Universelle in Paris, also singled Purcari out as an especially prestigious producer. Of all the wine regions in the Russian Empire, the document, which described the wine regions in the countries participating in the exhibition, applauded Bessarabia for its wines from the same region – the bank of the Dniester in the Purcari area – as well as the Swiss colony of Shabo, today in Ukraine. It also attributed the superiority of their wines to the experts of the day: colonists from the West – namely, the Swiss at Shabo and the Germans and French at Purcari. They are described as having knowledge and resources that the locals lacked: 'foreign colonists, the owners of the vineyards of Akkerman, extend their plantations and improve the system of wine production. Several colonist cultivators from Shabo move on the banks of Dniester, at Purcari and Leontievo, and bring celebrity to these localities through an exquisite wine obtained from peasant grapevines: *pomararanegra (serexia, malvoisie rouge)*'[29] (Paris Exposition Universelle, 1900: 345). An Agricultural School was founded in Purcari in 1893 by the Russian state in order to 'intensify and perfect production in vineyards and orchards'.[30]

The hill where today's vineyards are laid out has been put to the same use for at least two hundred years, but ownership changed in this time period. An important figure in the history of the winery and of the village was Iacov Ghermanson, a German colonist who in 1852 rented the Purcari estate, which at that time belonged to a monastery known as Căpriana (Bacalov 2013). Ghermanson, followed by his children, managed the winery at Purcari until the end of the nineteenth century. Brunovschi, another *boyar* (member of the feudal aristocracy), managed the vineyards until 1908. Up until the interwar years of the twentieth century, the winery developed and expanded along with other wineries in Bessarabia in order to supply the large Tsarist Russian market with wine.[31]

After 1918, when Moldova was under Romanian rule, properties larger than 100 hectares were expropriated, including the monastery that owned the Purcari estate. Now more peasants came into possession of land: from the territory of the Purcari Agriculture School, 150 hectares were split into plots of 3.5 hectares and given to First World War veterans. Small-scale agriculture continued to be practised in the village during these early decades of the twentieth century, but not to the same extent as during Tsarist rule.

However, it was difficult to find first hand data about production in Purcari as many local archives are said to have been burned by accident during the Second World War. One person whom villagers recommended as the 'encyclopaedia of Purcari' in the absence of official papers was the former mayor, Constantin Stețenco, born in 1925. He worked as an agricultural engineer at the Purcari *sovkhoz* and had held office as a mayor in the 1960s. When I went on a visit to talk to him, he took a pile of notebooks from his house with historical data about the village that he had saved from his father, 'who had an exceptional memory', and brought it out on to the balcony where I was waiting. Constantin shared details of land ownership, vineyard areas, ecology and the socio-economic situation in late nineteenth to mid-twentieth century Purcari from his father's notes. According to these files, winemaking stalled in Purcari during the interwar years:

> In the twenty-two years under Romanian administration, Purcari did not prosper. There was stagnation due to a lack of markets, and there was no demand for agricultural produce. High taxes did not allow peasants to develop their households. The unjust politics of the government, like the high taxes for education, did not give peasants an opportunity to educate their children in superior institutions. With this method of administration, only two sons of peasants graduated from a superior institution during Romanian rule, becoming engineers (Nistor and Ghizelea) … the agricultural tax, communal tax, wine excise, bonded work and unpaid work all slowed down household development. (Purcari, March 2017)

The interwar stagnation was followed by destruction during the Second World War. From 1940 onwards, the Purcari area was a front line in the war, and most peasant households were affected, with their gardens and vineyards being completely destroyed. A period of slow restoration of vineyards and other agricultural practices followed, and the village winery was also transformed towards the end of the Second World War. In 1944, the Purcari estate was taken under state ownership and started to function as a standalone state factory.[32] From 1944 until 1970, the arable lands in Purcari were organized in the 'Biruința' *kolkhoz*, with a surface of 470 hectares, and a *sovkhoz*, with a little over 300 hectares. Between 1970 and 1975, the two units were merged into a grand 'state household' (Romanian, *gospodărie de stat*) called the 'Purcari *sovkhoz* factory' (Romanian *sovhozul-fabrică* Purcari), subsuming around 800 hectares of land used for producing wine grapes, vegetables, fruits, grain, and raising cattle, pigs and fowl. The Purcari *sovkhoz* factory presided over this local association of factories. In total, seven villages were active in the association aside from Purcari: its neighbours Răscăieți, Tudora, Carahasani, Popeasca, Volintiri and Talmaza. The employees were peasant-workers who owned livestock and practised small-scale agriculture around their houses on personal plots of land.

During this time, dry wines were produced at Purcari, Tudora and Răscăieți – namely, Negru de Purcari,[33] still one of Moldova's best-known wines to this day, which was bottled at Purcari. However, the fortified wine that typified Soviet consumption habits was also an important part of the production in the association's wineries: *Moldavskii belii krepkii*,[34] known colloquially as 'MBK', was made from white grapes, and *Moldavskii krepkii rozov*,[35] or 'MKR', was a rosé (both similar to the aforementioned *kriplionîi*). These wines were never bottled and were made from grape wine to which distilled alcohol was added. The wine was usually bottled outside Moldova (across the USSR in one of the Moldovan bottling plants mentioned earlier in this chapter). Bottles were reused, being picked up from collecting points and sent to a 'washing line'. At Purcari, the 'Roșu', 'Negru' and 'Purpuriu' wines were bottled locally or in Chișinău, while the rest of the wine made there was sold in bulk to various Soviet republics.

Between 1990 and 1991, winery production in Purcari was reduced drastically, and the little work that employees carried out was not paid or was paid only in wine. Over the following years, wine continued to be produced – but, again, in smaller quantities than in the previous decade. While the winery had 658 hectares of producing vineyards in 1990, in 1996 it had only 197 hectares. The wine made was sold both domestically and abroad until 2002. In the early 2000s, immediately before privatization, the factory was officially working but practically almost unused. One of the older oenologists in Moldova recalled one of his visits to the winery in an interview:

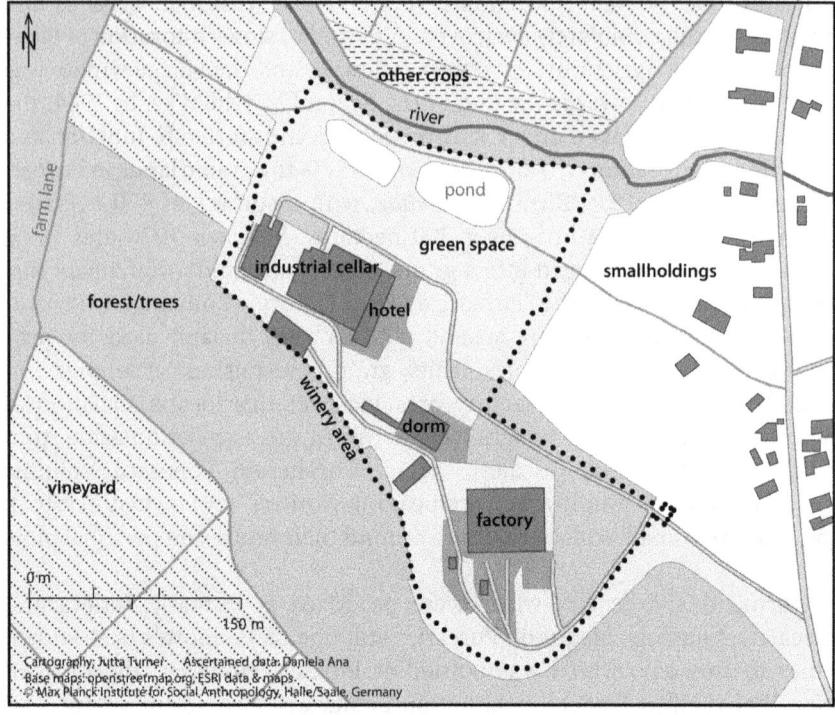

Map 1.2. The Purcari Winery perimeter. © Max Planck Institute for Social Anthropology, Halle/Saale, Germany.

> I remember that in 2001 I was part of an inspection commission to the Purcari wine factory, to prepare it for the harvest. It was mid-September and basically in the old factory's laboratory no one was working, at the processing section there was a trailer tractor with two tonnes of grapes in it, and mid-way in the harvest season they had processed a hundred tonnes of grapes.[36] Practically the factory was not working. It had neither grapes nor workers. All I saw were two women in the lab eating walnuts, and I asked them 'What are you doing?' They said they had nothing to do. This was the situation in the Purcari Winery in 2001. (Chișinău, December 2016)

The Purcari Winery was privatized in 2003, and it was now the main provider of jobs in the area. Some of the communal land has been privatized with the endorsement of a former *sovkhoz* engineer, who later became mayor of the village. Some of the older workers considered the privatization of this land somewhat abusive. One of the workers put it this way: 'Now the boyars came. Until 2003, there was more grazing land, and in the village there were around 1,500 cows. People did not have jobs then, so they had more animals'. The pasture land in the village is made up of meadows located on the right bank of the Dniester valley, together with a smaller area on the hills towards Olănești. In the past, there was a greater number of animals in the village and also a larger area of grazing land. There was thus resentment expressed at the fact that many villagers had become more dependent on wage labour and had fewer opportunities to carry out subsistence agriculture. But the privatization of the land was seen more positively by other villagers, as some celebrated the commercialization of the village economy through the expansion of viticulture (cf. Creed 1998: 47 on Bulgaria).

The former collective-farm workers received a share of the collectivized land through the national decollectivization programme. The plot that each former worker received was of around 1.5 hectares; these plots are colloquially called *cotă* (pl. *cote*), meaning 'quota'. Yet more than mere legal ownership, it is the power to control or access land that is important (Hann 2003a: 24). This was also noticeable in Purcari after workers received land – as, following independence, the technical equipment needed to work the land was lost, stolen or simply deteriorated, and only a few could afford to buy new machinery later on. Some farmers chose to work the land themselves without mechanized help, but it was usually unprofitable to do so given the low value of agricultural products and the small size of the areas cultivated by households.

Some sub-lease the land to companies or the so-called 'land leaders' (Romanian, *lideri de pământ*) in exchange for agricultural products.[37] Household gardens and *sote* have been other modes of providing household means of subsistence.[38] By cultivating these small plots, important quantities of vegetables, greens and fruit for household consumption are harvested. In gardens, in addition to grapevines, tomatoes, cucumbers, chickpeas, potatoes, peppers, garlic, onions, berries, cherries, melons, watermelons, pumpkins and fava beans are usually grown. A household in Purcari normally relies on wage labour, animals and vegetables produced for home consumption; sales of homemade products; remittances; and state benefits (pensions or unemployment benefits). Consuming products from one's own garden has both economic and social significance, as later chapters in the book will show.

The vineyard land (Map 1.2) is owned by the Purcari Group, which has mixed ownership. When the winery was privatized in 2003, the main owner was Victor Bostan, a Moldovan oenologist. He is the CEO of the company, and at the start of the business he had the largest share in the winery. The World Bank lent the winery five million dollars in support in 2005, after which the American–Ukrainian private-equity fund manager Horizon Capital invested eighteen million dollars so that the winery could buy the best equipment, and also to support the construction of a tourist centre.

Working capital is owned by the company, with some exceptions in the case of vineyard technical equipment: at harvest time, the company subcontracts tasks to people who own a tractor – most of which date back to the Soviet years, having been acquired when the *kolkhozy* and *sovkhozy* were dissolved. The winery owns six tractors and subcontracts eight more old ones at harvest, when fourteen are needed daily. The subcontracted tractors are usually provided by people in Purcari or a neighbouring village, as some former collective workers received technical equipment instead of land through the decollectivization process.[39] This is necessary during the busy harvest period because it would be too expensive for the winery to own a large number of tractors, which are used only for a limited period. Also, supplying hoes, secateurs, protective gloves, shoes and clothing are the responsibility of the agricultural workers, not of the winery. Inside the factory, some protective equipment is provided by the company, some is supplied by the workers and what is left is altogether ignored by everyone.

As it was organized during my fieldwork, Purcari Winery was an industrial production unit. Production of a single commodity was carried out in different sub-departments of the winery, which separated the production process into distinct parts carried out by different workers, who, in an annual cycle, repeated the same operations – such as filtering, oxygenating and decanting – over and over again.[40] The workers in Purcari Winery are mainly villagers from Purcari and Viișoara, the neighbouring village, but a few also come from other areas close to Purcari commune. Specialized and technical staff come almost exclusively from outside Purcari and live in the 'employees' dorm' during the working week, returning to Chișinău or other urban centres at weekends. The ages of the workers ranged from seventeen to sixty-six, and therefore included both teenagers and retired workers. The factory had around forty permanent workers all year round, in addition to eight to ten administrative staff. The vineyards require some 120 employees permanently year-round to work its 260 hectares (vineyards require care for nine to ten months of the year, from winter pruning until the harvest) and the number doubles during the harvest, being supplemented by seasonal workers. While the majority of workers in the factory come from Purcari, the vineyards have workers from six different villages – all grouped into 'brigades', according to village of residence. Each brigade has two or three *zvino*, or teams. The reason the workers are separated according to village of origin is that transportation is provided by the winery, each village being visited once a day by bus or an old truck. The salaries that vineyard workers receive through this seasonal work average

The Making of an Export Industry ➤ 53

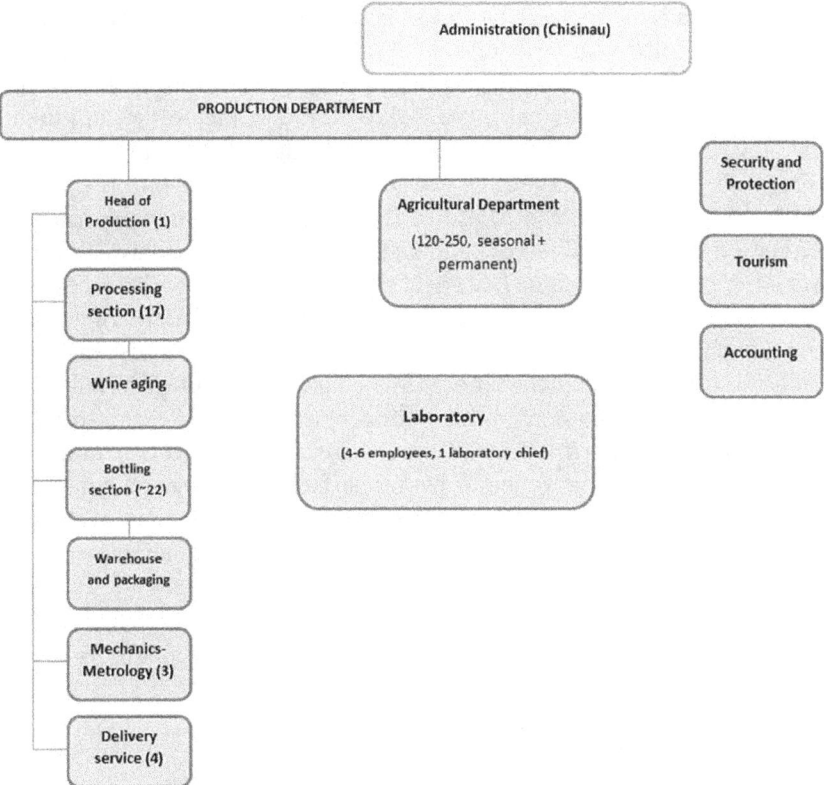

Figure 1.2. Organization chart of the production department at Purcari (2017). © Daniela Ana.

200 MDL a day or around 100 euro per month. Salaries for the factory manual workers varied from 2,700 MDL (ca. 130 euros), the smallest, to 5–6,000 MDL (ca. 270–300 euros). White-collar workers did not disclose their salaries, but they vary between 300 and 600 euros. Figure 1.2 provides a simplified organizational chart of the winery's employees excluding those in the Chișinău office, who work on marketing, finance, etc., for the whole Purcari Group.

Conclusion

The aim of this 'journey' through different regimes of sociopolitical organization was to show how winemaking has developed in the Moldovan space, with a focus on the Purcari community, but also to show how wine production and circulation have been encouraged, supported, attacked and mobilized – both voluntarily and involuntarily – by Moldova's centuries-old main trading partner, Russia. Winemaking has been practised for millennia on the territory of present-day Moldova, including the Purcari region, yet the modern development of the craft and its industrialization were closely linked to Moldova's relations of dependence with the Tsarist Empire and, later, the Soviet Union. The Moldovan wine industry has been configured by historical factors and access to resources, archival research providing insights into how historical political and economic forces have influenced Moldovan wine quality and prestige by deconstructing an image of quality and value as being intrinsic to a region, a grape variety or a specific technology. Furthermore, this chapter has shown how historical, political and socio-economic contingencies have converged to create the commodities and imaginaries that are exchanged and consumed. By attending to this convergence of historical factors, the chapter has shed light on the power relations that led to and constitute the present value of Moldovan terroirs on the market and in consumers' imaginaries.

Notes

1. *Viticultura și vinificația în Moldova*, No. 5/2006.
2. *Viticultura și vinificația în Moldova*, No. 2/2006, pp 30.
3. Gurin, A. *Viticultura și vinificația în Moldova*, No.6/2006, pp 20.
4. The territory annexed to the Russian Empire in 1812 included the part between rivers Dniester and Prut, and southern Bessarabia or Budjak.
5. Grapevine cultivation has a long history in Eurasia, with the earliest evidence of domesticated grapes and winemaking coming from the sixth and fifth millennia BC. In Moldova, the earliest records of cultivated grape come from the Cucuteni-Trypillia culture in the first half of the fifth millennium BC in the form of compression fossils and the seeds of cultivated grapes (Iarovoi 2007). Further material remains from winemaking come from the ninth–eighth centuries BC, when Greek colonies flourished around the Black Sea. By the seventh century BC, the Greek settlements at Tyras (today's Bilgorod-Dnestrovskyi) and other ports at the Black Sea intensified trade with diverse goods, including wine. In antiquity, the tribes populating the present-day territory of Moldova from the Bronze Age until the early Middle Ages also made wine, as Strabo's testimonies of the reign of the Dacian king Burebista (82–44 BC) show. When the Romans colonized Dacia in 105–106 AD, local wine production continued (Gusti et al. 1940). Later, during the late Middle Ages when the Principality of Moldova was emerging, winemaking developed and was exported to the Polish court until the Ottoman occupation of 1538. Dimitrie Cantemir writes in *Descriptio Moldaviae* (1716) that before the Ottoman occupation vineyards flourished in Moldova, but afterwards many were neglected or destroyed during wars. The wine that was still produced was seen as a

source of income, as the Ottomans gathered taxes on it (Gunyon 1971). Also, some table grape varieties were introduced during that period.
6. While in 1837 in Bessarabia there were 13,000 *desyatins* (see note 7, below) of vineyards, producing one million *vedro* (1 *vedro*=10 litres), in 1900 the vineyard surface was 74,000 *desyatins* producing fifteen million *vedro*. Most of the wine was sold across the Russian Empire (*Viticultura și vinificația în Moldova* No.5 [17]/2008).
7. An archaic land measurement used in Tsarist Russia; one *desyatina* equals 1.09 hectares.
8. 'Hybrid direct producers' or, shortened, 'hybrid' grapes are a cross between *Vitis vinifera*, the common grapevine, and other species of vines, which are usually more resistant to disease than *V. vinifera*, but also produce less aromatic grapes. Criticism of the quality of hybrid grape wines has lasted until the present: only a very low number of hybrid grapes are approved for cultivation within the European Union. Most hybrids were outlawed by the European Commission in 1979 because of the 'gustatory defects' of the wine produced from these grapes but in the recent years there is a revival of interest in them. This is due mainly to climatic changes – hybrid grapes are more resilient to climate change and they require less pesticide and fungicide.
9. At the beginning of the twentieth century, modernization in winemaking in the region meant homogenizing grapevine plantations, favouring the varieties that were best adapted to each region, respecting origin names and delimiting surfaces for each recognized region, keeping a registry of vine surfaces and varieties to ensure traceability, working with specialized staff (Romanian *pepinierist viticol*; Gusti et al. 1940: 412), organizing credits for winemakers, providing insurance against natural disasters, taxing, state price controls to ensure that retailers did not raise prices, protecting national production by taxing wine imports and reducing taxes on viticultural and winemaking equipment.
10. There were 60,000 hectares planted with hybrids and 30,000 hectares with 'noble' grapes in Bessarabia (Dölkers 1974: 107). However, the Romanian government decided on 29 February 1928 to ban the multiplication of hybrid-grape plantations and the trade with hybrid wine.
11. Source: *Pomicultura, Viticultura și Vinificația Moldovei*, No. 19 (228) 1984, 16/19. Production figures from the Soviet period might not be exact because they are part of the 'virtual economy' of the USSR, in which false production and profit indexes were frequently published (cf. Humphrey 1983; Visser and Kalb 2010).
12. At the time of my fieldwork, this wine, renamed *Kosmiceskoe bal'zam* ('Cosmic balsam'), was still being produced. The balsam contained high-quality wine, concentrated grape juice and a medicinal-plant infusion. This secret food production 'on the side' also provided an important boost for food research and exports of foodstuffs (http://www.buketmoldavii.md/kosmichesky/en/, accessed 8 August 2021).
13. See Rajković (2019) for a fascinating blog post about the view of the peasants in Yugoslavia in relation to the Apollo 8 spaceflight in 1968, questioning the issue of 'technocapitalist space' and asking where the share of the peasants was in the story of the (capitalist) conquering of space: 'Tell me Mile, my cosmic brother/Is there any salad on the moon?' (Rajković 2019).

14. In the 1990s, after the fall of the USSR, only 4% of Moldovan winegrowing surfaces were over twenty-five years old, while in France the figure was 47% (Mircea Blajinu, 'Vinul de poamă rară [The wine made of serexia]', *Literatura și Arta*, 8–9 May 1991.
15. Ibid.
16. 'Visuri franceze in viile Moldovei si vinurile Moldave in piata mondiala. Probleme din economia viticola din Moldova [French dreams in Moldovan vineyards and Moldovan wines on the world market. Problems of the viticultural economy in Moldova]', *Vocea Poporului*, 13 March 1990.
17. *Moldova Suverană*, 1985.
18. Isabella is a direct-producing hybrid grape of American origin, which is still common in Moldovan gardens and used in producing homemade wine.
19. Zefir was a Russian/Soviet confectionery popular in the former Soviet republics made from fruit puree, egg white, sugar and a gelling agent.
20. The 2003 festival programme stated that the aim of National Wine Day was to 'increase the culture of wine-making, to consolidate national traditions in the most important parts of the national economy, to maintain the prestige of the wines, as well as to attract foreign tourists to Moldova with interesting cultural programs' (Bîrlădeanu 2013: 48).
21. Paragraph 2 in Government Decision No. 1313/2002.
22. Organoleptic refers to the characteristics of a food or drink as experienced through the senses: taste, smell, touch and sight.
23. Many wineries sold almost their entire production in bulk: one winery in the Căușeni district, which owned 1,500 hectares of vineyards, exported 90% of its wine in bulk in 2005 (*Viticultura și vinificația în Moldova*, No.6/2006).
24. It is important to keep in mind that scandals and controversies around fake and hazardous wines are not confined to the world outside the more prestigious wine regions; more or less recent and notorious wine scandals happened, for example, in Italy in 2008, in the so-called 'Brunello affair', in which it was discovered that large quantities of adulterated wine had been exported as the expensive Brunello di Montalcino. Another such case was the diethylene glycol wine scandal from 1985, in which Austrian wines mixed with antifreeze liquid were found on German shelves.
25. Interview with G. Arpentin, ONVV director (July 2017, Chișinău).
26. Excluding those selected in the laboratory. The 2017 Plant Varieties Catalogue of the Republic of Moldova enlists 92 registered grape varieties across the country. Table grapes are white – 23, red – 12; for wine: white – 29, red – 13; for food – 8; seedless – 7. The catalogue gives the year of inclusion in the catalogue and the year of reintroduction, when applicable. While for other cultivated plants the years are quite recent (in the 2000s), for grapes they go back as early as 1946 – the year when the first catalogue was issued.
27. Colonists started arriving in Bessarabia in 1814, but it was only in the mid-nineteenth century that they began to be successful in their communities, which were mainly agricultural and viticultural (Schmidt 2012).
28. The full quote: 'The picture of vinification is extremely desolate and it is not difficult to understand why. Vinification requires much knowledge, requires enough

money to run the household, and the Bessarabian has neither one nor the other. He's got only feet, with which he crushes the grapes, he has an old barrel, in which he pours the dirty must and still not fermented. With such rudimentary instruments, sure, you cannot make a good wine and you are still surprised that in some regions Bessarabians, only with their own forces, are making a good wine, if they succeed.' (Brockhaus and Efron 1891: 615, author's translation)

29. All references to the local grape variety *Rară Neagră*.
30. None of the villagers graduated from this school, however, as a Romanian agricultural counsellor deplored it in an official report. Camera Agricolă Cetatea Albă, File 46, 'Exproprierea stufăriilor com. Purcari 1922–1929'.
31. Production dwindled after the discovery of phylloxera in 1883 (Bittner 2015). Until the beginning of the twentieth century, the Purcari estate lost half its vineyards because of this pest (Bacalov 2013).
32. Moldovan National Library Archive, 'Steaua Roșie', 1974.
33. This was somewhat different from the version of Negru de Purcari produced today; the initial recipe was: 'Cabernet, Rară Neagră, with Merlot, Malbec added, and sometimes Saperavi', differing from its present composition of Cabernet, Saperavi and Rară Neagră grapes. SAPCA, *Dosar* 8, 12 August 1939, Coresp. financiar-contabilă (1939–1940).
34. Rus. Молдавский белый крепкий, or 'Moldovan strong white'.
35. Rus. Молдавский крепкий розов, or 'Moldovan strong rosé'.
36. At the time of my fieldwork, a hundred tonnes of grapes were being processed every day (the average was seventy tonnes per day from mid-September until the end of November).
37. The yearly payment that an owner receives from a 'land leader' for cultivating his/her 1.2–1.5 hectares plot is 580 kg of agricultural produce: 300 kg wheat, 200 kg corn, 80 kg sunflower seeds. These are processed by the household to make bread, polenta and oil respectively.
38. The number of households in Purcari was 801 in 2014 (household size in 2014: 1 person – 179; 2 persons – 207; 3 persons – 136; 4 persons – 145; 5 persons and over – 134) Source: primarii.casata.md, accessed 3 February 2019.

    One *sotă* consists of 100 square metres, and is land given by a city hall to villagers at their request in exchange for a small yearly rent of around 50 MDL per thirty sote, or one MDL per sota per year. *Sote* are usually requested by those who did not receive a *cotă*. Usually, ten *sote* are leased to each family member.
39. Individuals who worked on collective farms received village-specific sizes of land plots comprising arable land, orchards and vineyards (Cash 2014: 167), as well as state employees.
40. Except for the processing section, which is only open during the harvest, and the vineyards, where a sequence of different operations are carried out in the annual cycle.

2

The Value of Homemade Wine
Debates on Heritage

> Homemade wine is more useful for the human organism. If you go to work in the field and the sun strikes you and then you come home and drink a hundred grams of red wine, the organism gains strength so it can fight the radiation it received. This one from the factory, you drink it but ... look, if you drink one litre of homemade wine you will never feel sick.
>
> —Maria, 61-year-old Purcari worker

In early October on a day during the harvest, at the beginning of my fieldwork, the workers were taken back to the factory from the vineyard due to persistent rain. As harvesting was no longer possible on that day, the Purcari brigade was asked to check the grapes going to the press for shrivelled berries, non-uniformly ripe bunches or leaves. After lunch, we finished work entirely because even the grape checking, which was carried out under cover but outside the factory, was made impossible by the rain turning heavier. Being wet and cold, we went inside a glass hut where the grapes were weighed and the sugar level measured next to the main factory building. Here, the head of production brought us a bucket of red mulled wine made in the factory and two cups to warm ourselves up before going home. This sparked a wave of remarks about wine among the workers, which turned into an exchange about wine styles: the majority claimed the wine was tasteless, and one even implied that the factory administration was trying to fool them with this 'treat'. When the turn to drink came round to one of the women in the team, she declined it because she did not like factory-produced wine at all. Another worker said he was not drinking it because he knew 'how these wines were made' and that 'the stomach or the liver will hurt after three glasses or so'. The rest were also critical but not as categorical: they said they preferred homemade wine because 'it came in one piece [Romanian, *vine într-o bucată*] – you know what you're putting in it', referring to the wine produced in almost every household in the village.

This was one of the first in a long series of discussions about factory wine versus homemade wine that I held with workers and villagers in Purcari, which revealed the importance of the domestic counterpart of the commodity I had set out to study – namely, industrial wine. I follow the distinction between commercial (or industrial) wine and homemade wine as my interlocutors conceptualize it; the former – referred to most frequently as 'factory wine' (Romanian, *vin de fabrică*) or 'production wine' (*vin în producere*) – is wine that is produced in designated industrial or small-scale production units, following production processes that are standardized on obtaining homogeneity of taste. It ends up on the market either bottled or in bulk. Homemade is wine produced in the household as 'house wine' (Romanian, *vin de casă*)[1] made from grapes grown in the home vineyard, on plots varying in size from a few tens of square metres to over a hectare. This wine is mainly intended for household consumption, but it can also be offered for sale or given as payment in exchange for labour (see Cash 2015a, 2015b). In the post-Soviet period, homemade wine has remained a prominent aspect of rural life in Moldova and it has also strongly influenced the dynamic of the domestic wine market, becoming a controversial topic among people in the industry and wine scholars. In their turn, peasants saw industrial wine as a less safe product, and the majority still prefer homemade wine above any other type of alcohol. One study (Magenta Consulting 2016) showed that 72% of Moldovans preferred homemade wine. This is not to claim that the entirety of Moldovan society was divided strictly along lines of preferences between homemade and industrial wine, only that the two positions have resulted in polarities that have an impact on the respective structures of the domestic and export markets. In 2016, Moldovans consumed only 9% of the total volume of commercial wine production, the rest being exported (ONVV 2017).

This dynamic has disturbed the wine industry's plans to enlarge the domestic market share for commercial wine, especially since sector reforms were introduced in the late 2010s. In this chapter, I explore how, starting with the intensification of commercial campaigns to popularize wines in Moldova, the encounter between household winemaking and the modernizing ambitions of the wine industry have resulted in increasing friction between local and global notions of sociality, value and the taste of wine. Perhaps in the present ethnography this friction corresponds most closely to the difference between 'value' and 'values' in anthropology (Eiss and Pedersen 2002; Graeber 2013: 224), making this concept sensitive to use because value has a more exact (economic) definition and values can be anything of importance in one's life. These frictions have been intensified for several reasons: rural winemakers cherish household winemaking as an artisanal practice (i.e. they control the production process, and most of their product is not alienated from them) as opposed to commercial wine, a commodity that, throughout most of the twentieth century, has been intended for export. Homemade is associated with a way of life, and the preference for the taste of homemade wine is frequently stressed. It normally has a lower alcohol content (7–8%) and is held not to cause hangovers or headaches due to its 'natural' content: a fermented grape juice kept in oak or plastic barrels, without filtration or preservatives, although the latter are not always excluded.[2]

The sections that follow provide insights into the socio-economic meaning of homemade wine, through which a better understanding of the politics of wine in Moldova will hopefully be acquired. The voices of the peasant winemakers are followed by those of the wine industry, which depicts homemade wine as either desirable if it can be properly commodified (i.e. standardized so that it does not stay in an 'informal' market, which makes it impossible to predict sales for the domestic market) or as a backward activity that simply inebriates the countryside while harming the wine industry proper. Finally, I look at wine events in Chişinău that actively promote bottled wine in order to increase domestic sales.

Homemade Wine: Subsistence, Sociality and Ecology

Commercial wine has been produced in many villages in Moldova for centuries, but homemade wine has been produced for much longer by the majority of people inhabiting the countryside. After 1812, at the beginning of Tsarist rule in Bessarabia, each colonist family in the province was given an area of 1.5 *desyatina* for a vineyard in their backyard (Schmidt 2012) while during the period of Romanian rule (1918–40), private property was retained (Gusti et al. 1940) and household winemaking continued despite measures against overproduction taken periodically by the state. In the Soviet period, although most of the land was collectivized, households retained private plots of land that were cultivated and had great importance for the USSR's industrialization project (Humphrey 1983: 269; Mincyte 2009: 32). In Moldova, household winemaking was a fairly constant and unchallenged activity except in the years following the introduction of Gorbachev's 'dry law' in 1985.

Rural history has dealt with the dichotomous categories of capitalist agriculture and household production, debating whether one type will vanquish the other. The collapse of the 'household mode of production' has been prophesied, but it actually survives in many societies around the globe (Pratt 1994) and has been shown to play a crucial role in the reproduction of socialism as well (Hann 1980: 8; Humphrey 1983; Mincyte 2009). In Moldova, household production is in many cases a sine qua non for the survival of households alongside wages. In the post-Soviet period, household winemaking continued and came to be at times one of the coping strategies of households that were dependent on low wages. It became of major importance both for its use and its symbolic value in the community, and it was often referred to by the peasants as being an ecological, biological or 'clean' product. As the production of homemade wine by Moldovan households has been continuous across recent history, the socio-economic transformations of the post-Soviet period did not revive household winemaking as such, but in this new context the practice took on new meanings such as supplementing household income and resisting the industrialization of food production.

Ecological and organic agriculture have received a great deal of attention from anthropologists – with the most recent wave looking at alternative food networks, usually driven by manifest political considerations (Pratt 2007; Guthman 2007; Vankeerberghen 2012; Pratt and Luetchford 2014; Aistara 2018). Wine has its place in the food realm, and studies of natural or organic wine have shown that producers and consumers alike have similar concerns as in the case of food, and are joining 'natural wine' or organic-wine movements around the globe as a result (Black 2013; Black and Ulin 2013; Demossier 2018).[3] Mincyte (2011: 102) pointed out that the informal postsocialist food economy can be different from the alternative-food networks of North America or Western Europe. Although alternative-food networks reach important numbers of urban consumers and have less problematic environmental impact than their industrial-scale counterparts, organic production can, because of small-sized plots or lack of mechanization, be seen by policymakers and business as an obstacle to the development of competitive agriculture.

Anthropological research on organic agriculture in the European Union has shown that when new regulations for organic agriculture were enforced, only a simpler version of what 'organic' meant to farmers remained in the legal definition. Although such legislation is typically concerned with agricultural inputs, organic farmers in Belgium, for example, saw organic agriculture as a way of life and a 'means of expressing certain concerns and values' (Vankeerberghen 2012: 5). They became frustrated because, under the new legislation, one could produce organically 'without living organically': the 'new' organic products were only slightly different from the conventional ones in that they excluded some chemical inputs. Living organically meant producing food in a way that protects environmental values and expresses certain concerns. The parallel that I draw with my case study stems from the manner in which peasant winemakers in Moldova talk about and defend their wines and from their grounds for rejecting industrial food and wine. Household winemaking is a rural practice that is somewhat devalued in the state-level discourse, but it serves large numbers of rural and urban consumers with ecological and cheap products. My research in Purcari shows that a preference for homemade wine and an enthusiasm for household winemaking reflect more than just a desire to consume cheaply and 'healthily'; in addition, producers see themselves as expressing a diversity of social values and meanings in making and consuming their own wine.

Making Wine at Home

Although vineyards and winemaking are mainly the responsibility of the men in the household, as is the case in other wine-producing regions (see Ulin 1996; Lem 1999, 2002), I heard often enough of activities in the vineyards being done by women at men's request. In general, both women and men know how to make wine, and where the household is run by a single woman she takes charge of the whole process (see also Cash 2015a).

Viticulture at home follows the main vineyard operations as in industrial vineyards, but it importantly excludes the spraying of synthetic chemical pesticides and fertilizers and mechanical weeding. All operations are done manually: they start from winter pruning, dry trellising, hoeing, green trellising, and shoot and foliage thinning, and culminate in the harvesting from late August until November, depending on the grape variety and the weather each year. Starting in early spring, the vines are sprayed with a copper-sulphate and chalk solution every two to three weeks. After harvesting, different grape varieties are crushed together; typically, a grape variety is crushed and fermented separately only when making white wine. Most villagers believe that what gives the wine its quality in the first place is the grape variety. Second comes *păsudul*, or the vessel (from the Russian Посуда– dishes, tableware). The wine is put in a barrel that needs to be properly cleaned, otherwise the quality of the wine will be spoiled in a matter of weeks. A wooden barrel can be used for decades, but the winemaker needs to make sure it is cleaned every year. Washing the barrel is done with hot water in which walnut-tree leaves have been scalded as they have disinfectant properties. This water is poured into the barrel while it is still hot and is left inside it for one to two hours. During this time, the interior of the barrel is cleaned and the staves take up their proper shape (Romanian, *se umflă doagele*).

The grapes are crushed with a manual crusher. The notable difference from factory wine is that the stems are almost always kept in with the grapes, while at the factory they are removed. The grape juice is then poured into the clean barrel until it is not quite full, because the fermenting grape juice needs some empty space inside the vessel. Then the grape juice is stirred twice a day for a week. The wine is then sampled to see if its taste 'is going in a good direction'; if so, it is left to 'rest' for one day and then released into a basin, then poured into a different barrel and kept in the cellar for a week. Some parts of this sequence may vary from household to household, but these are the main steps that have been followed by peasant winemakers for centuries, as villagers repeatedly explained to me ('this is what I learned from my father/grandfather').

Highly relevant not only for the peasants' taste preferences and habits but also for the wine market, as I elaborate later in the chapter, indigenous varieties of grape are more common in home vineyards than in factory ones. At the same time, in Moldovan peasant vineyards there are still large numbers of hybrid direct producers and European (mostly French) vines. However, local varieties are more suitable for the villagers because they need low or no chemical inputs, while French varieties are more sensitive to both frost and disease. People keep different grape varieties in the garden, but the most common are French varieties such as Cabernet Sauvignon, Merlot or Chasselas, Georgian varieties like Saperavi and Rkatsiteli, and indigenous varieties like Fetească Neagră or Albă, Rară Neagră or Moldova.[4] Grapevine replanting is usually done by buying stocks from the market, which can come from different countries, predominantly Moldova, Ukraine, Romania or France. Those who cannot afford to buy stocks, or who have been cheated in the town market and want to make sure that what they plant is what they wanted, propagate their own vines either through cuttings[5] or, but much less frequently, through seeds.

In household winemaking, planting and caring for vines and processing methods are thus fairly straightforward activities, which do not depend on any advanced technical equipment. It is enough to have the land, the vine and the knowledge, a good cellar and a proper barrel – and to be an artisanal winemaker for the benefit of one's own household and social circle.

Good *Gospodari* Make Good Wine

Almost every household in Purcari that I visited welcomed guests with homemade wine. Wine is used as a symbol for welcoming guests and for honouring them (Romanian, *cinstire* or *a face cinste*) and, by the same token, demonstrating one's craftsmanship (cf. Bîrlădeanu 2013 and Cash 2015a). The habit of making a wish or offering a brief toast at every sip is rarely skipped and, unlike the slow drinking of wine that is encouraged at wine tastings, here the habit is to down the whole glass in one gulp. Cristiana (a 27-year-old vineyard worker) and Marius (a 35-year-old public-sector worker) are a couple in Purcari whom I often visited. On my first visit in mid-October 2016, after a day's harvesting, Marius invited me to have a glass of wine with him before dinner was ready, so he brought a 1.5-litre plastic bottle of homemade wine and a small glass – one of the 100-millilitre shot glasses that people in the area use for wine. Marius poured one glass, wished us well and expressed the hope for future moments like this; he drank first and then, from the same glass, gave me my share.[6] The wine was made from the grapes grown in their own vineyard, but it was not expressing its full potential because it was not 'quiet' (Romanian, *liniștit*) enough yet. Nevertheless, he was very proud of his wine: their house is located on the top of a hill facing south-east, and he considered his vineyard and those of a few other neighbours to be the best in the area as they did not have black soil but more clay and sand, which grapevines prefer. Later on, when I spent the 2017 Christmas at their house,[7] the wine was supposed to be at its best, and Marius compared it with Negru de Purcari (the dry wine with high acidity and fine tannins, dominated by black fruit, lavender and oak flavours produced in the factory) although this suggests a contradiction: Marius evaluated the taste of the homemade wine as superior to the factory wine, but in order to prove the quality of his own production he compared it with Moldova's wine superstar.

Cristiana, his wife, interpreted the preference for their 'soft', 'easy to drink' and 'tasty'[8] homemade wine as a matter of habit as well as of economic constraints: 'perhaps people would prefer the Purcari [factory] wine, sometimes people finish their homemade wine, but they go to a neighbour to buy, there is no way one goes to the factory.[9] Because it is expensive, it is not for the pockets of our villagers.' In 2016–17, a bottle of Purcari wine cost from 80 MDL to 400 MDL (4 to 20 euros) and in the village it could be purchased from the winery shop. The wages of the workers in the winery during the same period ranged from 1,500 MDL to 5,000 MDL a month (75 to 250 euros).

For Cristiana personally, it was important that she knew how to make homemade wine and what ingredients should be used in the process. She felt that everyone in the village tried to make wine because it brought them pleasure and joy, and it created occasions – usually for the men in the household – to demonstrate their knowledge and their openness: 'Also, I know that men like to brag. My husband, for example, when a guest comes in to our house – even if he does not want to drink, maybe he has a headache – Marius does not accept refusal, the guest should taste at least a sip of wine, so that he can boast, look what a *gospodar* (English, 'householder, master of the house') I am and what a good-tasting wine I make.' Cristiana's depiction was quite direct and accurate, as entering a house in Purcari meant almost every time a round of compliments to the winemaker unless one had good reasons to decline getting drunk, such as driving, taking antibiotics or being severely ill. In this way, homemade wine became a social event (Douglas 1972: 65) encoded as a demonstration of craftsmanship.

The villagers also considered the period of time during which a household consumed its wine as saying much about the worth of a *gospodar*. For example, on a visit to Dumitru's and Victoria's home in the summer of 2017, Dumitru, a man in his late fifties, offered to show me his sixteen varieties of grape from a well-kept vineyard as I was taking a walk in his neighbour's garden. Dumitru took me to his vineyard and explained vine-caring routines and told me where his grapes came from, recognizing the varieties by looking at the leaves and the shapes of the green berries; he had a mixture of table and wine grapes that he was fermenting together. After this presentation, I thanked him and said, 'I hope that next time we meet we may even taste the product of these vines together. Goodbye!' To which Dumitru replied, 'Oh, but why don't you come in for a while so we can taste the wine; it's midsummer, the wine might not be at its best, but we'll have a glass'. Because it was the middle of the summer, I forgot about the ambition of the good householder in Moldovan villages to spread a batch of wine over a year. Distributing consumption of the batch of homemade wine over one year, in order to have 'from wine to wine', is a badge of merit of good householders in the Moldovan countryside, meaning that they drink moderately but also that they prove their skills by making a wine that does not spoil throughout the year and can still be drunk or sold in the village. The expression for this practice in Romanian is *a avea de la vin la vin* – literally, 'to have from wine to wine'. Still at Dumitru's we went inside the summer kitchen, where his wife quickly laid a cloth on the table and set out a plate with goat's cheese, tomatoes and cucumbers from their own production, and tasted the wine. Dumitru excused again the lesser quality: the wine we were drinking had been made ten months earlier, so for homemade purposes this was an old wine. However, without any additives, and with only Dumitru's knowledge of winemaking, this previous-year's wine was balanced, full-bodied and, to my taste, still suitable for honouring guests.

Homemade wine is also a means of payment for day workers and a more affordable option than bottled wine or other commercial alcohol. Paying in wine has been studied by Cash (2015a) in Răscăieți, a village neighbouring Purcari. She showed a side of the rural economy that is so deeply connected to the wine ritual that the economy itself becomes part of that ritual. If payment in wine is an economic, rational action in the first place, the fact that it contributes to the image of a household in the village means that it transcends purely economic interests. For example, villagers in Purcari could just buy wine when, for whatever reason, they did not have grapes that year, but they actually choose to buy grapes to make wine themselves. This was the case for Iurii (a 57-year-old electrician), who, by mistake, had

had his entire vineyard uprooted by the helpers that he had hired several years before we met. His initial intention had been to renew first one half of the vines and a few years later the other half. He replanted the vineyard but could not harvest grapes from it for the first four years, so he bought them from others because 'going to someone's house and not finding any wine, you kind of look at them as if ... since I remember, my parents were buying grapes, but you cannot not have your wine'. When guests come over, going to the village store to buy alcohol is embarrassing. 'Maybe some can do without this wine, but I believe, like our forefathers, that if you have wine you are a good *gospodar*. What kind of *gospodar* can you be if you don't have your own homemade wine?' Like that of Marius and Dumitru above, Iurii's relationship with wine is deeper than the ultimate act of consumption. It is a framework in which knowledge and sociality – the recognition of being a good 'householder' – figure prominently in how hospitality is expressed. Using homemade wine when people are visiting is thus doubly coded, demonstrating respect towards the guest as well as confirming the host as a worthy and integrated member of the community. How and which wine is served is an important code in the village community, as it has a specific meaning in the order of social relations and consumption.

Sustainability and Safety

One warm early June afternoon in 2017, I visited Costea, who invited me to his vineyard to try his wine. We stood at an improvised table, an upside-down plastic barrel on which a plastic 2-litre bottle of wine had been placed. Costea was one of the *gospodari* to whom villagers referred most often when they wanted to direct me to 'good winemakers' (other than themselves) in Purcari. A former *sovkhoz* combine-driver, Costea launched a small private business after 1991 with a village shop and had increased his business to three shops at the time of my fieldwork. He owned 0.44 hectares of vineyards in total and made wine from all the grapes he harvested, of which half was sold in the village and half was for household consumption by Costea and his wife, their three adult children and a person helping them with household chores. The wine was sold in bulk, in recycled plastic bottles; it was never labelled even when it was sold in his shops. A litre of homemade wine cost between 2 and 4 MDL (10–20 eurocents).

Costea said he adhered to his parents' belief that the proportion between those who liked to drink and those who liked to make wine was in balance and was 'given by nature; the grape feeds itself, it pays itself off. We grow the grape, it makes the wine, we also offer wine for sale, and for work. Wine finds its place for any use, whatever you do. If your wine tastes good every year, people do not forget.' He considered that winemaking was 'a virus of the whole district' because the hills had the right degree of slope and there was enough sun, the conditions that should give the best grapes. He presented his wine as 'a product close to "bio"' because he had chosen the right varieties for his area, which meant that they needed minimal chemical inputs. He carried out bi-weekly spraying with copper sulphate, limestone water and sulphur against diseases such as oidium and mildew. Like the other villagers, Costea had learned how to care for grapevines from his parents – and he stressed that the relationship with the vines in organic viticulture required more attention to detail than in its conventional viticulture. Costea pointed to a young grapevine that was visibly sick, the berries being minuscule and shrivelled up, although the stem was developed. From just looking at it he could not know for sure which disease it was, but it was most probably caused by his 'careless spraying': when spraying with copper sulphate, one has to spray every bit of the foliage and fruits otherwise they will not be protected from disease. Although it required more effort, his 'organic winegrowing' brought him rewards not only socially but also in terms of health and safety, as concern at the increased consumption of highly processed food was a common topic in the village:

> I am that kind of person who says that yes, now nature makes us use products that are not clean, but at least we, who are from the countryside, who can consume at least 70% of clean production (Romanian, *producție curată*), let's leave only 20–30% for purchased ones. A bird raised at home, a good wine, homemade bread – we have flour – we make different pies. ... in wine there are so many chemical elements that are useful, especially in red wine. The organism has to consume them. Wine is like a pill – you take one [glass] daily, as the doctor says, and it is useful. (June 2017, Purcari)

The 'cleanliness' or 'naturalness' of homemade wine was perhaps as important as the social component that winemaking craftsmanship brings to a *gospodar*. Commercial wine in most cases contains other substances besides what appears on the label, which is fermented grape juice and sulphites (Black 2013). The production process in a winery requires additional yeasts, refining agents and acidifiers. Consumers know this, and perhaps the awareness in Moldova is higher because, on the one hand, the number of wine factories in the Soviet period was very high and a large number of people were employed in the sector or had someone in the family working in a winery; on the other hand, the knowledge of how to make homemade wine is even more widespread: a process that people know and can control, and that in most cases is additive-free. Very rarely did villagers add sulphites (SO_2) to their own homemade wine to make sure the wine lasted more than a year without turning sour.

SO_2, or sulphur anhydride (Romanian, *anhidrid/ă* or reg. *anghidrid*) was one of the main points of contention among both rural and urban interlocutors when it came to wine. Indeed, people occasionally referred to *vin fără anghidrid* ('wine without anhydride') when talking about their own wine. After more months in the field and discussions on this topic, it seemed that *anghidrid* was as much a signifier for the preservative itself (SO_2) as it was for any other potential chemical additives. Why people settled on this particular additive in wine was a puzzle to me for a while, because other food products contain significantly higher amounts of this preservative. Moreover, professional winemakers and wine researchers defended its use and stressed it was not toxic. Vlad, the head of production at the factory, suggested that the obsession with SO_2 was related to 'the incompetence of the specialists carrying out [wine] processing in the past'. He also found the emphasis on SO_2 to be inconsistent, not only because of its presence in other foods but also because other materials added in the factory winemaking process could stir up just as much concern. Apparently, people knew that a few decades ago, during the Soviet period, winemakers who were insufficiently prepared abused the use of SO_2 'to cover their incompetence'. In order to protect a sloppy wine from going bad, they added some extra preservative: as Vlad put it, 'they added a bit more SO_2 so they could sleep well at night'. But at the time of my fieldwork, the rules were stricter and professional winemakers followed them without exception – so the reference to *anghidrid* was just a synecdoche for a factory winemaking process that was perceived as untraceable.

Peasant winemakers, who usually worked small vineyard plots of less than half a hectare, saw themselves as the continuators of local traditions, having knowledge that had been passed down from their parents or grandparents. The Purcari Winery's professional winemakers defined themselves through the long-term studies that they had carried out during the Soviet period or later, and the value stemmed from the proper training of well-prepared teachers at least as much as from their own experience. In the winery, given its size, more than one winemaker was taking decisions over alterations of grape juice. First, the woman leading the winery laboratory, Maia, was the oenologist who was based in the village for at least five days a week and managed all the laboratory activity. The tastings and wine-management decisions were shared with Vlad, who was also trained as an oenologist but who was employed as the head of production. The third 'essential oenologist' in Purcari was Victor, the Purcari Winery CEO who was also trained as an oenologist and who took part in the decisions regarding wine taste, procedures, blends and innovations. In his early fifties, Victor is represented in the media as a man of both oenological and business knowledge, being responsible for raising Purcari wine to its present value. Although he shared his time between Chișinău and Bucharest, he paid monthly visits to the winery in Purcari to carry out administrative and oenological work. On some of his visits, he was joined by the fourth pivotal oenologist for Purcari: the Italian 'flying winemaker', who helped his Moldovan colleagues with information about global trends in taste and suggested alterations to Purcari wine so as to get the best out of its terroir while keeping an eye on what sells.

Decisions and control over the production process that have been practised by industrial wineries both past and present intensified anxieties related to safety among peasant winemakers. The experience of a craft has been described elsewhere in terms of mastery, control and therapy (Makovicky 2020: 6) – but also as a curse of compulsion. The paradox here is that while companies and experts promise control and safety in their products, the sceptical consumers who want to keep making their products at home are aiming for the same things – namely, safety and control of the process of production. In the production process for homemade wine, the winemaker can fully trace the process of winemaking from the operations in the vineyard over the year, which culminate in the harvest, to the processing and storing of the grapes. This ensures that viticulture is ecological, and winemaking 'natural'. There is also a degree of control over taste. On the other hand, in the factory, a more detailed type of control is sought: quality standards in the vineyard, in the processing section, in the cellar, on the bottling line, etc. In this struggle for the supremacy of the expert notion of safety, the emphasis is placed on crafting forms of personhood that are compatible with a product and its image, as I develop in the following subsections.

Homemade Wine as Valueless Wine

Household winemaking in the Republic of Moldova is not clearly regulated from a legislative point of view. Only in 2017 were all vineyard owners in Moldova asked to register their vine areas and grape varieties in a national database called the Vineyard Register, so that all activity related to winemaking can be monitored by the state. The wine law was modified at the end of my fieldwork in 2017 to introduce several new rules for peasant winemakers: if they want to sell wine produced in the household, they have to pay taxes for vineyard areas, to sell the wine in authorized places and to have trade authorization and complete information on the bottle label. Regardless of the social, economic and symbolic importance of domestic wine in Moldova, many specialists look down on household winemaking as holding back the peasants themselves as well as the entire wine sector at this point. This approach of the elites to peasant winemaking is in line with records over the last two centuries. For example, Brockhaus and Efron (1891) described peasant wine in the Tsarist *guberniya* of Bessarabia as being of very poor quality and the viticulture techniques of the peasants as inferior, frequently being compared unfavourably with those of the vineyards of Bessarabia's nineteenth-century German and Swiss colonists. Moreover, in the twentieth century much of historical Bessarabia was making wine from hybrid direct-producer vines, considered a product of lower quality (Ciocanu 2015). Today the grapes and tools of the Moldovan peasant are still perceived as symptomatic of the country's poverty by many in the wine industry.

Among the voices that were most uncompromisingly critical of homemade wine was Veaceslav, a university professor in his mid-fifties and an important figure in the country's wine-research field. He has worked as a consultant to all the important wineries in Moldova throughout his career. The topic of homemade wine came up as we were talking about what 'socialist wine' meant in the past and today and what the Soviet legacy meant for Moldovan winemaking in the present. Veaceslav traced the attachment of Moldovans to homemade wine to practices during socialism: back then, wine was predominantly an 'economy class wine', and that has become a big problem for the sector in post-Soviet years, when many winemakers were still prioritizing price over quality.[10] This search for low-cost wine became the norm, and in parallel it led to what Veaceslav called 'something that is worse: when they make their own homemade wine … to avoid going to the supermarket after cheap wine'. Although Moldovan consumers can find cheap wine in supermarkets and in village shops (that is, they have the option to drink cheap industrial wine), this is a rather rare choice. Supermarkets provide cheap vodka and beer, but wine and *samagon* come normally from the household. This dynamic, in Veaceslav's opinion, was responsible for the very low consumption level of bottled wine in Moldova:

> And it is low not because Moldovans do not drink wine, it is low because Moldovans drink homemade wine. Every *gospodar* gets grapes in autumn. In makeshift conditions [Romanian, *în condiții de garaj*], in countryside conditions, in cellars, they make three to five hundred litres of wine for the family. And that is why they do not enter the circuit of bottled wines, … they buy do-it-yourself [Romanian, *propria confecție*]. And this is the biggest problem with the wine sector in Moldova: the lack of an internal market for wines. … No winemaking country has such a commercial balance between export and own consumption. Even Romania keeps 90% of its wines for domestic consumption. France has [a ratio of] 60–40%: it consumes 60%, it exports 40%. We consume a maximum of 10%, exporting 90%. Basically we do not have a domestic market [for bottled wine], and we depend on external markets; this is our tragedy. (Chișinău, December 2016)

A desirable domestic consumer, after successful educational initiatives, would be what Veaceslav saw in his daughter and her husband: the intelligent, curious buyer who takes time to analyse the different options that wineries put out on the market. These are people who engage with wine to 'enlarge their knowledge horizon', whereas the typical Moldovan consumer buys neither economy bottled wine nor premium wine but only wants 'homemade wine'. Veaceslav said he has been 'struggling with this issue for a long time', and in the mid-2000s he made a television show specifically with the aim of 'promoting wine culture'. The expression 'wine culture' means different things to different people; while peasants and the defenders of homemade wine as a form of cultural heritage include it in the 'wine culture' of the country, the critic refers only to non-domestic production – excluding 'popular taste' (Bourdieu 1984: 16) from 'culture'. The approach to 'wine culture' in Moldova is similar to that described by Jung (2013) in Bulgaria – that is, as 'lacking' – especially by the experts in the sector. In Veaceslav's view, Moldova should aim towards establishing a 'high culture':

> We tried to raise the [issue of] culture with scholars, university professors, academics, even medical doctors, we were trying to overcome the homemade wine problem [Romanian, '*încercam să depășim problema vinului de casă*']: [the claims] that homemade wine is more useful, that it does not contain sulfites, and so on. Every week we were filming in restaurants, factories, we had meetings with people. I did it for a year. ... people indeed understood that the anhydride that everyone feared was a myth that did not exist. We are talking about sanitary norms, which are very small; we use anhydride in normal limits. This is the struggle I have with those who consume wine in home conditions to this day ...why did I say that our traditions pull us back...if it weren't for these traditions we would have been somewhere else today. (Chișinău, December 2016)

Peasants, by being able to control part of the means of production and by themselves being competitors with commercial producers of reproductive plant materials, fertilizers and produce for their own consumption, slow down the encroachment of capitalist producers (Lewontin 1998: 76). This is why the aim of the industry is to integrate as many small producers as possible into the market. In 2009, Veaceslav carried out a study to prove his point regarding the damage that homemade-wine production was inflicting on the industrial-wine sector. He did not provide me with access to the report on the study, so in the following two paragraphs I refer to the numbers and the findings of this analysis that he shared with me during the interview. Homemade-wine production, or what Veaceslav called 'an underground wine industry', caused other problems besides obstructing the market for bottled wine: it did not pay taxes and it affected people's health. No clear data were collected on alcohol consumption per capita in Moldova because homemade wine and moonshine were not counted. Annual wine consumption in Moldova in 2016, for example, was 2.7 litres per person (Magenta Consulting 2016), but this figure did not include homemade wine. However, Veaceslav believed that the levels of liver disease in the country were high because of the very high consumption of homemade alcohol, which he linked to the fact that the state did not regulate its production. Based on his own data, Veaceslav calculated that 200,000 tonnes of homemade wine were produced annually in Moldova. That meant forty litres per capita – 'and that only in home, illegal conditions'; then one adds the officially declared alcohol consumption of wine, beer and spirits (thus, not including the homemade wine and moonshine), the result being that 'the conditions for alcoholism thrive'. Indeed, World Health Organization studies in Moldova revealed some of the highest rates of alcohol consumption in the world in the decades after independence. In 2010, the adult population consumed 18.22 litres of pure alcohol per capita (ranked first in the world), then 16.80 litres in 2013 (second place after Belarus) and 15.10 litres in 2015 (in third place after Lithuania and Belarus).[11] Such levels of alcohol consumption have resulted in a high incidence of chronic alcoholism in the country.

Although my observations of household winemaking in Purcari pointed to a more celebratory image, as the first part of this chapter showed, the darker dimensions of alcohol consumption – like addiction, related health issues and personal unreliability – were occasionally brought into discussion as well. Virtually the entire Moldovan countryside had been struggling for decades with poverty, massive outmigration and the unravelling of family ties, and precarity in social protection. Resorting to alcohol was common in disadvantaged communities, and sticking to domestic alcohol production and consumption was one of the coping strategies of dispossessed peasants and workers.

In relation to wine consumption, the issue and the solutions lie with the state and its policies in Veaceslav's opinion. Because vineyard areas were larger in the south of the country, people produced large quantities of grapes that could be sold only very cheaply. If the state bought an average of two tonnes of grapes, the peasant would earn 10,000 MDL (about 480 euros), a significant income for a Moldovan household. However, as this did not happen, the peasants transformed these grapes into wine and drank it, so that 'he [the peasant] does not earn anything, no money and no health'. Veaceslav's very firm position about the damage that homemade wine was doing to individuals, the community and the market point to a concern about value in both use and exchange terms. The use value of Moldovan homemade wine for the peasants lies not only in the beverage produced by grape fermentation but in the entire production and consumption processes. Less important for them is the marketization dimension: the rich web of meanings in the peasant community is rendered valueless in the view of the expert, for whom the value of a wine depends on its regulation and commoditization – producing wines that are safe (or generic) enough to be sold legally.

Finding Value in Heritage

More than ten months into my fieldwork, after discussions about homemade wine with wine specialists and peasants alike, two large camps emerged whose views seemed entirely predictable: most peasants cherished their homemade wine and the rituals that surround it while the experts criticized its high production volumes, its taste and its impact on the domestic market. Yet an encounter with the then-director of the ONVV, Gheorghe Arpentin (56 years old), an appreciated oenologist in Moldova, revealed a different position regarding homemade wine on the part of an official – namely, as a legitimate part of Moldovan culture and as heritage. Arpentin's appreciation of cultural products was based on 'field observations' in the villages, where he witnessed the dynamics that exist among peasant winemakers and tasted their products. He referred to homemade wine firstly as important economically: wine made in the household should be a source of income and potentially should protect grapevine biodiversity. Secondly, homemade wine had socio-symbolic value, being an artefact indicative of the villagers' skills and virtues and the taste of the place. Yet the difficult coexistence of the two modes of wine production does show that, once more, in integrating small producers into capitalist agriculture some of the social relations that are embodied in the commodity are destroyed (Lewontin 1998) in order to make it suitable for its purposes.

Gheorghe Arpentin was recommended to me many times by people working in the Moldovan wine sector as being the most knowledgeable person about Moldovan wine, past, present and future. Arpentin had over thirty years of experience in winemaking; had lived for a few years in France; and at the time of my fieldwork, besides directing the ONVV, he owned vineyards in the Purcari area – in the neighbouring village of Olănești. Although he represented the wine industry, his position was unlike that of the majority of his colleagues when it came to homemade wine. While he too believed that homemade wine could be a disadvantage for the industry, he argued that this did not have to be the case. If the peasant winemakers could be integrated into the market and the tourism sector, this could be a major advantage as consumption of strong spirits would fall. The idea of integrating the country's peasant winemakers into the market is no different from Veaceslav's solution, yet the manner in which Arpentin depicted them and their sociality showed a less firm division between 'modern' and peasant wine:

> They [peasant winemakers] are always isolated, everyone tells them they do bullshit [*sic*], that it's not good, but I think that's not right. There are some who make normal wine, and they ought to be helped. Let them become economic agents, at least to sell their wine in the region, in the district, in the village, each one with his barrel, to earn something. And the wine tourism…once we had a delegation of tourists from Europe, and they visited people's homes, they liked it more than going to a factory with a luxury hotel. Some appreciate this, so why not integrate them? If we say that they have bad wine, they hide and sell in miserable plastic bottles, but if we say 'come with us, look what you have to do to register' – because no one is registered in the Vineyard Register – and they are a big part of the puzzle that is missing. We [the ONVV] do not have the statistics to know what our potential is. We are thinking about how to integrate them, maybe not all of them, but when we go to the villages they do not have bad wines, and we can help them a bit to raise the quality. When you go to Georgia, they have a *qvevri* in the ground, but also the wineries.[12] Here, everyone does what they can. If they respect hygiene, let them even come with hybrids, maybe in time they will change. I don't see any other solution: you uproot the vine, and then what do you do? (Chișinău, July 2017)

Although one yearly contest for peasant winemakers is organized by the Chamber of Commerce in Chișinău, called the 'Golden Barrel' (Romanian, *Polobocul de aur*),[13] this event includes a few hundred winemakers across the whole country and is not widely representative. The systematic mapping and understanding of the diverse methods and wines in the Moldovan countryside was necessary but still missed in 2017. Gheorghe continued by suggesting that making niche wines from either local or very old vines would make it possible for peasant winemakers to add value to their wines. First, this could be done by pushing for policies that protect the diversity of local varieties of grapes – which have nevertheless declined consistently over the last century, leaving only a handful of indigenous grape varieties in Moldovan vineyards. But old vineyards still existed in the country that could be used in this way. Another idea for a niche wine market, he suggested, was wines made from vineyards more than thirty-five years old. Gheorghe recalled that he once attended an exhibition of wines from South Africa in London made of grapevines that were at least forty years old. This impressed and saddened him at the same time, knowing that in the Moldovan countryside there were many vineyards like that, some of them even made of indigenous varieties, but there was no incentive for the peasants to keep them. As they grow old, the vines produce fewer and fewer grapes. Even if they are of better quality, peasants are discouraged from keeping them because they never get a good price for these grapes –

so uprooting old vines to replace them with younger, more productive ones is the usual response.

This was one of the reasons why Gheorghe saw domestic winemaking as a potential biodiversity haven, with an emotional twist besides the quality of the wine: 'the emotional side itself sells, it is different when you hear the vine is eighty years old and they show you a photograph of it'. The initiatives that Gheorghe envisaged resembled the origin-labelled products combined with heritage-based tourism that lie at the heart of the European Union's concept of 'multifunctionality', an initiative protecting heritage and traditions associated with agricultural products (Bowen and De Master 2011: 73). Essentially this means that in order to be saved, nature first needs to be conventionalized or 'tamed' (Aistara 2018: 139). Similarly, pointing to the fact that species are evaluated based on their potential for commodification, Dempsey (2016: 2) argues that 'biodiversity … must be made relevant to the Ministry of Finance for it to survive', and this is precisely how the value of grape varieties is settled. The initiative to assess which categories of grapevines are valuable in export markets, identify the vineyards and then create an institutional or bureaucratic framework through which peasant winemakers can access niche markets would be costly, which made Gheorghe pessimistic because it would be the responsibility of the state to evaluate and conserve its agrobiodiversity. He thought that the state would respond negatively to his project because other issues were considered more urgent in the country.

Another option for saving these vines without relying on public funding would be to involve the Moldovan Small Wine Producers in this project.[14] The small commercial winemakers would purchase grapes from these peasants, and instead of paying them 4 MDL (roughly 20 eurocents) per kilogram, the average price at the time, would pay double: 8 MDL. This second idea was only at feasibility stage; it was a thought that had occurred to Gheorghe recently out of the worry that in five years all those old vineyards might have disappeared.

The Purcari area and the villages by the Dniester were the ones that should particularly be researched because there, unlike in several other districts in Moldova, people did not have so many hybrid vines and important indigenous exemplars could still be found. As a defender of agrobiodiversity, Gheorghe emphasized that by losing this heritage of grapevines of diverse types and ages, producers would become stuck with a limited number of grape varieties and, hence, tastes:

> In Purcari-Răscăieți, and down the Dniester there were [non-hybrid vines] also during the USSR. Many people in Moldova had hybrid vines at home, but these villages by the Dniester were unique, around Purcari, Olănești, Crocmaz, where

people did not have hybrids. Among them you can encounter Rară Neagră, but also Cabernet, Saperavi, everything. These are interesting to investigate. I once found one in Răscăieți: the bush was 110 years old, I think. There was one man, Ungureanu– I guess he died by now – he was eighty years old, and he remembered that the vines had been planted by his parents [before he was born]. So these expeditions would allow us to identify them, because a very important part of diversity in Moldova is disappearing, and all we'll have will be those clones[15] that we got from Europe. I am against clones. I say, if humanity were to be cloned and everyone will be like Arpentin, it's not interesting; you'd go out of your mind. You drink a Pinot Noir 777, and everyone praises it. … it's sad, everyone's the same. I tasted it from Australia, from New Zealand, from us … In Burgundy, no, they are smarter. They say they do the cloning, but they don't. This is how nature does it: one bush is weaker, one is stronger, and this diversity gives a different output. Here it is all one and the same. (Chișinău, July 2017)

The history of this process of crop standardization is related to mechanization and monoculture agriculture but also to the tendency to mimic products on international markets, which is also another form of product standardization. The state structures responsible for funding these conservation initiatives seem oblivious to real needs: at the Moldovan Institute for Vine and Wine, for instance, which is the main academic institution for wine research in the country, a small collection of old vines was maintained, but Gheorghe said that what was actually precious was what exists in people's gardens. Yet 'what exists' is still unsure: the vineyard areas are known, but the composition and age of the vines are not. In spring 2017, the Vineyard Register was launched, in which any wine producer, commercial or not, was expected to list details about their vineyards (vineyard area, grape varieties and wines made on the territory of Moldova are required, among other details), but only a small number of people had registered at the time of writing.

Wine Education in Action

In this context, in which the domestic market for Moldovan bottled wine encompassed a maximum of 10% of national production, the initiatives carried out by the main actor representing and organizing the wine sector – the ONVV, together with development agencies such as USAID and the Government of Sweden – mobilized to popularize bottled wine in Moldova and boost its sale. The 'Wine Friendly' events that resulted varied in their themes – such as food-and-wine pairing, terroirs, Moldovan PGIs and sparkling wine – and appeared under the umbrella of the country brand 'Wine of Moldova'.[16] They were presented as a larger project for the 'education of the Moldovan consumer', who presumably lacked the knowledge to appreciate the finer products available on the market. During the winter months I was in Chișinău, 'Wine Friendly' events revolved around the theme of terroir through a series called 'Descoperă terroir în pahar' ('Discover the terroir in the glass'). A total of twelve tasting sessions with wines produced by Moldovan wineries were organized in Chișinău in the course of four weeks to introduce consumers to the concept of terroir and to explain the newly adopted Protected Geographic Indication system. At each presentation that I attended, the attendees were told what to look for on a wine label with a PGI: they will know that these regions are responsible for certain characteristics in wines given the pedo-climatic conditions (the elements of terroir), the grape varieties and the technology, and can be sure that certain standards of quality in production were respected.

In order to promote these events, the 'Wine of Moldova' Facebook page posted messages and invitations in English with the following description (besides information on the sommelier and the food and wine to be tasted): 'Terroir is a balanced combination of the soil, climate conditions and millennial winemaking traditions, which ensure uniqueness and typicality of the wines produced in a separate geographical zone. Wines with protected geographical indication or protected designation of origin are products of a terroir, filled with emotions and fluids of the land of their origin, wines of the highest possible quality' (post on the 'Wine of Moldova' Facebook page on 24 January 2017). The fact that this message was posted in English was indicative of the target for these events: if their prices were not easily affordable for the average-waged Moldovan (they cost 10 to 20 euros), the English-language call to wine connoisseurs was further proof of the existence of discrimination among potential consumers.

While the system of recognizing terroir in the Soviet space used to be different from that in France (Walker and Manning 2013), acknowledgement of the elements of terroir – climate, slope, soil, grape variety and technology – in making a good wine were present in the discourses of the peasant winemakers themselves, yet it did not carry the same name. In fact, it did not carry any specific name – but in Purcari, people talked about the differences in taste. Without me needing to ask specifically about these elements, villagers told me about the difference in the taste of wine from village to village, and even the difference between one part of a village and another, and that the grape variety should have an important say in wine quality along with the structure of the soil. One worker, Anastasia, explained how Negru de Purcari meant 'this hill', pointing towards a slope in the factory vineyards. She said the soil there was drier and gave a specific taste to the wine. She could see the difference from her home: she lived downhill, closer to the Dniester, 'in the swamp' (Romanian, în *baltă*), and said that her wine was different: because of that soil, it seemed to smell like the swamp (Romanian *noi suntem pe baltă și parcă și vinul miroase a baltă*). Another interlocutor said that the things that make a good wine are the soil, the winemaker and the slope. Soil and water made the difference: 'what kinds of minerals does the vine find?' The presupposition that winemaking during Soviet times and the early post-Soviet period meant a lack of knowledge about terroir does not seem to hold true when discussing the matter with Moldovan peasant winemakers. Overlooking similarities between local knowledge and 'expert' concepts confirms that manifestations of taste among the upper classes strive for distinction, being defined 'against the aesthetic of the working classes' (Bourdieu 1984: 58).

The presentations of wines were often interactive and richly informative, with the specialist answering questions about the history, concepts and proper consumption of wine. One of the events, led by an experienced Moldovan sommelier, took a journey through the definition and history of sparkling wine, talked about the production methods and explained the differences between traditional methods and the newer Charmat, or tank method, as well as the three most common grapes used to produce sparkling wine: Chardonnay, Pinot Noir and Pinot Meunier. While going through the tasting, references were made to countries that are more famous for wine production, such as France and Italy, and the sommelier emphasized the poorness of the local varieties on which Moldova could build a name on the international market: while Italy has over five hundred indigenous grape varieties, Moldova can boast only six: Rară Neagră, Fetească Neagră, Fetească Albă, Fetească Regală, Plăvaia and Busuioacă. He was referring to the local, pre-phylloxeric varieties and was not including local grapes that had been selected in laboratories – except for Fetească Regală, which was created in the interwar period in Romania by crossing two local Romanian/Moldovan varieties. Because the strategy of a peripheral wine-producing country seeking to increase its value on the market today does best by promoting indigenous varieties, this is a major obstacle to Moldova's plans. He explained this loss first with reference to the phylloxera epidemic of the late nineteenth century and secondly through the nationalization of land and the *sovkhozy*; during this time, many technical varieties were introduced and the local ones were forgotten, as the new ones promised greater productivity.

Five wines were tasted, for each of which the sommelier presented a short history. For example, the third wine was a 2013 Cabernet Sauvignon from the Purcari Winery, which was presented a little more ceremoniously for two reasons. First, it was suitable for demonstrating 'the wine ritual' that sommeliers carry out to guarantee the best serving of the wine (mature, red wine is best drunk after around thirty minutes spent in a decanter, to ensure that the sediments are removed). Second, in the words of the sommelier, Purcari was a name that everyone had heard of in Moldova, and it represented the top-quality sector because of its history and production technology. Moreover, 'people all over the Soviet Union knew about Negru de Purcari, it even reached Kamchatka'. He praised the 'heart of the man who chose to continue the beautiful tradition of Purcari' and emphasized that we could feel 'that special history in the glasses'. While the sommelier was enthusiastically sharing these details, the discussions between him and the attendants drifted inevitably towards the presence of SO_2 in the wines. The two women next to me (in their early thirties and from Bardar, a town fifteen kilometres from Chișinău) were whispering that the best wine was that from their cellar, which was made using ecological grapes and without SO_2 (Romanian, *'Parcă tot a' nostru din beci merge mai ușor, nici nu pui anghidridă'*). I found myself in a similar situation in March 2017, while leading a tour of the Purcari factory for a group of four people. They were from Moldova and were asking many questions about history and production, the wine that I liked and what I would recommend, because they would like to buy a few bottles. To be provocative, but also telling the truth, I said I liked factory wine better; the reply was, 'That is because you are not Moldovan! It's a matter of taste; you would have preferred homemade wine had you been Moldovan.'

Conclusion

This chapter has analysed a controversy that is ongoing in Moldovan society over the value and meaning of homemade wines in the countryside. Household winemaking is a prominent activity in Moldovan villages, encoding a multitude of social and economic aspects: the winemaker displays skills, knowledge, virtues and feelings to those who share the fruit of her or, more frequently, his labour. It also has economic importance, in various ways: it is a means of payment, a product for petty trade and an affordable alternative to more expensive commercial alcohol. It is a product born out of cleaner agriculture, tied to a flow of local knowledge and having a particular taste that can be reproduced at will – not industrially, but inside the home.

On the other hand, industrial wine is an important product of Moldova, but historically it has been associated with its export markets, and still is to this day. Attempts on the part of the industry to create a domestic market for bottled industrial wine have encountered resistance, which was a matter of choice as much as necessity. As has been evident throughout this chapter, the reasons Moldovans reject industrial wine are related to historical feelings of distrust and are sometimes due to differences of class. The rejection of industrial wine by a majority of Moldovans is partly linked to a global tendency to reject industrial foodstuffs: there is distrust of industrial food, but organic or ecological products are rarely the pricey, exclusive alternatives that they often are in the older capitalist states. Homemade wine is cheap, unregulated and socially embedded. Even at the 'educated consumption' in action of a winetasting in the capital, homemade wine was still an important topic.

The discussions over homemade wine also show how globalization creates different local responses in local contexts. Although this is already a commonplace in globalization theories and anthropology, showing how this dynamic works in the case of the Moldovan wine sector serves several purposes: it provides a context for the discussions that follow in this book about producing value in industrial winemaking and about the 'reinvention' of the Moldovan wine sector in accordance with international ideologies of value. On the one hand, discourses and stories are crafted for the faster and more effective integration of Moldovan wine into the global market. On the other hand, the painful experience of the country's dependence on exports is nudging wine-sector decision makers to increase the domestic share of the consumption of this commodity. This can only happen by denying the qualities of homemade wine or by adopting a benevolent yet still civilizing and transformative approach, such as that espoused by Gheorghe Arpentin. For the experts and the industry, although homemade wine reflects a bundle of meanings and social relations in the minds of many Moldovans, it should be changed so that it can produce value on the market. Usually this means the regulation of hygiene standards and producing a taste for a more predictable palate.

Finally, a reflection on the binary opposition analysed in this chapter. It is not a complete one: in the end, the two products have enough features in common – and peasant winemakers were not always dismissive of stabilized, filtered and bottled wine. The reverse is true for the stauncher industrialists who want a market for their wine. As will become clear later in the book, these apparent dualities – unique/generic, natural/technological – are not disjunctive but in fact constitute each other. In the context of market relations, features such as 'naturalness' or 'uniqueness' tend to be appropriated by producers in order to add value to commodities, and, as this chapter has shown, some of the social relations surrounding these products need to be destroyed if their circulation on the market is to be made smoother.

Notes

1. Also called 'natural wine' (Romanian, *vin natural*), bio wine (*vin bio*) or 'wine without sulphur anhydride' (*vin fără anghidrid*).
2. This was the predominant discourse that I encountered during my research among peasant winemakers. It contrasted with the discourse of almost every professional winemaker or wine scientist whom I interviewed or discussed the matter with.
3. The practices that distinguish organic from conventional viticulture predate the industrial era; however, modern organic viticultural movements date back to the 1940s (Goode and Harrop 2011: 50–51).
4. Although 'Moldova' is a table-grape variety, it is often used in vinification by peasant winemakers.
5. The cutting method, called *la svoicorini* (from the Russian свои, 'their', and корень, 'roots'), is done by burying a vine stock in the ground and waiting for it to take root. From this stock, a new plant grows.
6. Two or more people drinking from the same glass is a common practice in Moldova. The host starts, and then the glass is refilled and offered to guests in the direction of the movement of the sun; in order to 'gather the people at the table, you start from the host and you go around the sun' (Elena, 58-year-old worker).
7. The Julian (or old-style) calendar celebrates Christmas on 7 January each year.
8. The taste descriptors for homemade wine used by interlocutors from the village are not very precise. A wine is appreciated as 'tasty' (Rom. *gustos*), strong (Rom. *tare*), light (Rom. *usor*), soft (Rom. *moale* or Rus. *myagkiy*), hardened (Rus. *tertyy*, for tannin), sweet (Rom. *dulce*), sour (Rom. *acru*), fragrant (Rom *aromat*) or strawberry (Rom. *de capsuna* or *foxat*). I give the transliterated Russian words, which are used frequently too.
9. This is what I often heard from workers in Purcari and avoidance of this practice might be primarily related to the price of the Purcari wine, which is higher than in other local wineries. For example, people in the neighbouring village of Răscăieți would buy sometimes larger quantities of wine from a winery (Jennifer Cash, personal communication). Buying commercial bottles of wine in the Moldovan countryside is, in any case, habitually not the first choice.
10. A similar view explaining the narrowness of the domestic market was found in the Moldovan wine-science periodical *Viticultura și vinificația în Moldova* (2008): the article states that Moldovans acted unilaterally as taught by the Soviets, focusing only on exports and forgetting about the internal market. Because around 90% of the wine produced by Moldovan wineries was going to Russia, 'the shelves started to be filled with other drinks – vodka and beer' (2008: 27), or alternatively with homemade wine. In 2008, when the article was published, the author considered it was too late for industrial wine to find its place among Moldovans' first choices (2008: 27–28).
11. Ministry of Heath, Labour and Social Protection in the Republic of Moldova, 2017. 'Notă informativă privind progresul implementării Programului național privind controlul alcoolului pe anii 2012–2020, pentru anul 2017' (Eng., Informative Note regarding the progress of the implementation of the National Programme for alcohol consumption between 2012 and 2020, for the year 2017), Chișinău.

12. A *qvevri* is an earthenware vessel in which Georgian traditional wine is made and fermented – and it is also the name of the winemaking method, which is part of the UNESCO Intangible Cultural Heritage of Humanity as of 2013.
13. The contest started in 2002, in the same year as the Moldovan Wine Day festival, in an attempt to institutionalize various dimensions of traditional practices in Moldova. The categories for prizes do include an aspect that is excluded in the professional wine contests: red and white wines made of hybrid grapes. However, the loss of the vines and practices described by Arpentin tends to diminish in the absence of financial support.
14. Their website is www.winemoldova.com (accessed 25 June 2021). The members of this association – small wineries, which have increased in number in the last decade – were described by my urban interlocutors as representing a more progressive, flexible and experimental side of Moldovan winemaking; Gheorghe Arpentin and his small winery were part of this trend.
15. Grape clones are cuttings taken from a grapevine with traits that the winegrower wants to reproduce (disease or frost resistance, yield, fruit qualities). The clone is genetically identical to the mother vine. It is the predominant method of grapevine reproduction around the globe, but there is a difference in how clones are selected from a population of grapevines – and this is an issue that Gheorghe is also referring to: selection for cuttings can be clonal or massal. In the former, all the cuttings, and hence the future adult plants, will be identical to the mother vine. In the latter, cuttings are selected from several plants exhibiting similar traits, in this way creating an opportunity for genetic diversity to multiply. In clonal selection, critics like Arpentin see an overly homogeneous product. On the other hand, Veaceslav was highly critical of massal selection because in his view it created variation in fruit traits, hence lowering the market value of the wines due to a level of intra-varietal heterogeneity of taste.
16. 'Wine Friendly' was a programme launched in 2015 by the ONVV aiming to 'promote wine culture'; it gave the 'wine friendly' distinction to restaurants that offered a diversity of Moldovan quality wines and the food to match them.

3

Labour Force Reproduction
Economic Strategies in a Post-Soviet Winemaking Village

> A man had two dogs; he fed them and kept them locked up. One day he did not have enough food to feed both dogs, so he released one of them – he 'gave it independence'. While the locked dog continued to be fed, the free one was going around the village to people's houses, begging for food. Sometimes it would get some food, sometimes some rocks, and at other times some kicks. Freedom, independence! We're like that free dog now.
> —Iurii, 57-year-old electrician

One freezing day in February 2017, Valentin (60), the driver who transported workers to and from the Purcari Winery, set aside some time to show me around the village. He drove outside the winery perimeter and pointed towards the River Dniester: in that corner of the country 'three borders meet' – those of Moldova, Ukraine and the separatist unit of Transnistria. We were in a border zone, and we were going to choose the road closer to the river because 'there, it is wilder, and what is wilder is closer to the soul', he said. He was referring to an area consisting of a large river plateau in the direction of the Dniester, with the crumbling clay walls of houses left behind by people emigrating or passing away, and the rusty carcasses of what appeared to be outdated industrial facilities. Plots of cultivated land and some houses that were still occupied interrupted this 'wilderness'. The road was not paved and went up to the higher part of the Purcari village, where the majority of the people lived. Along the road, there were also deserted rows of grapevines that had been cared for until the late 1980s but left abandoned ever since.

Despite its hint of wilderness, the river plateau mostly consisted of arable land. During the Soviet period, this land used to be cultivated with vegetables that went to the Olăneşti canning factory, which closed entirely in 2013, or to a few other canning factories in Transnistria. A smaller area of land had been used for producing vegetable seeds but was now leased to local entrepreneurs, mainly to grow cereals. The cultivated land in Purcari was decollectivized in the early 2000s. With some frustration, Valentin mentioned that the plot for each Purcari villager at decollectivization was 1.5 hectares: in Antonești, a neighbouring village, more plots were given because the Purcari *sovkhoz* produced vegetable seeds and wine while the Antonești farm bred animals, for which larger surfaces of land for grazing and haymaking were allocated. In the end, Antonești villagers had more land to share between them while the Purcari *sovkhoz* was given 'these scraps', Valentin said, pointing towards the slopes with deserted vines on the left-hand side of the road.

Many of the discussions I had with villagers in Purcari began or ended with this need to survey what was 'then' (under the Soviet Union) and what was available now. The comparison left many with a bitter taste in their mouths as they pointed to the loss and injustice caused by a fallen 'empire' that everyone had thought was too big to wither away, and then by leaders perceived as corrupt and selfish. At that time, people either worked at the Purcari Winery, whether just seasonally or permanently, or, to a considerable lesser extent, in the vineyards of four other companies producing grapes or wine in Purcari, none of which processed the grapes in the village. Others had jobs in education or the public administration, or they emigrated – such were the job opportunities in Purcari. Although post-Soviet political leaders had promised Moldovans a better life and a different kind of modernity than the Soviet version, in the end the majority of them felt excluded from this modernity and found themselves looking for diverse coping strategies to supplement very low wages or to subsist in general, or watching the collective spaces and infrastructure become inaccessible through either privatization or neglect and decay.

As I also showed in the previous chapter, some of the household activities that contribute to the reproduction of the workers are integrated into processes of capital accumulation, but this is not clearly recognized as a productive activity contributing to capitalist production – and even less so in the field of quality winemaking, which is enmeshed in romanticized depictions. Social reproduction theory (SRT) can help us most fittingly in making sense of these changes as it shows how labour power as a commodity is fundamental to the whole system of capitalist production (Harvey 2006: 163), although it involves non-capitalist processes of production such as women's care work, subsistence gardening or resting; in capitalism, these become 'naturalized' and taken for granted (Mezzadri 2019: 33) under the illusion that only wage work produces value (Graeber 2013: 224). Drawing on SRT scholarship arguing that capitalism relies in part on agricultural communities for the reproduction of labour power (Meillassoux 1972; Edholm, Harris and Young 1978; Harris and Young 1981; Bhattacharya 2017), and that household work is one of the forms of 'cheap nature' (Moore 2015: 63) that contributes to capitalism's reproduction, in this chapter I explore the social and economic processes that are necessary in the reproduction of workers in the wine region of Purcari.

The Reproduction of Labour Power

SRT scholars explore the social processes and relations that produce the conditions of existence for workers by addressing the relationship between exploitation and oppression (Bhattacharya 2017: 2–3), and the theory stemmed from the debates around the subordination of women and the reproduction of capitalism through their role in biological and social reproduction. Feminist theorists (Edholm, Harris and Young 1978; Harris and Young 1981) have argued against the conflation of different forms of reproduction in society in a catch-all understanding of the concept. They criticized the way in which the concept of 'reproduction' has been used by Marxists interested in transcending the static mode of production and also by theoreticians of women relying on their biological tasks. This critique is convincingly supported through the breakdown of the concept of reproduction into three types, which are more distinct than the previous use of the concept ever allowed: social reproduction (referring to the reproduction of adequately socialized labour, i.e. within a specific ideological apparatus); reproduction of the labour force; and human, or biological, reproduction (Edholm, Harris and Young 1978: 102; cf. Graeber 2013: 223, on production – it is created and recreated similarly on these three levels: the production of material goods, social relations and human beings).

Here I look at the second type – the maintenance of the labour force – more precisely, at how the workers making wine at Purcari get by. Reproduction of the labour force can refer either to the maintenance of the labour force or to the allocation of workers in production processes over time (Edholm, Harris and Young 1978: 106). The material reproduction of the labour force that I focus on here is the former: the maintenance of workers through 'the day-to-day performance of domestic labour' (Harris and Young 1981: 125). In capitalism, this part of reproduction has been performed predominantly by women but in Soviet republics this work has been split – not equally – with men. Anastasia, whose example I analyse in a section below, is here in the role of the main breadwinner and this is not uncommon for families in which women are wage workers. The role of women as producers outside the reproduction sphere of the household is prominent in the Purcari workers' community, as women are as present in the labour force as men.

But my present focus is predominantly on processes related to class rather than gender, ethnicity or race, to show how two types of work – wage and domestic – are part of the same socio-economic process (Bhattacharya 2017: 5). Labour power is reproduced not solely in the home but also in public institutions and infrastructures such as schools, hospitals, leisure facilities or elderly pensions (Bhattacharya 2017: 7). For the Purcari workers especially, leisure, travelling and collective local infrastructures are listed as lacking. Food provisioning from one's own garden became an urgent necessity in different periods of the 1990s and 2000s. The areas of social reproduction in the households of Purcari Winery workers that contribute to the circulation of capital in the winery that I analyse here are food provisioning, inhabitable/functional space and rest options (i.e. vacations, free days, socialization outside the work space). I examine these areas comparatively, just as my interlocutors framed them: their experience or memory of socialism, as in other postsocialist countries, continues to inform evaluations of the present.

Comparisons

Purcari used to be a 'rich village', and its past glory was quite quickly brought into the discussion whenever I talked to the workers. On a workday in the winery's industrial cellar, Ileana (50 years old) came up to my bottle container and started recounting her memories of her childhood with her grandparents in the village. One of the things she remembered from those years was that Purcari and the 'villages on the Dniester' were seen as more affluent by villagers in inner Moldova. She recalled how her relatives from these other parts of the country came to village celebrations, staying for two or three days and looking on in admiration at the prosperous winemaking village of Purcari. Another worker, Elena (58 years old), added that Purcari was indeed rich, as were the villages in the *sovkhoz* association: they used to be called 'millionaire villages' (Romanian reg., *sate milioner*). The whole Dniester Plain was full of fruit trees, vegetable fields and vineyards. After the fall of the USSR, she said, a large number of these activities ceased and what followed was the 'enrichment of the few' at the expense of the region's welfare. Not only was there a lot of activity back then, but the work of those involved was recognized through meaningful payments and all sorts of prizes for deserving workers. By the 1970s, the countryside in the USSR had become more affluent than urban areas, and positive memories from those years were frequently brought up by the elderly in my site in Moldova, like elsewhere in the post-Soviet space (Annist 2016: 93; Aistara 2015). Dzenovska (2018: 20) pointed to a similar affective attachment to Soviet 'stability, sociality, and a promise of a future' among Latvians. My interlocutors had fond memories of the Soviet years, while only a few workers thought that they had been better off since independence as more possibilities had opened up for them in terms of mobility or entrepreneurship. The Soviet experience was the remembered or imagined state of 'normality'.

Indeed, a quite undisputable fact is that during socialism job security was almost never a problem for the proletariat, a fact that increased the distress felt in the period of labour dispossession that followed the collapse of the Eastern Bloc. If the politics of the postsocialist decades meant reductions in employment, migration, a deepening of inequality and stagnant incomes for many, in the planned economy of the Soviet state the daily experience of the workers was a more secure and calculated one (Verdery 2003; Kalb 2014). The notion of security travelled through the discourses and evaluations of my Moldovan interlocutors, like the anxiety-free, or *spokoino jivot*, way of life under socialism encountered in other East-European countries such as Bulgaria (Jung 2019: 84). The Soviet years meant more than daily security, but memories of deportations or of the failure of the Soviet modernization project were brought up less than the positive memories of this period.[1] In people's immediate, daily experiences, memories of the last decades of the Soviet system seemed to prevail in the face of capitalism, when people started to 'talk about money', as Anastasia (47 years old), a worker in the processing section for fourteen years, remarked. At the beginning of my fieldwork she said:

> My mother kept telling me that when we were with the Russian [sic], it was easier to live (Romanian, *când eram cu rusul, era mai bine de trăit*). There was everything you needed in the stores. This is what she was saying, that I did not get to live the easy times [as an adult]. But yes, when we were with the Russians it was easier. We received 90–120 roubles per month, but this would suffice, we were buying sausages, meat for the children – this was until 1991. We did not feel what children feel nowadays, we were not asking for so much money. (Purcari, November 2016)

The increased dependence on money for daily reproduction caused anxieties and meant that many of the previously perceived advantages ceased to exist in the years after independence. It is not that dependence on money was seen as being bad in itself, but aspects of basic consumption in the country-side – electricity, heating, processed food, clothes, toys, vacations – were considerably harder to access after the collapse of the Soviet system.

While following the emic comparative view, it is important to acknowledge criticism of the tendency in the anthropology of postsocialism to make 'mirror comparisons' between capitalism and socialism that render 'socialism as the Other of capitalism' (Petrovici 2015: 84). By replicating this divide, anthropologists researching former socialist countries have tended to measure these societies against Western paths to modernization (Hann

2002: 8). There is more overlap between state socialism and capitalism than the emic narratives acknowledge, but nevertheless there is a substantial difference in terms of how resources were allocated in capitalism and how workers experienced time; how they consumed, and what was available to them at the end of one month of work in a capitalist winery; and the extent to which they needed to find alternative provisioning strategies to supplement the normalized, insufficient wage.

Food Provisioning

As the advantages left over from the socialist system increasingly disappeared in the post-Soviet years, the villagers in Purcari developed a series of economic strategies that were meant to supplement their insufficient or absent salaries. Their reliance on resources other than wages is what would be referred to as a 'coping strategy' in the anthropological literature. Such resources may come from the land or other private property, or consist in trade activities, informal employment, networks and mutual aid or stealing (Artiukh 2013). In Eastern Europe, the economic reforms of the post-1989 years deepened inequalities and led to a diversification of coping strategies. Despite the presumption that socialism integrated rural households into a wider, industrial division of labour and replaced the household as the main unit of production and consumption, subsistence agriculture and petty trade were present during socialism. In the capitalist system, household production is actually still very important in some areas in Central and Eastern Europe (Gudeman and Hann 2015a; Kofti 2018: 128). Moreover, outside the former Eastern Bloc too, household production and kinship solidarities are important in the reproduction of flexible labour regimes (Mollona 2009: 7), some reproductive work within the household being appropriated through the relationship between capital and unpaid labour (Moore 2015: 70).

In Purcari, similarly, workers have relied to an important extent on products made in the household in order to make ends meet throughout the postsocialist decades. Anastasia's household constituted one such example. Her husband was a retired farm worker and they had two sons, Artur (20) and Petru (29). While Artur was living in the village, Petru had moved to Chișinău to study, had found a job there and got married. It was common in Purcari households with more than one child that one child would choose to stay in the village or would return after studying in order to support their parents, while the rest lived abroad or in the city. Anastasia was the only member of the household with a full-time job, her work schedule at the winery varying between eight and twelve hours, thus challenging the male bread-winner's prominence as the main wage earner.

In the household, they raised one pig and fowl for meat as well as a cow that provided them with dairy products: butter, milk and cheese. The animals were mainly taken care of by the husband and the son during the week, and by Anastasia on Sundays. Anastasia sold some of these products to her neighbours and winery colleagues. Other food for the household was grown in a vegetable garden: potatoes, onions, cucumbers, peppers, beans, garlic, corn and chickpeas. The family owned another plot of arable land of around 3.6 hectares consisting of three *cote*, quotas of land that former *sovkhoz* workers were given at decollectivization. They received three plots for the three members of the family who had worked in the Purcari *sovkhoz*: Anastasia's husband, her mother-in-law and her father. They cultivated a small area of it with potatoes and leased the rest to a so-called 'land leader' (Romanian, *lider de pământ*), who provided them with grain to feed the animals and to make flour and oil.[2] What they still needed to buy was rice; chicken fodder; or, when they 'want to eat sausages or olives', imported or industrially processed foodstuffs – but the last-named figured very little in their diet. In many households in Purcari, bread is baked at home from the wheat received from the land that villagers cultivate or lease, and in almost every village there is a grain mill. 'And from this flour we make everything, *învârtite* [a type of pie] and bread', remarked Anastasia when I visited her home, in front of a table full of food. She baked almost all the bread they ate in the household for a week on Saturdays, and she bought bread only in the summer when there was more work in the fields and time was scarcer. Sustained by these strategies, capitalist companies can keep the cost of labour down, which, as Meillassoux (1972: 102) argued, becomes possible through 'the super-exploitation, not only of the labour from the wage-earner himself but also of the labour of his kin-group'.

Anastasia's salary varied between 4,500 MDL during the harvest season and 3,500 MDL the rest of the year (200–170 euros, roughly converted), while her husband's retirement money was around 1,800 MDL (ca. 80 euros), the average pension in Moldova. Artur's income varied: some months he would work at the Purcari Winery as a day worker, some months he was in Poland working in the construction sector, and there were some months when he was without work. On average, Anastasia's household had a monthly budget of 7,500 MDL (370 euros), which was used for paying bills; buying clothes, processed food and medicines; and travel or recreation and leisure expenses. Based on the calculations of the National Bureau of Statistics (BNS), in Moldova the minimum monthly expenditure required was 1,800 MDL/person. This sum represented the poverty threshold in rural areas according to the BNS calculations, an assumption that is easy to dispute. Research in the textile industry in Moldova showed that the living wage – covering actual needs such as food, energy, medicines and transportation –should be around 11,000 MDL (570 euros) per person monthly (Nenescu and Sprînceană 2018). Thus, Anastasia's household is located on the poverty line based on official calculations and had far below the level of income necessary to meet its real needs – yet proper nutrition was not a problem. As Cash (2019, 2015a) also showed for Moldovan households, poverty is defined as a lack of income rather than a lack of food. The importance of food produced in the household becomes even stronger in this context. To return to the initial question raised in this chapter, in this way workers who rely on household production contribute significantly to the smooth functioning of a capitalist enterprise that needs or chooses to cut its labour costs.

Looking at household food-provisioning practices further back in time shows how crucial they were for the reproduction of Purcari households. From the 1990s until the late 2000s, producing and selling food from one's household was central for subsistence purposes. The main coping strategy against the poverty of those decades in Purcari was petty trade with homemade products in the largest food market in Odessa, the Pryvoz. Just about everyone in the village sold things in Odessa during those years, as my interlocutors repeatedly recalled – some with nostalgia, others slightly embarrassed. Looking more closely at the role of this trade gives us a glimpse of social and economic life in Purcari in the 1990s. This petty commerce was also carried out under the USSR, but it became more important afterwards. Anastasia recalled that in the 1990s a bus from Purcari transported people to Odessa, where, after selling their products, they would go to the grand 'Seventh-Kilometre Market near Odessa and dress their children'. She 'even found [her] husband there': Anastasia is originally from Olănești, while her husband is a Purcari local, and they first met on this occasion in Odessa. During Anastasia's seven years on maternity leave, she produced household produce and sold it there: 'I was selling everything. Flour, grapes, I was digging out the horseradish in the garden, stealing peaches from the hills.' She liked doing it because the payment was good, and 'many people in Purcari built houses out of that money'. At the time of my fieldwork, Anastasia was selling milk, cream, cheese and butter either to work colleagues who did not have a cow or in the closer market in Olănești on Sundays, having given up going to Odessa because her factory schedule no longer left time for it.

The embarrassment felt in discussions with other interlocutors was due to the fact that, apart from homemade food products, for a few years during the 1990s one of the main products made by villagers in Purcari was counterfeit *divin* (the Moldovan name for brandy), a combination of chemicals and alcohol made at home that they sold in Odessa. Many people in the village were involved in this. An employee at the hotel, also a villager from Purcari, told me: 'I remember when the minibus stopped here, we got in with all this cognac. I gave up after a few years, when I got the job here, as it wasn't [appropriate] for me to ask people in the market whether they wanted brandy. But we had to survive somehow'. Another worker at the factory – Dan (63 years old), the forklift driver – recounted that when the USSR was unravelling 'money disappeared' for some time,[3] creating ambiguities and abuse from employers. 'In the 1990s, when they leased the factory to Cotnari,[4] my son returned from work in Russia and worked in the winery for a year. [The winery management] was deceiving people, laying them off. And who could people complain to? The whole country was being run by bandits. At the entrance to the winery there was a cistern, paying people in wine'. One solution to the difficulties that Dan's family found itself in was fishing and harvesting fruit, which they sold: 'I was waking up at one o'clock, going to Odessa to the market to stand in the queue, and selling fruit or fish. This area [the villages near the Dniester] was better off: Odessa fed a lot of people. Everything was sold in Odessa!' At the time of my fieldwork, villagers in Purcari were relying on this trade to a much lesser extent but, as in Anastasia's case, most families needed to produce food in the household in addition to wages and other sources of income to get by or to be able to keep a child at school in an urban centre.

Vova's (29 years old) example showed the kinds of hardship that younger families were facing. He was a former migrant worker in Moscow – where he had lived for four years, after which time he returned to Moldova. At home, he did various manual jobs in Chișinău, Ștefan Vodă (the administrative centre of the *raion* to which Purcari belongs) or his native village of Olănești, and at the time we met in October 2016 he was working in the winery for two months. Although he did not complain very much about his current job, he was hoping to acquire Romanian citizenship soon so that he could work in the UK, where some of his friends were living already. But until that plan came off, he would work in the winery because he had a family to feed: a wife and an eighteen-month-old son. He always tried to maintain a modest and positive attitude, but in fact I saw him many times in the course of the year looking very tired and overworked. One day, we were transferring aged Chardonnay from the barrels to the blending cisterns, which allowed us to converse for longer. He started reflecting on how society was organized: 'It's some sort of a maze: I give the money, I need food, I work here to give the money for someone else's work [who works in my garden so I can have enough food]. The idea would be just to work your land and be happy with what you get, because "through the sweat of your face you shall earn your daily bread", as the holy writings say.'[5] Paying someone else for one's food – be it helping hands or supermarkets – would perhaps not come across as so absurd if the wage sufficed, but for many manual workers it is impossible to save something from their salary.

This is a decades-long tendency in fact, as during the process of switching to a market economy wages fell dramatically and many people migrated. In the 1990s, because of the devaluation of the Russian currency, the average wage fell from around 220 dollars to less than 50 dollars (Cantarji and Mincu 2013). With fluctuations throughout the 2000s, in 2011 the average wage increased to 271 dollars. A 2014 report gives an average salary of 291 dollars, though for those in agriculture, forestry and fishing it is only 192 dollars (BNS). A monthly report for February 2016 gave average earnings as 236 dollars (around 200 euros). The fall was most probably related to the catastrophic economic situation caused by the theft of a billion dollars from local banks in autumn 2014, accounting for about 15% of the country's GDP, which Moldova's citizens are supposed to pay back over the following decades.[6] In the winery, in 2016–17 manual workers' salaries ranged from 2,700 MDL (130 euros) at the low end to 5–6,000 MDL (250–270 euros) at the highest.

In this political and economic context, Moldova had one of the highest rates of outmigration in Europe. Temporary labour migration is the most common form of emigration from Moldova.[7] In Purcari and the surrounding area, many people leave for work abroad despite the fact that they have family at home and talk about the pain that comes from leaving their children behind and the emptying of whole villages. Working abroad earns substantially more income than would be possible in Moldova, but some villagers, after experiencing work as migrants, now prefer to stay at home.[8] Yet, the emotional costs of this decline have been significant regardless of the option chosen – doing factory work or going abroad.

The Value of Wage Work

In the post-1989 decades in Central and Eastern Europe, workers have suffered a decline in their social recognition both financially and symbolically (Kideckel 2002; Dunn 2004; Heintz 2006; Vodopivec 2010; Grdešić 2015; Kofti 2016). The service sector has been growing across the region, while industries have been dismantled. In his research on labour relations in Romania, Kideckel wrote about the fall in the position of worker as creating a condition of 'worker subalternity' (2002). In Moldova, the high unemployment rate and the exclusion of workers from the economy through privatization, the subsequent dependence on fewer employers and the weakening of the labour unions led to a comparable and durable form of subalternity after 1990. As a result, exclusion became systemic, backed by those in power, and former workers had to resort to migration for work or develop coping strategies outside waged employment at home.

The fact that wages were often extremely low also created a sense of decline. In Purcari, for example, workers in the agricultural department earn the lowest salaries for their back-breaking work. At the time of my fieldwork, the highest salary earned by workers in the vineyard was 200 MDL per day (around 10 euros) during the harvest. Other operations were paid at a rate of 14–15 MDL (60–70 eurocents) per hour. Manual weeding, one of the hardest types of work carried out in the vineyard, was paid at a rate of 12 MDL (50 eurocents) per row of sixty to seventy vine stocks; each worker could manually hoe ten to thirteen rows a day. Although these wages were low and insufficient to cover individual monthly expenses, they were higher by one to two lei than in other wineries in the region and the workers were paid regularly. Sometimes workers in the vineyard would compare the present time quite positively with the first years after the privatization of the Purcari Winery: at the beginning of the 2000s, workers in the vineyard did not receive their salaries for months. Claudia (56), a vineyard worker from Purcari, had been working in the vineyard ever since 2003 when new vines were planted by the newly privatized winery. Regarding the unpaid salaries, Claudia recalled that the local *nacealnic* was not paying the wages and was hiding this fact from his managers in Chișinău.[9] When the managers from Chișinău visited the winery, the *nacealnic* tried to keep them away from the workers in the vineyard so that the latter would not raise the salary issue. However, at some point the workers met with one of the managers, told him about the situation and a few weeks later received their money, which had been delayed for months. The *nacealnic* and two other employees who helped him were fired. This case turned out all right in the end, but the overall situation for workers in the agricultural sector has been among the hardest, as this is where the lowest salaries in the country are paid. Legislation did not help the workers either. Although when I started doing fieldwork agricultural workers in Moldova were already struggling with genuinely precarious positions, in October 2016 the Moldovan government approved a draft law to exclude seasonal and day labourers from the system of health and social protection, even though they have to contribute to the state budget in these sectors. Furthermore, such workers would need to obtain their own health insurance, and there would be no obligation to sign a work contract between owner and workers. While this legislation still needs to go through to the Parliament, it is an example of the extreme flexibilization of work and of the decline of basic social and health insurance further increasing the precarity of these workers.[10]

After independence, therefore, waged work became even more insecure and dependent on private owners' desire for profits – and some workers became superfluous. The trajectory of Ileana (mentioned earlier in the chapter), born in Purcari, was poignant in this sense. She had worked in the Olăneşti canning factory as a laboratory technician for more than ten years. Ileana had wanted to become a French-language teacher when she was a teenager, but her mother had not allowed her to do so because of the length of the study time and the low income. This was not only a matter of money, because in a canning factory workers would 'at least go home with a couple of jars of food; a jar of peas, of peaches, of apricots every day', which was legally allowed besides one's salary. She eventually went to study food technology in Tiraspol, not languages. She was satisfied with this choice in the end, not least because the *konservnii zavod* was, as she emphasized, a very beautiful factory. She described the interior and the technical equipment as complex and efficient, giving her a sense of fulfilment to think of herself as a worker in such an environment. As a laboratory technician, she had a fairly easy job in terms of physical effort or exposure to 'dirty places', as she put it. However, in 1994 both her children fell seriously ill with influenza, and the factory management would not allow her more than two weeks off. When, in the end, Ileana found that she needed to stay home for more than a month, she lost her job. Afterwards, she earned a small amount of money as a day worker in the village – and between 1994 and 1995, she worked in the industrial cellar of the Purcari Winery, replacing a worker on leave. She started working again at the winery in the spring of 2016, but she was at a disadvantage because she was not recognized as a technically skilled person despite her ten years' of work experience in the laboratory. Although she had been hired for a permanent worker position at the time of my fieldwork, Ileana was asked to do various jobs, which she was unhappy about because she wanted at least to belong to a team, to feel like she was 'doing something of her own'. Instead, she filled in slots when others went on leave or when the department was short of people – doing everything from sweeping the lawn around the château to turning bottles, filling barriques, bottling or night shifts in the bottling section. She was not happy, but she tried 'not to make God angry' and simply accepted what was available. Religion or god were frequently invoked by Purcari workers when talking about work, good fortune and hardship, although very few villagers attend Sunday masses regularly.[11]

A common view on work in anthropology is that it is 'a physical and mental activity performed for a purpose that is external to the activity' (Spittler 2008: 143). The performance of work can be explained in terms of 'the learning process, immediate benefits, the earning of wages, and the positive and negative sanctions which are part of the institutional framework of work' (Spittler 2008: 18). But work, besides its performance related to these aspects, includes a human aspect that is related to the degree of a worker's closeness to the activity that she carries out. She can identify with her work or experience alienation from it, she can find meaning in her work or not, she can see work as joy or as toil, and it can be a purely instrumental activity or may have other motives. Ileana's story conveys ideas about the centrality of work as a meaning-making arena besides being a fundamental necessity for workers' reproduction.

Holiday Travel

Manual workers decried the loss of the opportunities from the past that came from the employer and covered a substantial proportion of the expenses necessary to go on a holiday at least once a year. Leisure time and vacations were topics frequently brought into discussion by workers of all ages, either trips within the USSR as workers or with reference to the number of years since some workers have taken a vacation. They missed the opportunity to see new places and relax. At the time of my fieldwork, some workers agreed to take their days off officially, but actually worked and received their wage on top of that.

Chiril (62 years old) had been a tractor driver in the Purcari *sovkhoz* for twenty years, spraying the vineyards and transporting materials. After the *sovkhoz* was liquidated, he continued doing various jobs and for a couple of years had been responsible for cleaning pumps, filters and the walk-in refrigerator. Born in Purcari, he completed his military service in 1974 in Moscow and then returned to his native village. He then went back to Russia for three months in the year in 1977, 1978 and 1979, working in the construction sector, and found it easier to do so: 'Back then it was normal [to travel]; now they search you to see how many kopeks you've got with you'. Although labour mobility was occurring at an unprecedented rate at the time of the exchange, Chiril's memory pointed to the fact that when one travelled within the USSR there were almost no restrictions, while today's former Soviet republics and EU countries imposed various conditions on migration and travel for Moldovans. His daughter lived in England and his wife sometimes travelled there to see her, but he did not travel anymore because, as he put it, he had seen the world when he was younger and he thought that there was nothing more out there for him to see. As Chiril was recalling the places he had visited when he was young, Nicoleta (62 years old), one of the oldest employees of the factory, who has worked there since the late 1970s, came over and started to recount that she had also travelled with the '*turisticheskaya putevka*', a free holiday package received by deserving or lucky workers during the Soviet period.

Nicoleta had officially retired, but she still continued to work in the factory to supplement her retirement money and to help her younger daughter's family.[12] From Purcari, she had been working in the winery for over thirty years with a break in the early 1990s when she gave birth to her second daughter. Once during the *sovkhoz*, she won a three-week trip to Moscow as a member of the Komsomol (the Young Communist League) in a raffle: the boss put a number of tickets in a rubber boot and wrote 'Moscow' on two of them. One of the winning tickets was Nicoleta's; 'Natasha, my daughter upstairs [a cook in the workers' kitchen] was four, and I didn't even think of not going. I left her with my husband and my sister and was off!' She saw significant places, such as 'Alla Pugacheva's two-storey house,[13] the Red Square, what not'. Chiril added that he had travelled 'across a large part of the USSR': Sochi, Sukhumi, Batumi, Yalta – 'I saw the whole of Crimea!', as well as Moscow and Minsk. He reached Georgia by sailing with a ship across the Black Sea, one of the *putevka*s he had won as a tractor driver. Chiril was very happy remembering his time in Georgia: it is not usual in temperate climates such as Moldova's to see orange or mandarin trees bearing fruit and just to eat them from the trees, but in Georgia this was possible. These stories may have stemmed from a mixture of nostalgia for youth, the real economic depression of the present and the pressure one feels to consume in late capitalism. Options for consumption and possibilities to travel grew but socio-economic inequalities grew along with them, and those who have been left out of some consumption chains feel the exclusion particularly acutely.

Collective Infrastructure

Investment programmes in rural areas during the Soviet period facilitated the modernization of villages, introducing facilities comparable with those in urban areas – ranging from infrastructural upgrades like electrification to secure social systems providing wages, pensions and medical insurance (Hann 2003a: 10). Discussions with workers frequently slid towards these topics, the quality of village life in the past being evaluated positively. Infrastructure in Purcari – transportation and cultural or general utilities for the community – was almost invariably presented as superior 'during the *soyuz*' ('union'). One afternoon spent at Ioana's (31 years old) and Grisha's (36 years old) home in early 2017 brought together themes that had appeared scattered in conversations with workers over the year of my fieldwork. They were both employees of the winery and had been married for thirteen years. Ioana had worked in the industrial cellar for three years while Grisha had been a bottling-line operator since the winery was privatized in

2003. Their home was in the village neighbouring Purcari, Viișoara, with its little less than 400 inhabitants, which belongs administratively to Purcari town hall. Ioana prepared a late lunch for my visit, and on this occasion I met her two children and her mother-in-law, a former accountant at the Purcari association of *sovkhozy* until 1990. Memories about the Soviet years arose from us talking about street lights – it was turning dark, and on my way back to Purcari I would have to go on foot for a kilometre out of the total distance of five kilometres. At that time, Viișoara, Purcari and other villages in the area were not equipped with street lights, and the town hall was not planning to change the situation.[14] From street lights to the streets themselves, they were much better maintained during the Soviet period, said Grisha's mother. When it was snowing, a tractor cleared the snow so that people could move around – and on the country roads there was levelled gravel, making roads more functional. Now, when there was rain, some secondary roads became unusable as they were full of deep puddles or slippery dirt (jokes about *glod*, or 'dirt', in the villages are commonplace). In the years after independence, country roads were maintained less and less frequently. In the winter of 2016–17, when I was in Moldova, parts of Purcari were inaccessible on several occasions because of snowstorms.

An unusual feature of the rural infrastructure was the cloud-breaking system, located in the neighbouring village of Talmaza but dismantled at the time of my fieldwork. Upon entering Talmaza, one could see deserted factories, former farms and other traces of Soviet agricultural infrastructure. But one unusual structure stuck out on a hill in the village: a spherical building that had served as a launcher for rockets to disperse clouds of ice that produced hailstorms. Workers in the winery who were originally from Talmaza told me that in the past, when the system was working, the families of those managing it moved on to the hill and were regarded as 'families of scientists'. The cloud-breaker in Talmaza had been discontinued because of restrictions on the border with Ukraine and Romania, where there was a fifteen-kilometre limit. On the border where I was, the rockets had been forbidden – especially after the 1992 war with Transnistria, when explosives had been attached to them so that they could be used as weapons. While many villagers in the region stated on several occasions that hailstorms had become more frequent and destructive in recent years, affecting what they grew in their home gardens, some said that perhaps the cloud-breaking system did not make any difference. Nevertheless, this device was a meaningful symbol for the villagers, and its dismantling seemed like an allegory for what went wrong after independence: first there was stagnation and loss because of the war; later, communal goods were dismantled.

These images of a loss of functionality in Purcari reveal a sort of practical nostalgia for forms of organization, infrastructure and possibilities for spending leisure time that are no longer available today or available only to a lesser extent. The fact that these opinions should not necessarily be understood as nostalgia for Soviet ideology needs to be emphasized. Nostalgia among workers resembles what was described by Berdahl (1999: 202): less for reproduction of a past, and more for 'the production of the present'. While some employees articulately expressed their longing for the egalitarian and transformative approach of socialism or communism (like Dionis, in the following chapter), many were concerned primarily with the insufficiency of income for a basic but dignified everyday life. The rural proletariat in more advanced capitalist countries had gone through comparable situations: for example, the land-reform plan in Tuscany, shifting from the *mezzadria* type of tributary relationship (a share-cropping system) to capitalist family farming, was felt in the first instance by the ex-*mezzadri* as freedom – but soon they felt like 'a bird loosed from a cage, only to find [themselves] in the aviary', because 'capitalism … always put men where they were needed while making them feel free' (Pratt 1994: 60). I see that the manner in which my interlocutors felt about the end of Soviet socialism is similar. Many people in the countryside now had land, but wages did not suffice and agricultural machinery was unavailable for the new smallholders; the promised freedom had not brought palpable advantages to more than a minority.

Since the fall of the post-Soviet communist government in 2009, the state has been under the rule of different 'pro-European' parties, the strongest being the oligarch-led Democratic Party of Moldova. In this period, in the national media and in political debates, one of the most frequent notions used to describe present-day Moldova is that of a 'captured state' (Romanian, *stat capturat*) – a phrase mentioned for the first time in a 2000 World Bank study (Marandici 2016). The concept of 'state capture' is normally used in the context of states in the Global South and the former Soviet republics. It designates 'a lack of economic performance, openness and transparency among corrupt countries that are dependent on the export of a single crop, commodity or mineral' (Visser and Kalb 2010: 181). As Marandici (2016: 71) notes, '[o]ligarchs, deindustrialization, poverty, migration and remittances are the defining elements of the new economic order'. The Moldovan state was also characterized earlier as weak (Heintz 2008). The privatization of companies and land was accompanied by either the decay or the privatization of public infrastructure, the renewal of which in Purcari and the neighbouring villages depended throughout the post-Soviet years on individuals like politicians in electoral campaigns and philanthropists, or so-called 'external donors' such as USAID or the governments of some EU countries.

Nostalgic Capitalists

Earlier, I discussed how the weakening of social institutions and the exclusion and devaluation of workers' status was experienced by the workers at Purcari in the first two decades after independence. Throughout these years, intense work in the household in order to supplement one's wages was necessary for Purcari's villagers to make ends meet. However, a smaller number of them experienced these decades differently. For them, the freedom to set up a business and to accumulate financially without restriction were the great benefits of the fall of the Soviet Union.

Costea, whom I introduced in chapter 2, was one of the more affluent villagers in Purcari, having worked as a driver and then as a manager of the *sovkhoz* machine park in the final Soviet decade. Since the 1990s, he and his wife have opened three shops in the village, thus taking advantage of the newly opened possibilities for entrepreneurship. They owned two houses, two hectares of vineyards, industrial harvesting machinery and a car. Although an example of villagers who prospered after independence, Costea preferred the 'Russian communist regime', which had managed to modernize Moldova: 'imagine that in Moldova there were some peasants roaming around, with sheep, without [any research] institute, university; all there was, was poverty. And look at what they've done: farms, sugar factories, metal factories, wine factories'. He was opposed to the idea of Moldova being alone, because 'Moldova cannot even afford to pay itself salaries'. To his mind, the country should have kept open the factories that were dismantled and privatized after 1991, taken the small gifts that came from Europe as well, but also mended the country's relationship with Russia: what Russia gave to Moldova was incomparably better than what Europe had given: 'whole trains filled with wood, iron, coal, oil'. During the conversation, I wanted to draw his attention back towards the present and asked Costea whether he really believed that now, when Russia no longer had a socialist government, it was possible to have the cooperation and exchanges of the bygone Soviet era. He cut me short and told me: 'let's not look at ideology but at facts: how much does a KW of energy cost in Transnistria for a citizen financed by Russia in comparison with us [Moldovans]? For us it is six MDL, for him it is sixty kopeks. ... our pension – 700 MDL, for them it is 1,500 MDL'. He emphasized that for him there was no real issue at that moment, because his income was high enough and his children had migrated to Germany and were earning good money. He could even move to Germany and 'sit like a boyar there' and be taken care of by his children, but his complaint was about the many Moldovans who did not have that chance. The latter had had no help from the Moldovan state, and when Europe gave Moldova funds 'there were conditions attached'. That, to Costea's mind, was not a proper social state (Romanian, *nu este garant in sfera socială*).

Another local entrepreneur whose remarks also acknowledge the worsening situation in the community – albeit less nostalgically than Costea – was an electrician from a village neighbouring Purcari: Cristian (65) from Carahasani. A former worker in the Purcari *sovkhoz*, Cristian had also benefited from the implementation of free-market policies. He was introduced to me by a Purcari villager, and Cristian welcomed me into his house with ease. He showed me his son's house – a residence with many rooms, richly decorated – so that I could see that 'people in the Moldovan countryside can live well too', that they had a proper bathroom in the house and oak floors. I understood later that he was politically and socially active, and proud of being a hard-working man.

Cristian started working as an electrician in the winery of his village, Carahasani, after he returned from serving in the military in 1973. In 1974, he received an order to transfer to the Purcari association as a head mechanic, where he worked until 1978. He had a brigade of locksmiths under him, responsible for maintaining the association's technical equipment. In 1978, he returned to the winery in Carahasani, where he worked until 1985 when he quit and started working for the irrigation association in Olănești. He remained there until 1987, then worked in the *kolkhoz* at Carahasani until 1989 as a 'security, technology and work protection engineer' and from 1989 to 1991 worked at a cooperative in Carahasani as a locksmith. He therefore experienced the security of the Soviet factory as a mechanic and the decline of the working class in the 1990s, when his retirement money was reduced by half – but then he was happy about the new freedom and his success as an entrepreneur from the late 1990s onwards. As he explained, because of his more privileged position in the former collective farm, at decollectivization he received twenty hectares of land. He leased another twenty hectares and started cultivating vegetables and cereals, which he sold in Romania or Moldova. This small business in grains brought him financial stability and dispelled the nostalgia for the Soviet period that is common among his covillagers.

Cristian therefore sought to establish a private business for himself rather than rely on his winery job, as he saw Russia becoming less amenable to Moldova in the 2000s – especially in relation to its wine, the embargo being put in place in 2006. Despite the hardships caused by the wine-export crisis, living conditions were better now in Cristian's opinion. The twenty-five years of independence 'put the brain into motion', he claimed, and those who said that life was better under communism were 'those who did not work, those without skills and knowledge'. Yet he admitted that it was more difficult for the village, 'for the community, as not all are doing well'. Salaries were low, prices were high and villages had only weak infrastructure. He explained the poverty in Moldovan villages as due to faults in the Soviet modernization project: 'During the USSR in Moldova funds were allocated for production, for factories and farms. And infrastructure was developed around these facilities, but it was not a priority to develop infrastructure for people's use, around houses, for example. This is why poverty is even deeper in some rural areas.' The winners of capitalism frequently explain inequalities through the lens of meritocracy and place individual responsibility at the forefront, downplaying systemic injustices.

Although pertaining to a quite different political system, Ferguson's (2013: 226) observations that in South Africa hierarchical dependence was not a problem, but on the contrary a main method of personhood-making, illuminates a side of Moldova's relationship of dependence with Russia too. The network of dependence at both state and local level provided the recognition, support and stability that shaped the dignified person of the Soviet years. Not being submissive to the Party had harsh consequences, so hierarchy was enforced in this way. When one accepted the Soviet rules of the game, one became a recognized member of a social order that supported dignified livelihoods for workers. With this background in mind, whether experienced or imagined, the individualistic discourse that came to accompany the post-Soviet years proved unconvincing for many workers in Moldova. Those like Cristian or Costea, who became successful local entrepreneurs, defend the competitive individualism of the post-Soviet years only in part. Cristian was aware that the market economy did not manage to create sufficient collective benefits, while Costea believed that maintaining a paternalistic dependence on Russia while Moldovans pursued private initiatives would stabilize and support Moldova again as it had in the past, in the first wave of modernization.

Conclusion

Departing from the assertion that value is relational and is produced through the exploitation of human labour (i.e. human labour is undervalued in order to create the surplus value necessary for the survival and reproduction of a capitalist producer), in this chapter I have examined the impact of the reduction in the costs of necessities among workers in the Purcari Winery. Besides the amount of labour time socially required for the production of commodities, the notion of value also entails a basis of invisible reproductive work. The primary aim of this chapter has been to describe the kinds of additional productive and reproductive work that contribute to the making of Purcari terroir wines. This part of the productive process is perhaps the least visible or recognized, and it is hardly celebrated in the production of prestigious wines around the globe. Thus, finally, the chapter also aimed to contribute to taking social reproduction theory further by considering it from the vantage point of the production process of wine, one of the most highly fetishized commodities in contemporary capitalism (Ulin 1996; Black and Ulin 2013; Crenn 2016; Demossier 2018). In my usage of the term 'reproduction', I have drawn on feminist Marxist anthropology to distinguish between biological reproduction and the reproduction of the labour force. The latter is an essential component of wine; its laborious production process from the vineyard to the glass requires a permanent and seasonal labour force that is often unable to feel any difference in their pockets even if the winery is a successful one.

In order to understand the social relationships and dispositions of people as they are experienced in the present, I went further back than the year of independence in 1991 to the last two decades of the Soviet Union, the 1970s and the 1980s. Those were the decades that older workers associated with security and better recognition at the workplace, as well as a richer life in the village. While entrepreneurs and employees in leading positions in the wine sector often tried to break from the Soviet past, which they saw as rather retrograde, manual workers experienced things differently. Analysing the data in this comparative framework aimed to reveal alternative, vernacular imaginaries of social organization in a post-Soviet society (cf. Creed 2011). For many workers, the fall of the Soviet Union and today's labour conditions created a sense of having been let down by both the state and private companies. After thirty years of independence, during which immersion in the global capitalist system created socio-economic insecurity, my interlocutors recalled the experience of Soviet socialism and saw it as a better alternative. In their desire for social services and economic stability, villagers tie the values of the community in the present to their memories of the socialist experience.

Notes

1. During Stalinism, especially in the years 1940–41 and 1944–51, several waves of deportations of 'class enemies' took place in Moldova (see Conquest 1986 on the entire Soviet Union and www.deportari.md [accessed 25 June 2021] for the experiences of deported Moldovans).
2. The '*lider*' farm was the commonest type of corporate farm in Moldova at the time of my fieldwork, made of plots that had been distributed to former state-farm employees. These plots either proved too costly for the owners to farm or the latter were simply not interested in working the land.

3. Between 1992 and 1993, instead of money Moldovans used coupons, which had been introduced as part of the transition from the Russian rouble to the Moldovan leu.
4. Cotnari is a Romanian winery and the name of a popular wine region in north-east Romania.
5. Romanian, *'prin sudoarea feței tale vei câștiga pâinea de toate zilele'*. Vova was paraphrasing Genesis 3:19: 'By the sweat of your brow you will eat your food until you return to the ground, since from it you were taken'; he had been exposed to religious texts in his youth, when his mother became a Jehovah's Witness.
6. Ernu, Vasile, Ovidiu Țichindeleanu and Vitalie Sprînceană. 2017. Jacobin, www.jacobinmag.com/2016/03/moldova-chisinau-protests-russia-eu-ukraine (accessed 25 June 2021).
7. The International Organization for Migration (IOM) registered 753,800 migrants from Moldova in 2015, out of the country's 3.5 million inhabitants. The unofficial number in the media and public discourse is around 1.5 million migrants in total, almost half of the country's population. See https://moldova.iom.int/migration-profile-republic-moldova. In 2016, the IOM wrote, 'The main push factor for Moldovan migrants is economic: poverty, lack of adequate employment opportunities and low salaries, while higher living standards abroad act as a pull factor.'
8. Here, I make only cursory observations about how deeply the phenomenon of migration affected Moldova as this was not the focus of my study. Extended anthropological accounts of migration experiences among Moldovans can be found in Demirdirek 2006, 2007; Keough 2016; Roșca 2017.
9. From the Russian начальник/nachalnik, this word is used frequently by employees to refer to their superiors and translates as 'boss' or 'commander'.
10. The agriculture sector also suffered from significant delays in the payment of subsidies. On 27 September 2016, the government announced the suspension of agricultural subsidies for 2017 because of budget cuts related to the almost one billion dollars that had been stolen from three Moldovan banks. Meanwhile, the 2015 subsidies had not been paid either.
11. At Easter in 2017, I was invited to stay over at Elena's (another worker in the bottling section) and Valentin's house, and before midnight on Holy Saturday we went to church for the resurrection mass. My hosts emphasized that the church was only full on this occasion in the year; otherwise, people only went to church to commemorate the dead. Other workers in the winery expressed the same view, some of them decrying the emptiness of the church, others seeing it as reflecting a justifiable attitude on the part of the villagers because the priest and the Moldovan Church were seen as corrupt and untrustworthy. Nevertheless, villagers frequently mentioned their fear of God and prayed or observed religious celebrations in the household by not working.
12. In 2017, the retirement age for women in the Republic of Moldova was 57.5 years. For men it was 62.4 years (lex.justice.md/md/313291 [accessed 25 June 2021]).
13. Pugacheva was a Russian singer already famous during the Soviet period.
14. This observation about street lights was one among many; when my second roommate in the Purcari dorm started working as a tour guide, she was shocked to

see how little of 'Soviet modernization' remained in the village. She came from a village in Transnistria, a few tens of kilometres from Purcari, and mentioned frequently that, regardless of other deprivations, rural areas of Transnistria were incomparably better equipped. It was 'enough to look over the Dniester and see how brightly illuminated the villages are' – as was indeed visible from the high, dark bank of the Dniester on the Moldovan side.

4

Sending Wine around the World
Globalization and Work Rhythms in the Bottling Section

> My father was a tractor driver during the USSR. When the harvest was starting, one would see him at home no more than once a week [during the day]. Then on Saturday and Sunday they [the workers in the *sovkhoz*] were getting head over heels: one was getting a haircut, others were playing cards. I cannot say they were drinking too much: they could spend one day with 1.5l of wine, and they had time to get some rest as well. Now we do not have this time. I don't know if the whole world is like that, but we are on the run now. Compared to them, who lived in peace, we have to run. We get home on Saturday, and we do not know what else to do, there is always something to do. You arrive at, say, a birthday party, and it's gone. There is a lot of work … maybe this is why people are more jittery. The world has changed.
>
> —Iurii, 57-year-old electrician

The largest part of the time I spent working in the factory was on the bottling line. Although my first workday in this section happened quite late, after I had spent more than a month in the Purcari Winery it came to be my favourite factory space because the activity there allowed me to work at the same pace as the other workers – and at almost any activity: putting bottles in containers, packaging, sticking 'medals' on bottles, unfolding cardboard boxes to prepare them to take the bottles, etc. But more importantly, the bottling line was the space where the pressure of the orders was most visible: it was the activity in the entire wine-production process in which the presence and rhythm of the market could be grasped through different signifiers and patterns (cf. Kofti 2016: 440). Orders could be urgent or they might need a sticker in Chinese to be fixed manually to every wine bottle, or the bottles needed to be wrapped in paper by hand because American consumers saw this as a sign of extra care, as the production director explained. If in the other segments of the winemaking process the biology of the grapevine, the sun activity for grape ripening or the fermentation pace of the must guided the human actions and their work rhythm, in the bottling section it was principally the transnational wine markets and the winery's place within it that set the pace.

In the bottling section, or the *rozlev*,[1] as it was usually referred to by the employees, the two teams worked in twelve-hour shifts with a break of an hour in the middle, switching weekly between night and day shifts. *Smena* was the word used most frequently to refer to 'shift'.[2] On the November day that I went to *rozlev*, the daytime *smena* for that week welcomed me rather unexpectedly from the very first moment: one of the younger workers gave me a ribbon of medal stickers, and another showed me where to stick them on the bottles and how to hold the ribbon so that I could work fast. Half an hour later, I was already integrated into the chain of actions that the bottle-labelling process required. The hours spent working and chatting here quickly revealed the various tensions and transformations that had emerged in work rhythms and sociality over the last four decades. In the previous two chapters, I touched briefly on the main ways in which sociality among villagers was expressed in the Soviet period – namely through food, homemade wine, exchanges of money between households, life-cycle rituals and through workers' gatherings on the banks of the Dniester for barbecues and drinks. In my discussions with the workers on the bottling line, a more particular point for them – one that was felt less acutely by other winery workers – was recent changes in their relationship with time. When Vlad began directing production in 2015, shifts were increased to twelve hours, night shifts were introduced on a permanent basis and Saturday shifts in the bottling section became a regular feature.

These changes to the work schedule indeed coincided with Vlad's arrival, but they were not directly related to his particular style of management. The new rhythm was a consequence of the fact that at around that time, the Purcari Winery was becoming more successful in the wine markets of Central and East-European countries as well as the USA and China (in total, the Purcari Winery exported wine to twenty-eight countries in 2017). After the last embargo imposed by Russia in the autumn of 2013, the Purcari Group relaunched wine brands in all its four individual wineries and started what the marketing director, Maxim, referred to as 'aggressive marketing campaigns', which led to a substantial increase in sales.[3] The commercial success of the winery was translated into more irregular or longer hours for the workers in order to cover the higher number of orders. The everyday experience of time for the workers changed in both industrial and domestic work, as well as in how they socialized. While in Soviet days workers socialized at work and at home to comparable extents, in recent years socialization has been dominated by the workplace. Since 2015, the increasing number of orders needing to be fulfilled and the supplementary workers on the bottling line have been just enough to cover two shifts with prolonged work hours, leaving little time for leisure and social events outside the workplace. Focusing on ethnographic observations on both the shop floor and in workers' households, in this chapter I show how the entry of the winery into the globalized wine market led to conflicting transformations in the lives of the workers: while work time was extended and produced new forms of alienation and of the degradation of certain aspects of the quality of life, industrial work time also began to be enriched through rituals of commensality and socialization.

Flexible Capitalism and Brands

In flexible, or postmodern, capitalism, time and space are compressed – being driven by the development of technology, which reduces distances and makes possible a greater circulation of goods and people around the globe. Harvey (1989: 147) considered postmodernism to consist primarily in a shift in the experience of space and time, and he conceptualized the way in which space-time compression came to manifest in the social order as 'flexible accumulation'. This is an umbrella term capturing a series of responses to the rigidities of the postwar years before the early 1970s, the decades when Fordism kept labour and capital in balance. Flexible accumulation implies structural changes to the regulation of labour that translate into flexibilities on multiple levels – production, trade and consumption – and it is 'oblivious to constraints of space and time that normally pin down material activities of production and consumption' (Harvey 1989: 164). Kjaerulff (2015) has shown that flexible capitalism, despite bringing loss and precarity, also brought new forms of relations that cannot easily be classified as either deleterious or beneficial for workers. Nevertheless, the capitalist system is based on the creation of surplus value that requires different forms of alienation. Alienation in Marxist terms refers to the separation of the product from the person producing it (objectification) and appropriation of the product by someone who did not contribute to its production (exploitation) (Narotzky 2018). The alienated consciousness fosters a willingness to be exploited.

The number of working hours in a production unit can increase for a number of different reasons; one might indeed be the tendency in capitalist relations of production to extract more surplus value from labour, but the lack of technology in production can put similar pressure on workers – even in precapitalist times. What makes the increased number of working hours specifically a consequence of the extraction of surplus value here is the logic of flexible capitalism: working hours are moved around and stretched to benefit companies, and new products are introduced that require more effort from the workers. This is the so-called 'versatility' (Kjaerulff 2015: 5) that is induced by market competition and secured through labour codes that decreasingly protect the workers. In Harvey's view (1989: 285), this is an adaptation to the 'volatility and ephemerality of fashions, products …' of postmodernity. Volatility and rapid turnover are among the major changes in flexible capitalist markets, and even long-established brands make periodic changes to their products to 'surprise' consumers. Diversifying products, or periodically 'extending brands' (Foster 2007: 708), is a way of creating new value in the context of a highly diversified market for goods. What increased the pace of work and disrupted 'normal' practice in the Purcari bottling section were, apart from the increase in orders, the introduction of novel products in the Purcari Winery such as ice wine (a dessert wine made of grapes left to freeze on the vine and harvested late) and sparkling wine. The winery's concern with the reinvention of its products and the addition of new ones was a response to market competition: it made it possible for the Purcari brand of wine to be present on consumers' tables in more diverse contexts than would be possible with the ordinary wines: for example, ice wine is a dessert wine, while the three sparkling wines launched at the end of 2017 are suitable for festive occasions.

While in the capitalist West similar changes started in the 1970s, in the former Eastern Bloc the devaluation of labour and work skills, the upsurge in structural unemployment and the destruction of union power began during the later years of perestroika and increased after the dissolution of the Soviet Union in the early 1990s. It has accelerated until the present day in sometimes more extreme flexible regimes than in Western countries. Moldova experienced the devaluation of labour to a dramatic extent, resulting in one of the highest rates of workforce migration in the world. If one looks at the wine industry alone, the situation was slightly different from other productive sectors in Moldova, given the rather stable trade relations with Russia in the post-Soviet years until 2006. This is not to imply that the 1990s meant security and welfare on a par with Soviet days, but that wine produced in Moldova could be sold to Russia at any time without restrictions until the first embargo in 2006. The full inclusion of Moldovan wine-industry workers in the model of flexible accumulation happened once the country lost its trading ties with Russia and started preparing for its entry as a wine-producing country on the global wine market.

The example of the Purcari Winery eloquently shows how the implementation of flexible labour regulation worked, as this winery was one of the first in Moldova to take clear steps to distance itself from Russia after 2006 and to make progress in non-Russian markets. This meant that at the time of my fieldwork, Purcari was the most successful winery in Moldova in markets to the west of the country by sales and the number of medals that it won in international wine contests. It also managed to flexibilize work relations: work schedules could vary depending on peaks in demand, product designs were adapted, access to the labour market took new forms, and new forms of sociality emerged (see Kjaerulff 2015). The new forms of sociality that I analyse in this chapter can partly be read as revived practices: commensality and gatherings are usually initiated by older women workers who sometime refer to the lost socialization practices from the past. Their testimonies are comparable with others from the postsocialist space: *kolkhozy* are remembered in Latvia as traumatic in the beginning but more positively because of their sociality later (Aistara 2018: 37), while work and sociality also fulfilled both sides of otherwise necessary economic activities in socialist Poland (Pine 2007).

It might reasonably be asked whether the wine industry is actually an appropriate sector in which to observe these changes in models of employment given the fact that viticulture and winemaking are non-homogeneous themselves, having seasonal peaks in different periods of the year. For example, twice as many workers are needed in the vineyard at harvest time as in the rest of the year, while working hours in the grape-processing sections after the harvest, during fermentation, need to be longer. In agriculture, work from morning until sunset on non-rainy days can be seen as 'natural', as nature asks for grain to be harvested before it turns to rain (Thompson 1967: 60), while grapes have to be harvested before they become overripe or mouldy. In general, production in agriculture is a discontinuous process that depends on the biological cycle of the animals being raised or the plants that are cultivated (Pratt 1994). But some of the winery's activities over the year belong to industrial processing, and if the winery has a steady flow of orders it means that over the year these activities never stop. The bottling line in the factory is one such example, as it runs every day of the week except for Sundays and some public holidays (also from time to time some Saturdays are free). As I will show below, the bottling section has to deliver wine throughout the year – as a result of which, it is constantly bottling wine and labelling bottles.

At Rozlev

The main winery building hosts several departments: the grape-processing department, the blending section and the refrigerators, along with the offices of the production management and the laboratory. One floor below the offices, on one side of the white concrete building, is the bottling section, its presence revealed by the large number of stacked bottles kept at the entrance throughout the year.

110 ◆ *Wine Is Our Bread*

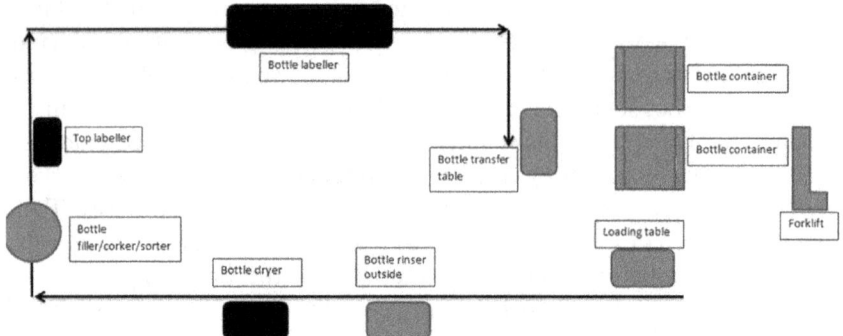

Figure 4.1. Diagram of the filling process. The parts in grey are active in the process, the ones in black are inactive. © Daniela Ana.

The majority of workers in the winery consider the *rozlev* to be the most comfortable and 'cleanest' of all the sections, as it is the least cold and least wet.[4] The space (Figure 4.1) is predominately metallic and bright, lit by a white neon light from afternoon until morning. Regardless of the task being carried out, if the conveyor line is on there is a constant overlapping of sounds: clinking bottles from the loading table at the end of the conveyor line; hissing and puffing from the rinser and dryer; the voices of the workers travelling across the hall to deliver messages or orders, or to make jokes; and, finally, the regular movements of the corker or the labellers (Figure 4.2), which echo like a metronome around which the other sounds gather, resulting in the end in an almost harmonious industrial tune.

Yet work here can be strenuous and spirits tense sometimes, as this section is the only one to work constantly in twelve-hour shifts. The other workers in the factory usually work eight to ten hours a day, starting at 8 AM. Yet, the activities here are also repetitive, and workers can get lost in their thoughts in a more relaxed monotony than is possible in the other sections. While doing these jobs, the women can be very quiet or brooding, or launch into joking or debating or singing depending on the dynamic of the group and its relations with the management on that day. From time to time there would be some jokes, or small moments of tension escalating rapidly and noisily, like little dust tornadoes playing around the workplace. They release some of the tension, as they do not last, and workers do not feel upset with one another for long. One example of such a moment is when the bottles that come along the conveyor line are not picked up promptly and start collecting at the end of the line, after which they start trembling under the pressure of the bottles coming after them. This is

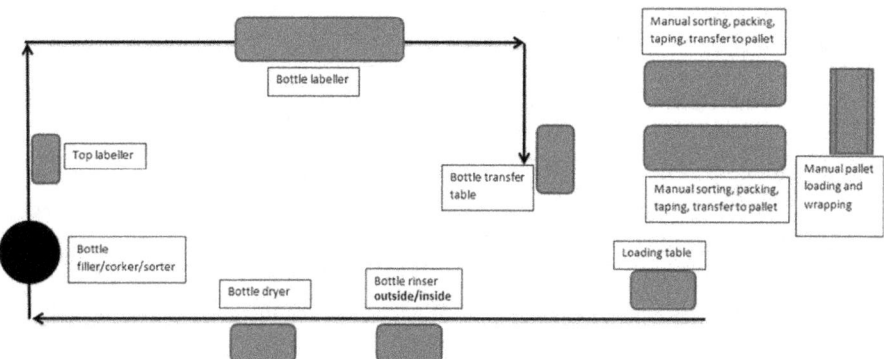

Figure 4.2. Diagram of the labelling process. The parts in grey are active in the process, the bottle filler (in black) is inactive. © Daniela Ana.

the phase just before the bottles might fall to the ground and break. One person is always responsible for picking the bottles up from the line and putting them on the nearby tables, but sometimes she is not at the line for different reasons – she is preparing boxes or has gone upstairs for drinking water. Then Maria or Alina would start shouting loudly, 'Those bottles are not going to pick themselves up! Come and take those bottles off the line!', or one of them would stand up angrily and start to move the bottles from the line to the table. There would be a moment of confrontation when the worker responsible for the line came back to her place, accompanied by a last round of shouted reproach and justification. In a matter of minutes, an earlier discussion would resume, and all the workers around the line would talk loudly and amusedly together without a trace of the earlier anger.

The workers in this department often obtained their positions through recommendations by acquaintances or family members, and employees at the factory and in the vineyard are frequently relatives. This may be the main reason why arguments do not last. Anthropologists of labour have shown in different settings that kinship 'ideologies' affect political and economic dynamics not only within the household but also in the factory (Mollona 2009). In the case of winemakers specifically, kinship ties ensure continuity in the family wine businesses (Lem 2013). The presence of this thick family network in the Purcari Winery leads villagers on the outside to see the *rozlev* as a fortress of kinship ties, making it hard for others to access vacant jobs. In *smena* 1 (Table 4.1), apart from Artiom, every worker was a relative of at least one other person in the team or in the company. The foreman, Alin, brought his cousin Grig into the team as a semi-skilled worker at the beginning of 2017. Maria and Bogdan were mother and son,

Table 4.1. Employees in *smena* 1 at the bottling section, Purcari Winery. © Daniela Ana.

No.	Name	Gender	Position*	Age	Salary November 2016 (net) in MDL	Employment (in years)
1	Alin	M	Bottling-line foreman	35	6,892.95	12
2	Bogdan	M	Bottling-line operator	35	5,445.87	7 (intermittently)
3	Elena	F	Worker 3	58	5,832.46	6
4	Maria	F	Worker 3	58	5,998.71	9
5	Alina	F	Worker 3	52	5,975.57	8
6	Grig	M	Worker 2	33	4,771.98	0.5
7	Livia	F	Worker 1	24	4,125.79	3
8	Simona	F	Worker 1	33	4,161.55	3.5
9	Nata	F	Worker 1	36	NA	0.5 (waitress at the hotel for five years previously)
10	Artiom	M	Worker 1	44	3,373.23	3

Note:

* The workers' positions are split into three wage categories. 'Worker 1' stands for unskilled worker, 'Worker 2' for semi-skilled worker and 'Worker 3' for skilled worker.[5]

and in addition Petra, Bogdan's wife, worked in *smena* 2 in the bottling section. Maria, Bogdan's mother, had been a widow for several years and lived together with Bogdan and Petra and their two children, aged three and eleven. The three workers in the family split factory shifts in such a way that there was always a parent or other adult at home to take care of the children. Elena and Nata were mother and daughter, and the workers' shuttle bus driver was Nata's father and Elena's husband, Valentin. Alina was employed through her kinship connection with the winery's accountant. Livia, who was divorced and lived with her parents, worked alongside them both in the factory: her father was a worker in the processing section, and her mother, Ileana, moved between sections as the management decided. Finally, Simona was the daughter of Iurii, the electrician, and her brother Florin was employed as skilled worker in the industrial cellar. The processing area was dominated by women so it is evident that the sexual division of labour in industrial winemaking in Purcari does not apply to any comparable extent to household winemaking.

The bottling-line workers' activities revolved around two main tasks: bottling, when wine was poured into the bottles; and labelling, when the wine had spent enough time in the bottles and was ready to be distributed on the market. I will describe these processes below.

Before the wine arrives in the bottling section through a pipe system to be poured into bottles, it comes from the processing section and rests in stainless-steel tanks in a walk-in refrigerator for cold stabilization – a process that prevents its further fermentation. From there, the wine goes through three filters and is then sent to the bottle filler (Figure 4.1). The empty bottles are placed manually on the conveyor belt by a worker at the loading table. These bottles go through the bottle rinser, which washes them inside and out. When they arrive at the filler, an exact amount of wine is released into each bottle. Until this point, the whole process is automated: the two bottling-line operators need only set the right data on the filler computer. The full bottles travel further on the conveyor belt to the corker segment, where natural corks are fitted into them. From here until the end of the line, no other action is needed at this stage. At the end, two workers stand by the line and pick the bottles up to arrange them vertically in a container on three layers separated by cardboard sheets, with 156 bottles on each layer. This task requires particular attention otherwise bottles come fast on the line, press against each other and fall, or the colleague at the second container gets overwhelmed and loses her rhythm. The most important thing is to learn how to keep a steady rhythm. The capacity of the bottling line is three thousand bottles an hour, and a bottling session takes eight to nine hours with some small breaks if something goes wrong on the line or if the bottles are not brought to the conveyor belt fast enough. The containers are taken by forklift to the industrial cellar. Depending on the type of wine, the containers stay in the cellar from three days to three years. When the wine is ready for the market, the bottle containers are brought back to the line to be labelled and packed.

For the other main task in the section – labelling – the bottles coming from the cellar are placed on the loading table, from which a worker puts them on the line. From there they go through the bottler rinser, which removes the dust that has settled while they were in the cellar. The bottles then go through the drier, next to the top labeller, where a top plastic cap is put on each one. The final stage on the line is the bottle labeller, where the front and back labels are glued to the bottles. As the bottles are now deprived of their anonymity, they are picked up from the line by one worker and put on two tables nearby where two teams of two–three workers take care of the necessary next steps: sometimes stickers advertising the most recent prizes are put on the bottles, sometimes they are wrapped in paper and sometimes decorative collars are attached to the bottles depending on the country to which the wine is to be delivered. Fully ready, the bottles are now put in cardboard boxes of six. Prior to packaging each box, the bottling date must be stamped on it and a sticker showing the bottling series and the type of wine needs to be ticked on the list of Purcari wines that is printed on the side of each cardboard box. These tasks are all done manually by the workers.

Another thought might come up: the tasks just described have a rather monotonous sequence of actions that do not require any obvious creativity or attention, only vigilance in carrying out repetitive and half-automated processes. This contrasts with the image of making terroir wines, which is normally represented as an artisanal activity in which the winemaker is present and may contribute at any point in the commodity's production process. In a larger facility the 'artisan's' presence is conveyed through periodical moments of supervision rather than an exhaustive accompanying of the product.

Working Days in the Winery and the Household

Workers from Purcari and Viișoara arrive at work every morning at a quarter to eight on the bus provided by the winery. The workers go to their dressing rooms (separate ones for men and women) and put on their overalls or simply change into work shoes. The workers from the *rozlev* go downstairs to their section, meeting the workers from the night shift coming in the other direction and preparing to leave work for the next twelve hours. The day shift could either pick up from where the night shift ended or start a new task. The work pauses at noon for one hour and then continues until 8 o'clock in the evening, when the night shift comes back. *Rozlev* workers disliked the lengthening of the shifts, but if the work time were reduced to eight hours they would receive a little over half the wage they got now – not enough even for the monthly bills. Before 2015, any work time over eight hours used to be paid as overtime (the normal hourly wage plus a quarter). Since the beginning of 2015, however, the twelve hours in these shifts have been paid uniformly; depending on the skill level, the hourly wage is 12, 14 or 16 MDL (or something between 50 to 80 eurocents). Monthly salaries rose more because of the increased number of working hours. Although three eight-hour shifts would have allowed a healthier rhythm of life to be followed, having only two shifts saved labour costs because of the smaller number of employees needed.

The shift to a flexible regime – stretching working hours and exploiting labour force, employing more seasonal workers than usual, bypassing work-protection regulation – would perhaps not have been as easy if there were more functioning factories in Purcari and its neighbouring villages. Many wine and canning factories in south-east region, which used to employ the large majority of the villagers, had been progressively closed since the dissolution of the Soviet Union. In the late 2010s, there were fewer jobs available and, because workers did not have many employment options locally, keeping the job at the Purcari factory was important – unless one was open to searching for work abroad. Thus, the low income and the lack of alternatives for jobs in the area became tools in manufacturing consent for exploitation (Burawoy 1982), while in the public discourse the message to the workers is that they should be grateful that they have jobs at all. Turner (2008: 52) considers these to be the most important social relations in the reproduction of capitalism, in that they represent exploitative production relations as fair and natural. In any case, the workers themselves observe and interpret the changes to their daily lives. The stories of two workers in the bottling section show firstly how the enhanced competition and success of the winery in export markets has reshuffled workers' sense of worth and well-being, and secondly how the same dynamic is complicated by gender relations.

Alina (52) has been working in the winery since 2009. She was a shop assistant in the village from 1985 until 1994, when she went on maternity leave until 2000. From 2000 until 2006, she was one of the many Purcari villagers who sold homemade wine and counterfeit brandy in Odessa. From 2006 until 2009, she again worked in a shop in the village but, through a new family connection (after her daughter married), she managed to get a job at the winery and since then she has been working in the bottling section. She recalled that when she started working the winery did not have very many orders, so they worked from 8 AM until 5 PM in her section, and Saturdays and Sundays were always free; these were the years after the first embargo imposed by Russia in 2006, when Moldovan wineries were slowly (re-)establishing export-trade partnerships. In the Purcari Winery during the late 2000s, sometimes no bottling or labelling would be required – and from time to time the workers were asked to stay at home for one or two weeks in a row. Alina recalled that in 2009 orders for Russia started to come in again, and production increased somewhat. During this time there were two shifts, but 'when Moscow was causing trouble' – she was referring to the 2013 embargo – 'we changed to work in one shift' for one year.

In 2015 – when sales started to grow again, and more quickly than before – night shifts were introduced and soon became permanent. Alina adapted easily to the change, but her time outside the shop floor shrank considerably. One day we were sitting and unfolding boxes at the *rozlev*, and she described her and her colleagues' new lives expressively: they come to work twelve-hour shifts because they need an income; when they go home during the day, they go work in the garden so they can produce some food for the household. But then there is a drought or a plant disease, and they see that their tomatoes are dying or their garlic is turning small, so then they go to the market and buy what they could have harvested from their own gardens. She said that this means that all their 'life is work and small money'. Sleeping was also an issue, given the structure of the weekly shifts. She took comfort in the fact that, being older, she did not need to sleep so much, four or five hours being enough; 'the younger ones need to sleep more, but they will all damage their nervous system anyway'. Talking about the quality of life inevitably brought up comparisons with the Soviet experience. For Alina, while when working during the Soviet period the sense of time was different, 'it was better, working from 8 to 12, with a break until 5, then from 5 to 8 again, work. With the master [*la stăpân*], we work from 7 till 10 in the interests of the owner.' Alina added the hours spent preparing for and travelling to work and back again: she left the house to go to the bus station at 7, and by 8 she had started work. In the evening, after going to the locker room, she would leave from the factory at 8:30–8:40 and she would be available for her household after 9:30 PM. This was the normal schedule on a day shift.

Working *la stăpân* (for the master) makes a difference not only in terms of working hours, it actually has a cluster of meanings for the winery employees. It changes whose interests one serves and who takes responsibility for worker protection. In the Marxist view, this system of ownership is the source of exploitation, being opposed to the longer experience of collectivization that rural Moldova went through. Private property is also the source of alienation: the worker sells her labour to produce commodities that are later alienated from herself. For Alina, working *la stăpân* meant that one person decided the rules because 'everyone now belongs to a master' and the workers carried out transformational activities in the interests of the owner, while the senses of dignity and power that came from a collective model have been lost. The way in which Alina reflected on object ownership – of labour, land and technology – substantiates the relational view of property put forward by several economic anthropologists (Hann 1993; Verdery 2003). Property is a relationship between persons, and expresses the sense of practical entitlement that emerges from that relationship. Memories of the past tend to be depicted in a more positive light than its actual experience, but the mere fact that the present is overwhelmingly evaluated through references to the past experience of collectivized land and labour shows a continued trace of attachment to the Soviet system.

Almost one year later, on my last visit to Alina's home in July 2017, we spent some time in her garden. It was a week when her team were on nights, so she had a free afternoon – having slept in the morning. We talked about work, about the absence of bonuses for the work exceeding eight hours, the same wages being paid for Saturdays and the short breaks between night shifts. Many workers were aware of these aspects, but for different reasons they did not act against them. Some were just too afraid of losing their jobs and imagined that going to the managers or the CEO with such requests would result in their employment being ended. Others switched between jobs and had little interest in making efforts to organize better as a collective in the winery.[6] Alina's children were financially independent, and her husband earned enough so that together they made ends meet for a household of two – unlike many households, in which at least one spouse was unemployed or the children were still at school. We were sitting on a bench in her garden when she pointed at the lilies in front of us: 'Look, we leave home at 7:15 in the morning, we return at 9 [in the evening]; I look at these flowers, they are blooming, and I don't even have time to look at them [before] they are gone. We don't even know when the seasons change, when the weather changes.'

Some of the younger workers indeed suffered more from desynchronized circadian rhythm. Simona (33 years old) had been working in the bottling section for three years. She was a single mother living with her parents and her brother's family, and her situation was quite particular as she was given far too many chores in the household. She had to wake up at 5:30 every morning during day shifts to milk the extended family's two cows and to take care of the milk – setting it correctly to make cream, cheese and other dairy products. She then took the cows down to the Dniester, a thirty-minute walk both ways. She would then get ready for work before 8, go to the winery and come back twelve hours later. Sometimes, she then had to do more work in the household. In the evening, she said she fell 'asleep at 9:30 while [her] daughter is talking to [her]'. Simona would sometimes wake up with swollen, numb hands after the long shifts, which involved hard, repetitive effort using her arms. Her monthly salary was pooled in the household, and her mother controlled the money because 'our young ones want a car.' In addition, Simona's mother took the dairy products to Odessa, selling them to buy foodstuffs that they could not produce in the household. This happened once a week, and the profit they made was very small compared with the work that they put in to make these products.

Overall, Simona spent most of her time awake working. The workload was not constantly felt to be miserable, as on some days the winery work could be less demanding. Longer breaks to change the bottling-line segments (if the bottles had different sizes, for example) and not having agricultural work to do at home counted as more relaxed days.

The effects of poverty were also felt in the self-perceptions of the workers. Artiom, a worker on the bottling line, said to me one day as I was walking out the section, 'Tell to your compatriots that Moldovans are not really that stupid!'[7] I stopped and asked him, 'But who says you're stupid?', to which he answered, 'Who does not feel stupid when he is poor?' Probably this moment also had to do with my position in the field as a Romanian – I was unavoidably interpellated at times as someone in the position to judge and mock the Moldovan society[8] – but nevertheless, poverty and dispossession contributed to a self-image of inferiority among the workers.

Despite the obvious hardships that these workers experienced, only rarely did the bottling-section teams voice their concerns. I witnessed one such occasion in *smena* 2 during a day shift on a Friday, when the workers were not allowed to take a break for a quick snack at around 6 PM (after eating at 1 PM). The *smena* foreman told them that they should work and not take a break before finishing the bottling task that they had started. This released a storm of anger, and one worker told the foreman that they were underpaid and overworked. He said that if the company wanted them to work on the following day – a Saturday – at least one boss should have stayed in the village over the weekend (most of the employees in leading positions came from Chișinău, lived in Purcari from Monday to Friday but returned to the city at weekends). The topic of the day was the rumour that the canning factory in Olănești might reopen. All the workers were aware that active companies in the region could afford to pay low wages because there were many unemployed in Purcari and the neighbouring villages. If the Olănești factory reopened, it would give the workers more leverage. But these moments did not last long and, as I gathered over the year, they were never discussed with the management in Chișinău.

The Strain and Sociality of Long Shifts

The night shift started at 8 PM and ended at 8 AM, with a one-hour break after midnight when workers ate for thirty to forty minutes and rested for half an hour. The tasks in the night shift did not differ from those done during the day: there might be bottling or labelling and packaging to be done. Sometimes there were requests to 'make presents' (Romanian, *să facem cadouri*), which were special boxes containing a combination of two or more wines, or wine and a Purcari-stamped glass. The teams working in the bottling section were the only ones doing night shifts, so no other workers or managers were around. Only rarely during the harvest might one or two persons be needed in another section overnight and one person worked periodically overnight when the walk-in refrigerator needed to be cleaned, so normally the factory was empty during night-times. Although the weekly alternation between night and day shifts was very tiresome, workers enjoyed some aspects that were missing on the day shifts. Most of the bottling-section workers said they preferred working at night because it was quieter and no one bothered them with orders or checked on their work process. They did not think that the presence of managers changed the quality of their work, because they could not 'cheat' the conveyor belt by slowing down the process.

Although the workers found a way to deal with the long working hours, these took their toll occasionally when household work was at its peak and a day spent toiling around the household was followed by a night of work. One of the workers in the bottling section was Bogdan (35 years old), married with two children. He had been a forest ranger for a few years in the early 2000s, like his father, but was removed from his position and had to pursue other jobs, so he had been shifting for some years between working in Russia as a construction worker and seasonal work at the winery. At the beginning of 2016, he decided to work permanently at the winery and was employed as bottling-line operator. He now preferred the work in the winery despite the lower pay, as during his time as a ranger he was constantly worrying about wood being stolen, his friends asking illegal favours or unannounced inspections. Working abroad was also something he wished to avoid in the future because he no longer wanted to be far away from his family. Over one year, I witnessed various moments in which Bogdan seemed strained by the twelve-hour night shifts. One night in May, he showed up at work not having slept for more than two hours in the past thirty-three – and he was going to work a full night on that day as well. He had been helping his mother-in-law building a new house until 2 PM, and then at 4 PM he had gone to school for the parents' meeting at the end of the school year (his wife Petra, who was part of the second *smena*, was working on the day shift). He approached me during a smoking break and said, 'I don't know what you are going to write in your book, but here it is chaos'. He was also aware that when it came to night shifts and work over eight hours, the pauses were too short.[9] Bogdan had been doing this switch between weeks of twelve-hour day shifts and nights of twelve-hour shifts for a year, and said that he would look for a different job soon. He had been 'a good forest ranger' and 'was very good with paperwork and schedules';

Table 4.2. Cost advantages at the Purcari Group level compared with other European wine-producing countries, reproduced from the public document 'Purcari Corporate Presentation 2018'. © Daniela Ana.

Purcari Group Costs of Goods Sold, 2016			Input costs assessment
28%	Agriculture	Labour	Significantly cheaper labour
		Chemicals	No cost advantage in chemicals
		Land	Vineyard prices in MD, RO at lower costs than Western Eu.
		Fuel	Fuel, cheaper in RO, much cheaper in MD
33%	Production	Oenological materials	No cost advantage
		Labour	Significantly cheaper labour
		Energy	Cheaper energy
		Equipment	Moderate cost advantage on locally built eq. + reparations
39%	Finishing	Bottle	Significantly cheaper bottles
		Labels	No cost advantage
		Cap &Cork	No cost advantage
		Labour	Significantly cheaper labour

Note:
MD = Moldova; RO = Romania; Eu = Europe.

he had received a diploma for being the best employee; and Dionis, the bottling-section director, was 'like a stone': he did not listen to the workers or take note when they had organizational skills beyond their manual tasks. A couple of weeks later, however, we again talked about the schedule and Bogdan was rested and content. He was talking differently now, showing understanding for Dionis and, along with the other workers in the team, agreeing that the bottling director had a lot on his mind and could not take decisions about the schedule. It was *comanda* ('the order') that decided the workers' working rhythms. If the market demanded Purcari wine, it was imperative for everyone not to miss the chance to provide it.

Later on that summer, Bogdan again complained during a night shift that the workload was too high. He felt that the managers should show more solidarity with the workers and take care over their workloads: 'they sit all day and think work is easy, but it isn't...lifting things day by day. Let's not count me in, but there are women, men who lift things for eleven hours, a single boy puts ten thousand bottles on the line, you get tired automatically. At night it is very hard to work.' The fact that the bottling line was overused caused occasional problems, and it had sometimes to be stopped during labelling to sort out small issues such as the line not washing the bottles properly or not fixing the top label correctly. This and the rising number of orders put pressure on the workers, so working hours were kept long and included Saturdays on an almost constant basis. Like Alina and Simona, Bogdan brought into the discussion the fact that although the workers had land to work, it was very hard to find people to help them with this kind of labour. He said he was making an effort to figure out why, 'before Vlad', they had had more time: 'I worked with several [heads of production]. It's either that people were more united, or there weren't so many orders. ... and no young person will stay for 1,800 MDL per month (around 90 euros); you need at least 4–5,000 [MDL; roughly 200–250 euros]. Look, as a bottling-line operator I work for 16 MDL per hour, but there are others with just 12 MDL per hour.' Public information about production costs is available at the Purcari Group level (referring to the four companies) but categories in the breakdown of production costs show how interaction with the globalized wine market and the alignment with international quality standards are playing out on salaries (Table 4.2). Until Purcari is able to charge a much higher premium price for its wines, the mainstay of its competitive advantage is low labour costs at all stages of production.

Maria (58 years old), Bogdan's mother, was quite reluctant to be critical of the company in my presence. She was satisfied with being able to 'hold on to work, because money does not suffice; it would be desirable to work less and to receive the same money...it would be desirable...but I cannot say more.' Although it was sometimes obvious that she was not well rested and had periodic health problems with her pancreas and her back, Maria was one of the most cheerful workers in the winery, making time seem to go faster while working the night and Saturday shifts. She was the artist of the *smena* and often sang on these shifts, with the other workers joining in sometimes.[10] Maria liked to think of herself as an entertaining colleague, and from time to time she would say between songs or jokes that we had to remember we worked together with '*chea* Maria' (Aunt Maria). These artistic interventions in the industrial work schedule occurred mostly on Saturdays and outside the 'normal', non-extended working hours during my stay, when supervisors and tourists were not around.

In this way, Saturdays had something of the mood of the night shift; the workers could relax more and the atmosphere at lunch was different: while during the week the workers sat at separate tables with three to five seats, ate their meals and continued the lunch break by lying down in the dressing rooms or outside, on Saturdays workers brought food from home and put two tables together so that the ten-worker team could sit together. These meals were richer and more diverse, being brought by the women: if during the week there was mostly soup, a second course made of chicken and a side dish, on Saturdays there were local cheeses, *siliotca*,[11] baked potatoes, various sausages, eggs, salad, *babka*,[12] pie, pickles, stews and salads – a veritable feast. Eating took a little longer than half an hour on Saturdays and the workers got only a quarter of an hour rest, but they interacted with each other more. Food from home brought to the factory showed continuity with practices of commensality and socialization that had been more frequent in the socialist years. It was the older women workers who brought most of the cooked food from home, while the younger ones brought cold cuts or canned food.

Elena (58 years old), one of the workers on the line, had worked as a kindergarten instructor for twenty years, then as a shop assistant for a further eight. She had been working at the winery for six years at the time of my fieldwork. I asked her whether this activity was more strenuous than her previous jobs. She said at first, referring to factory work, that 'this is what became of me' in a self-depreciatory manner. But after a few more seconds she said that as she grew older, she found taking care of children more exhausting – and being either a teacher or a shop assistant came with more responsibility. Here at the factory, '[y]ou come, you do your thing, and then you can go home and just put your head on a pillow and you're done'. Like Alina, she looked at the work schedule from the standpoint of an older person, one who 'does not need that much sleep anymore'. She used to like sleeping long hours – but now, even if she wanted to sleep for long, she could not. This was ultimately the reason why she did not complain about the night shifts, though she realized that they could be hard on the lives of the younger workers. Elena cherished nights and Saturdays in comparison with other working times because of the extra freedom for play and commensality, as well as the potential to plan their tasks more efficiently in the team:

> When they make food for us, we all eat the same food; it's like we're on a diet. But on Saturday everyone brings what they can, and it feels tastier, it is like with kids when the mother is not at home, we climb on to the table. We simply feel freer, we are not afraid that someone will come and tell us to work faster. Our *smena* is in such a way that … last night we made twenty-one euro-pallets, this is a record. When we started

[the shift] the girls marked boxes for *Rară Neagră*, and we quickly made 15 pallets. In this time, three women were sitting at the line, picking the bottles and packing them, but I and Alina made another 1,260 boxes while these fifteen pallets were being made. We then marked the 1,260 boxes for rosé. You know, we make time to work, rest, eat, and then work again until the morning. (Purcari, March 2017)

The more closely the workers could control their working relations and the production process, the less alienating wage work appeared to be – as for the workers in the previous chapter. Anthropologists of work have shown for different work settings that playfulness and commensality are important aspects of workers' communities. Kofti (2018) showed that in Bulgaria, commensality and mutual aid decreased in the postsocialist period among non-family neighbours. In the bottling section of the Purcari Winery, the social aspect of communal work is exemplified by meals, jokes, singing and occasions for doing favours. The workers who contribute value to global capitalism are often not just passive victims of relations-of-value extraction (cf. Durst 2018), they are also social actors who are reproducing their households and finding or creating new rituals and meanings in their everyday lives.

Factory 'Natural' Time

On Saturday shifts at the *rozlev* I had more time to chat with the women workers, and on the day before Purcari *hram* I asked them how they usually celebrated this event in the village.[13] They raised their voices to say that nowadays the *hram* was not as elaborate as those that they had experienced during the Soviet years, and that the changed work schedules had also altered the manner in which village rituals were carried out. There was an artistic programme with children from school and kindergarten, and some people would go out into the centre of the village, but in the past people from other villages had also come and a big celebration had taken place – 'for three days with the harmonica' (Romanian, *se stătea trei zile cu garmoșca*), added Maria. But people no longer had time for this. A brainstorming session started around the reasons why villagers celebrate the *hram* differently: 'People just don't have time now', 'People are dependent on money! They cannot do without money as they did in the past' or 'They had more spare time, workloads were not as bad!' The workers recalled how weddings used to last for three days as well: there was the wedding of the bride, of the groom and then *colacul* ('knot-shaped bread'), which was for the godparents. Before the 1990s, people could go to more than one wedding per evening and they could afford it because they did not have to give money all the time. People offered cows or chickens (Romanian, *se juruia vaca sau cloșca*) and animals for consumption generally. Now, one could barely afford to go to one wedding a month.

In the afternoon of the day of *hram* on 25 May, I went to the centre of the village. The celebration took place on the school sports field: sports competitions and artistic events took place with the children from kindergarten up until eighth grade. After the artistic performances had ended, food and wine were offered to the people by the town hall, the music continued to play and many people started to dance. During this time, I met with around half of the employees from the winery. Many of them had been allowed to work shorter shifts on that day of six or eight hours, and only a few were permitted to take the entire day off, but the workers in the bottling section had to work the full twelve-hour shift because a bottling session had started on the previous shift and this could not be stopped. This was one of the operations in the winery that appeared as 'natural' in E.P. Thompson's (1967: 60) understanding, whereby once it had started its momentum could not be stopped. Besides this, waiting in the line were some urgent orders to be sent to Romania, which had to be completed after the bottling session had ended.

Dionis and Labour Organization: The Middle-Management Perspective

The experience of Dionis (55 years old), a union leader during the final Soviet years and the current bottling-line director in the winery since 2013, adds another layer to the story of sending wine around the world and how this activity is perceived by him, a skilled worker with experience covering the critical decades on which this research focuses.

Dionis grew up in a village in the south-east of Moldova. From 1979, he studied winemaking in a specialized high school in Chișinău – and in 1982, he graduated from the Technical University in the same city with a diploma in the technology of white wines. Dionis took a break from winemaking between 1982 and 1984, when he completed military service in the Soviet Army. After that, he chose to go further with his studies and, between 1984 and 1989, he studied at the Polytechnic Institute in Chișinău. Before finishing, he was assigned by the state to work in a sparkling-wine factory in the capital. The positions that he occupied ranged from supervising the blending section to being the president of the factory's works council for a couple of years until he was promoted foreman of the bottling section. He then moved to another winery in Chișinău, and from 2003 until 2009 he worked as a bottling section director. Between 2009 and 2013, he was unemployed but did not want to tell me whether or not this was related to the crisis in the wine sector.

In 2013, Dionis saw an announcement in a newspaper that the Purcari Winery was looking for a bottling-section director. He was selected and has been heading the Purcari bottling section ever since. He was responsible for drawing up the monthly plan and preparing all the technological processes in the bottling section, including bottling wine, labelling and delivering, ordering auxiliary materials and organizing the schedules for each shift. He also had to make sure that the consistently large number of orders were completed on time to be delivered to twenty-eight countries around the globe. Dionis had to be at the factory from around 6 AM until late at night, sometimes after midnight supervising the night shift, but not continuously. His office was on the floor above the bottling section. This was where workers came in the morning to get their *nareada*,[14] or daily plan, and then Dionis would go downstairs to the bottling line from time to time to check their progress.

His passion for wine had begun in childhood, as he had grown up in a region in the south of the country where winegrowing is ubiquitous. During the Soviet years, there were vineyards in every village in his *raion*, and on average every fourth village had a winery. He worked in the school brigade from fourth grade, weeding and harvesting in the vineyards, and this was when he started to like 'wine culture'. While studying at high school, he grew to like the field even more through his professors, whom he found very inspiring and fair to the students. Over time, student internships in wine companies convinced him to specialize as a winemaker, to be part of something important to society: 'the grapevine is a fundamental companion to human civilization', he stated. But although he initially specialized in winemaking, he came to focus later on one segment of its production – namely, bottling. Regardless of the effort and fragmentation of his work, he was able to find an anchor in the final product, for which he felt responsible, while connecting himself to a history of the place in order to put together a narrative of tradition and continuity:

> Grapevine is the most important for man. To make a good wine is a huge thing; a good wine is made when you make an effort. I learned winemaking and went on with supervising bottling because this is how I started. And I did not change the section because I strove to do well what I started. Here, we deliver 240,000 bottles monthly and 2 million annually. This year we aim for 2.5 million. This position asks a lot. (Purcari, June 2017)

The Eurocentric discourse on the significance of wine for civilization is very common in representations of wine (cf. Guy 2003: 2). These equate winemaking with civilization and civilization with winemaking communities –

which, for the majority of human history, have been communities located in Eurasia. The link that Dionis makes between civilization and winemaking is a common trope among winemakers and consumers around the world, which usually goes no deeper than acknowledging the historical presence and relevance of wine in consumption, ritual and agricultural knowledge in Eurasian and, later, other societies as well. Although it is not the case here, it is important to note that wine has been reclaimed in chauvinistic discourses in the past (see Hamvas 2003); equally, as Ulin (2007: 49) eloquently shows in his critique, nationalist discourses did not shy away from the 'anthropomorphizing of viticulture' in the past, resulting the conflation of national purity and the vinification of local grapes from a single property. The task of an anthropologist to understand the system of values and meanings of a winemaker while being able to grasp the undertones of exclusion is not always easy – first because some of these discourses do remain at the level of an innocent local pride, while others can shed light on how discourses on difference and exclusion are made.

The long history of winemaking in the region and the prestige of the Purcari Winery provide a cultural identity to the worker, who does not understand his work as purely instrumental, even though the tasks are repetitive and the final product is alienated from him. There is a cumulative view of something that is bigger than individual activity, mediated by the local socio-historical context as described by Ulin in the Dordogne (2002: 694): 'the culturally formative activity that is entailed in wine-growing work and identity unfolds in a social arena that positions winegrowers both literally and figuratively in fields of power and that should be seen as both historically and socially mediated'.

However, in Dionis' opinion the Soviet years were better in terms of the quality of working life and because there was great hope ahead for a Communist society: 'Before, we were heading towards something better, we were waiting for communism. But now it is chaos.' Thinking about the differences in practices between then and now, Dionis recalled that when he worked in factories in the 1980s there was a monthly plan – and this was the ultimate priority. It was certainly not always followed, but it had a regulatory or stabilizing function for workers and planners alike. It is now widely accepted by scholars that the Soviet system was not necessarily well planned and controlled, was full of contradictions and had a large shadow economy, but that in their daily life many people perceived it as orderly planning that made stable life possible (Visser and Kalb 2010). Dionis held this latter view too and claimed that planning made work different from what it was in the present, when private companies asked for larger amounts of work to be done unpredictably, 'because now wine is delivered everywhere, and this is why there is more production'. At the first wine factory where he worked in the 1980s, Dionis was elected labour-union president. Back then, he argued, labour unions were fighting 'for human rights, they were doing a lot for the citizens, for the people'. They provided free holiday tickets (Romanian, *foi de sanatoriu*), and the collective contracts brought advantages to the workers. If workers had over five years of work experience, they had a raise in salary and their amount of holidays per year was increased. He no longer followed the activity of labour unions. The trade union representing the workers in the wine industry in Moldova is Federația Națională a Sindicatelor din Agricultură și Alimentație 'Agroind-sind' (National Trade Union Federation in Agriculture and Food Industry 'Agroindsind'). Workers, owners, the ONVV and the trade union have regular meetings with regional and national foci, but the focus is more on developing collective production and market strategies than on organizing the labour force in factories and the fields.

Thus, in a way, direct benefits for the workers through trade unions diminished, and Dionis was disappointed that companies distanced themselves from these organizations (Romanian, *companiile s-au dezis de sindicate*) and that many of the priorities of the past had been lost:

> You don't have tourism for workers. Back then you paid a small amount and got tickets for tourism. Back then there was also the collective work contract. Every year there was an assembly of the employees, this thing was discussed. The questions raised had to be answered. While I was in the union I strove to get the management to be on the side of the workers. Every department had what was called union activism. Every month, in every department, the activist collected questions from the department and the union decided which of the questions would be taken to the management. I was attracted by this kind of work in which you could do something good for the worker; I felt pleasure when I was doing something good for the people. You can feel that there are no unions [today]. People always have issues to raise, and in the past they were all for one, [but] in capitalism each one is for himself. ... Everything was arranged then, cheap food, everything was calculated as a coefficient from people's salaries to suffice, and it was forecast. Every enterprise had its economic department, financial planning. They made the plan, and everything was settled for the individual for their eight-hour working day, [but] now it's not like that. Democracy is good, but not everyone understands it. This system will also end. [Before] there was Lenin, the initiator of the revolutions in 1905, 1917; he was for the rights of the people. He took from the rich to give to the people. Now it is the other way around; it is taken from the state and given to the few. The system will fall. What will follow, we don't know. We don't have Marx and Engels anymore; they took the system in a positive direction. But then, there were those who did not take the ideas further in a correct manner, which is why we are here. (Purcari, June 2017)

Labour-rights experts usually emphasize the less favourable image of Soviet labour unions (or the *profsoyuz*, as they are still called by Purcari workers): despite the positive image they have in the eyes of former workers, trade unions in the Moldovan Soviet Republic were heavily controlled by the Party and were top-down, hierarchical institutions. Indeed, organized labour did not have a prominent role in Soviet society. The *profsoyuz* were more concerned with holiday tickets than with organizing workers. Officially, the role of the unions was triple – firstly as the plan's 'transmission belt'; secondly as a subsidiary of management that distributed social benefits such as holidays, recreation facilities and apartments; and finally as a defender of the workers in cases of violations of work norms – a role that was less prominent (Kubicek 2002: 607–8). Nevertheless, the fall of the USSR entailed 'the end of a moral order' (Hann 2011: 29) in the sense that everyday practices and world-views suffered a major shake-up.

Conclusion

Bottling expressively reveals how the integration of the company into the market has determined working rhythms in some areas of the production. In this chapter, I have tied the flexibilization of labour in Moldova to the process of the global labour market neoliberalization. The example of Purcari Winery is especially revealing, because its conscious efforts since the late 2010s were directed at selling its wine globally and breaking away from the traditional export relationship that Moldovan wineries had had with the Russian market. What occurred in the post-Soviet years and accelerated in the post-embargo period was a change in the value of Moldovan wine. The ethnography in this chapter has shed light on the patterns of value extraction and the differentiation strategies of late capitalism by looking at the ways in which the lives of workers in the wine industry were transformed when the commodity that they produced took on a new value. The increase in workloads had to do not only with the rise in orders but also with the strategy of product diversification and the volatility of postmodern capitalist firms (Harvey 1989). In the winery, the repeated introduction of new products disrupted an already demanding work rhythm.

I have also focused on the daily and nightly lives of the workers in the winery and at home in order to show how they appreciate the recognition that they receive, as well as to explain why organizing collectively for better conditions is challenged from many sides – the scarcity of jobs in the region, the fear of retribution and the practice of economic coping strategies that take some of the pressure away from the wage job. New forms of alienation and sociality came about because of flexible work regimes. The different shifts led to important changes in the experience of everyday life in both the winery and the household. Women and men both periodically expressed distress regarding the shrinkage of time left that they could spend with their families, on holidays or gardening. But the new schedule could also create spaces of socialization and solidarity that are not possible during normal day shifts – especially among women. If visits in the neighbourhood had been lost to the workers who had to be present in the winery for longer hours, meal breaks at weekends or at night – with food brought from workers' households – represented re-enactments of the lost commensality. They were different in substance and duration to the latter, but they nevertheless signified the reclaiming of bygone practices.

After exploring the dimensions of production in the vineyards, factory and workers' households, in the next chapter I move on to a new dimension in which the value of Purcari wine is produced: outside the factory production site, in vineyard soils and laboratories, and on the desks of the marketing workers in the Chișinău office.

Notes

1. From the Russian *разлив*, meaning 'bottling' or 'spilling'.
2. From the Russian *смена*, meaning 'shift' or 'change.' I refer to them as 'team 1' or '*smena* 1' to differentiate them from the other team in the bottling section, team 2, with whom I worked less often but enough to have a sense of their work rhythm and social dynamics as well.
3. I was not provided with access to figures for production volumes and sales by the Purcari Winery alone for previous years, but it was noticeable from the sales at the Purcari Group level that the new marketing strategies had worked well, as their sales grew constantly from 2010 (except for a drop after the 2013 embargo and the 2014 conflict in Ukraine). In 2010, the Group sold wine worth 9.6 million euros; in 2011, 10.3 million euros; and in 2012, 13.5 million euros. In 2013, sales were still rising but the September ban led to slower growth: 14 million euros, falling to 12.8 million euros in 2014. Since 2015, group sales have been rapidly rising, to 15.2 million euros in 2015, 22.9 million in 2016 and 31.5 million in 2017.
4. For example, workers in the blending and refrigeration sections, regardless of the task they carry out, are exposed to a cold, wet floor and low temperatures throughout the year. In the refrigerator, washing stainless-steel vats involves the worker in spending time at -15 degrees Celsius, going out periodically and alternating between -15 degrees and 20 degrees Celsius. In the industrial cellar, the activity often involves manual washing of the barrels with air humidity at a constant 90%. Outside the factory, the workers in the vineyard are exposed to high temperatures in the summer and very low ones in the winter.
5. Moldovan salary law in units with financial autonomy, lex.justice.md/document_rom.php?id=335FE8DE:8C76B498 [accessed 26 June 2021]. For skilled and unskilled labour, the Romanian words used are calificat and necalificat. The definition

is narrow: regardless of the employee's knowledge, if he/she does not have a preparatory course or a diploma recommending him/her for the activity, that worker is categorized as 'unskilled' and therefore is paid less.
6. Like Bogdan, who was switching between winery work in Purcari and construction work in Moscow – or another worker, one of the forklift drivers, Alex (35 years old), who took unpaid leave for three to four months a year to work in the construction sector in Poland and the rest of the year worked in the winery. The company did not encourage switching from job to job, but more experienced manual workers were not sanctioned if they did it outside the peak season between September and December. My understanding was that for managers it was clear enough that it was difficult to get by on the salaries in industrial work in Moldova, so they were not in a position to judge workers who wanted to supplement their annual income. Besides that, this practice might have been the main reason why the workforce did not organize and why strikes were almost non-existent. Remittances and job-hopping took some pressure off the workers.
7. Romanian, *Să le spui la zemlecii tăi că moldovenii nu sunt chiar așa proști*. (He used the word *zemleci* (sing. *zemleac*), from the Russian земляк: 'fellow countryman').
8. See also Poenaru (2016: 81) on the 'civilizational impulse' common among Romanians towards their Moldovan neighbors, which is sometimes internalized by Moldovans in their turn.
9. According to the Moldovan Labour Code, in a company it is allowed to work 6 days a week with a day of rest, as an exception upon internal agreement in the company. It is also allowed in exceptional cases to have 12 hours shifts, but the break between the shifts should be of at least 24 hours (CP124/2003, T. IV, C. 1, Art. 100, Par. 6 https://www.legis.md/cautare/getResults?doc_id=110228&lang=ro, accessed 14 August 2021).
10. In her childhood and adolescence, Maria had participated in singing contests and had also loved sports. She had wanted to practise sport professionally but did not manage to because she did not have a chance to learn to swim, and this was one of the tested disciplines. Until she got married at twenty-two, Maria also took part in local folklore groups.
11. From the Russian *селедка*, meaning marinated herring. It was a popular dish in Moldova, eaten with boiled or baked potatoes, onion and oil.
12. From the Russian *бабка*, a sweet noodle cake.
13. A *hram* is the day of dedication of an Eastern Orthodox saint by which a village is celebrated once a year. In Purcari, it is celebrated on Ascension Day, which depends on the date of Easter; in 2017, it was 25 May.
14. From the Russian *наряд*, meaning 'duty' or 'order'.

5

Nature, Value and Globalized Markets
Articulating the Purcari Terroir

> Terroir is a term that [in Moldova] was not known until now. The global tendency is to ask you to research more deeply to see what is at the root of quality grapes, of quality wine. Maybe earlier there was something, but it was not precisely termed 'terroir'. There were microzones in which grapevine was cultivated, and they could obtain quality wines, yet I am not from that generation, and I cannot say what was then. But I believe that no one went more deeply into this matter.
> —Eugen, 30, chief production officer

By means of an ethnography of the relations of production in the village and the winery, the previous chapters of this book have shown how terroir and homemade wines are produced and also how their value has been constituted historically. Meaningful differences in the taste and qualities of wine are not denied but these realities are only part of the story regulating the global hierarchy of value in wines (Jung 2016), with economic inequality and dependence concentrated on one main export partner also having crucial importance in the recognition of Purcari wine – an argument that can be extended to virtually all commercial Moldovan wine. I acknowledge later that the first source of value is material production, the sale of the workers' abstract capacity to work plus his or her work carried out outside the workplace, for reproduction. I argue further that other sources of value in commodities come about through the reattachment of the product to a different person (Foster 2005: 11) and the extraction of surplus value from abstract characteristics of land in the form of monopoly rent (Harvey 2002: 94–95).

Reattachment works as a concept of desirability and the meaningfulness of a commodity; monopoly rent, as a seal for its uniqueness. A desirable, meaningful and unique wine is conveyed by Purcari through marketing work such as advertising and branding. This marketing relies on the scientific work of classification and the selection of vineyards' environmental features – and furthermore on creating wine brands by playing with concepts of uniqueness in extracting value from soil through agriculture (use value) and through monopoly rent (surplus value from exclusive property rights), but also with a desirable genericness achieved through a standardized taste following global trends suggested by international wine consultants.

First, the uniqueness of Purcari wine is captured through the scientific work of classification, selection or evidencing parts of 'nature'. Soils and yeasts, along with local knowledge, are brought together in order to define a Purcari terroir. In the world of wine, the main marker of distinction is often a 'unique' terroir, which promises in turn the unique expression of a grape through the terroir wine. Next, through marketing work that builds on the outputs of the scientific work, this uniqueness is conveyed to consumers.

In wine marketing, it is often in the framework of the Old World–New World dichotomy that the issues of uniqueness and the generic characteristics of wines are discussed. These two categories point to two rather opposing typologies of 'wine regimes' that are meant to help in understanding shifts in notions of place and locality, history, technology and taste. In the text that follows, I will first analyse the terms of the Old World–New World dichotomy to show that, although it seems to be a sound entry point in understanding uniqueness and generic characteristics in the wine world, it has only limited analytical value; I suggest instead employing theories of globalization and a critical political-economy approach in order to grasp not only differences of taste and prestige but also historical differences of power (see also Ulin 1996, 2013; Banks and Overton 2010; Harvey 2002; Itçaina, Roger and Smith 2016; Demossier 2018; Inglis 2019). A critical political-economy approach to terroir helps us to grasp the ways in which value in wine is produced by forging a product with a local identity that is at the same time adaptable to the discourses of the global wine market. I then show how scientific work is mobilized in order to develop coherent terroir-marketing strategies by classifying nature (soils and yeasts) and providing evidence of 'local knowledge' or the human component of terroir. Finally, I show how the articulation of the Purcari terroir eases its entry into transnational markets: helped by itinerant wine consultants reshuffling 'locality' for the sake of market competition, Purcari wines climb up the global hierarchy of wine taste. The analysis of the scientific and marketing work contributes to debates in economic anthropology by proposing new understandings of value creation, as well as showing how economic relations (marked by enhanced market competition) inform differentiation strategies in a Moldovan winery. At the same time, the chapter sheds new light on current debates on locality and identity in Moldovan society.

Purcari Terroir beyond 'Old World' and 'New World'

At this point, I will thus make a detour to discuss the role of the New World–Old World dichotomy in forging differentiation in the globalized world of wine. A loose definition of the two categories, in use since the 1970s, runs as follows: Old World wines are typically associated with West-European countries with long histories of wine production based around terroir wines made by artisanal producers, their quality being explained and marketed with reference to their strong connection to their place of origin (Banks and Overton 2010: 59). New World wines, on the other hand, are depicted as opposed to the conservatism of the Old World. Here, terms such as 'experimentation', 'development' and 'innovation' predominate (Banks and Overton 2010: 60). New World wines are not tied to the land – at least not in the framework in which European terroir wines made in old wine regions are – and differentiation between products is based on grape variety rather than origin labelling. Moreover, New World winemakers defend trade liberalism against the market protectionism enshrined in the legislation on place of origin. Critics accuse New World wines of abandoning the charm of traditional winemaking in favour of industrialization and promoting 'technological wines' (Garcia-Parpet 2008: 238) or generic wines that are oblivious to terroir.

From the 1990s onwards, however, these tendencies became less polarized although the terminology was retained. European countries started to incorporate so-called 'New World methods', and in their turn the 'New' winemaking countries tied their wines more and more closely to the land using the same increasingly developed systems of quality classification based on place of origin as the French 'Appellation' system. Banks and Overton (2010) proposed a reconceptualization of the world of wine going beyond the established Old-New dichotomy, motivated by the complexity of the wine industry around the globe today. They claim that the ultimate challenge to the dichotomy comes from growing production trends in 'Third World' countries. While the Old and New World vineyards may have witnessed little fluctuation in production in the last three decades, countries such as China and India have increased their vineyard areas to such an extent that they now surpass New World countries combined. Another dimension that renders this conceptualization outdated is that these 'Third World' producers are not only blind to power differences in the world of wine but also uncritically reproduce a categorization of winemaking countries that is rooted in colonial-style language. Moreover, from the vantage point of a post-Soviet winemaking country, the categorization suffers a further loss of meaning. My Moldovan interlocutors –

winemakers, workers, consumers, wine bloggers and sommeliers – used these categories to only a very limited extent and did not base their wine choices or evaluations on them. It is a language that is more commonly used among marketing professionals and at Purcari the New World–Old World categories appear in reports and documents describing the market differentiation strategies of the winery, but they are virtually irrelevant in marketing material meant for the consuming public. Apart from the wine marketeers, in my interviews and observations throughout the fieldwork year, distinctions based on 'Old' and 'New' winemaking practices were made very sparsely. This ethnographic finding further supports the contention that the New–Old divide fails to capture the material and political realities in various parts of the wine-producing world.

The main fault line, which Moldovan winemakers and consumers brought up very frequently, was that of a (post)socialist legacy in wine taste and presentation that was opposed to its Western counterpart. The most visible wine blog in Moldova, finewine.md, is run by Andrei Cibotaru, a trained journalist who became a wine enthusiast in recent years and started writing about wine. In one of our discussions, I asked him about the Old World–New World distinction and where he would place Moldova and other former socialist-country winemaking regions. To begin with he replied ironically, 'Thank God we don't have such subtle knowledge around here!' He recalled that at the beginning of his wine-journalism career, he sometimes felt embarrassed at international wine competitions when debates around this topic were launched because these were categories of importance neither for Moldovan winemakers and consumers nor for him either. Referring to Moldovan wines from a comparative point of view, Andrei said that '[i]f we're talking about before the embargo, these were socialist wines, sweet ones. I believe we belong to the Old World: geographically we are in Europe [and] wine has been produced here for thousands of years. ... There are attempts to make wine here like in the New World, like in New Zealand, Australia, Chile, but I think we are rather another world, that of the new producers who have some background in winemaking, but make new wines.' Andrei's view captured the main elements that make a country like Moldova a more complex producer than the traditional dichotomy allows – history and reliance on local knowledge, combined with changing wine styles, guided by both creativity and the search for profit (i.e. making wines that are to an important extent guided by what is profitable on the market) and implying that the Old World–New World division is oblivious to current political and economic realities.

The inclusion of certain regions under a specific label is indicative of market positions, and it supposedly helps marketers or consumers to orientate themselves in diverse markets. Also, the Old-New dichotomy speaks about local tastes and wine styles that facilitate wine-marketing messages. But it refers to something more than wine – wine categorization is also symptomatic of a socio-economic divide, no matter how 'cultural' its categories might seem. Like wines, societies as a whole are bottled as 'Old' and respectable, 'New' and experimental, or 'Third World' and poor. Anthropologists have explained the power of this 'play-like' practice of imagining (Graeber 2013) and naming, in the end assigning – externally or internally – a system of values to a group; or similarly, as Narotzky (2018: 32) argues, 'naming the world is a form of engaging with it that has practical consequences'. This works like an ideology of wine quality that comes to structure the social recognition of that quality.

To further substantiate the above argument ethnographically, I analyse the marketing and scientific practices that are intended to make Purcari wine a global commodity by relying on a critical political-economy approach in globalization studies that helps to unpack the power relations that structure wine production and circulation. They address different political economies of wine that have been developed historically and help in understanding matters of production, trading and consumption, and how policies shift from one institutional order to another. Itçaina, Roger and Smith (2016) show how the changes in wine politics that started in the 1970s led to changes in institutional frameworks in the field of wine through political work. By 'political work' is meant the connections between knowledge, science and power that come to allocate power to actors in the field of wine, and the terroir is the base from which claims for distinction as monopoly rent are made (Harvey 2002). I will proceed to deconstruct the terroir-making and terroir-enhancing practices used at Purcari in order to show how a Moldovan winery forges its identity as a terroir wine producer by 'imbricating' (Demossier 2018: 55) local and transnational resources and discourses in order to maintain monopoly claims within a globalized wine market.

Marketing and Target Markets

During acts of exchange, the value of commodities is abstracted even further so that 'qualitatively different objects of irreducibly distinct use-values become comparable in quantitative terms in the domain of exchange value' (Eiss and Pedersen 2002: 284). For quality wines, different characteristics and qualities evoked in the marketing discourses reframe the product – a form of objectified abstract labour – so that it can increase its market value. And this happens in relationship with other similar products on the market, which is why it is relevant to say a few words about the main target markets of Purcari Winery in order to understand why some specific differentiation categories are favoured in its marketing discourses.

In developing brands and advertising material, the company works with professional advertising companies in Chișinău – and within Purcari, the two main marketing strategists and decision makers are Victor, winemaker and CEO of Purcari Winery, and Maxim, the marketing director since 2014. Victor (57 years old) graduated in oenology in Chișinău in 1982; as a student, in 1981, he completed his student practice at the then state-owned Purcari Winery and, as he put it, got to know the place better. He worked as an oenologist for ten years and, after Moldova's independence, started several private businesses in the field of wine – most of them in Moldova, but for four years he also owned a winery in the Krasnodar region of Russia. He sold that business, returned to Moldova in 2002 and started four projects that became what is today known as 'Purcari Wineries' group: Purcari Winery, Bostavan and Bardar in Moldova; and Crama Ceptura in Romania.

Maxim (43 years old), who was born in Moldova, studied marketing in Romania and returned to his home country after graduation. He has worked in various advertising companies promoting medical equipment; information-technology products; and, later, food products. He was employed as marketing director at Purcari in 2014, and in his department there were a public-relations manager, two brand managers and a designer. Branding and marketing are collective activities, but the final decisions are made by Maxim and Victor. As Victor set his eyes on Purcari Winery's brand potential since its Soviet years, he harnessed the place and its history to articulate its terroir and thus 'exploit the Purcari heritage' first in markets in the vicinity of Moldova and, when the time is ripe, in the already saturated markets of Western-European countries.

The targets for the next ten to fifteen years in Central and Eastern Europe are more realistic markets for wineries from the still relatively unknown Moldova. However, these markets are not simply a given due to the aforementioned cultural closeness; a 'good business climate' (Purcari Wineries Plc. 2018: 12) is crucial too. Therefore, calculations about alcohol-consumption rates, consumption trends, unemployment rates, ease-of-doing-business rankings, economic growth, gross-domestic-product level, market value and volume or targeted marketing campaigns are done every quarter-year.[1] These calculations are meant to capture the trends of the moment and to insert Purcari wine on the list of popular drinks of developing wine markets.

The example of the country presentation at the wine vernissage in Prague in the autumn of 2017, the event to which I refer in the introduction to this book, serves to illustrate well how Moldova brings its unique biography while promising state-of-the-art quality in wines – i.e. continuity despite crises, and reforms 'towards quality and excellence'. Moldova is depicted as undergoing a 're-orientation' to its 'millennial heritage of winemaking' – a moment of returning to certain values, which were presumably innate to Moldovan wine in early times. The brochure for future business partners in the Czech Republic contained descriptions of the three wine regions and the 'divin' one (this is the trademark name for Moldovan brandy as of 1993), giving details about the soils and climate and about the grape varieties best adopted.

Similarly, also aiming at Western markets, the Association of Small Wine Producers in Moldova started to advertise their wine in Germany in an online shop – one of the markets in Western Europe with more potential for Moldova than France, Spain or Italy. In the leaflets that consumers receive from the winemoldova.de shop, Moldova is presented as a wine region with a long tradition, which developed its production to an industrial level through cooperation with the Tsar and, later, with the Soviet Union – and alongside the mass-consumption wine developed through these trade relationships, Moldova is placed on the same latitude with Burgundy and 'in parallel, in some niches, the production of wines of the highest quality has always developed' there. It is also mentioned that wines from Moldova were known in Western Europe in the nineteenth century, they took a break (not mentioned but implied that it was a break in the international world due to the very close relationship with Russia) and that now these surfaces are to be discovered again by its Western drinkers, they are filled with 'valuable wines from small producers and old autochthonous grape varieties'.

The value of the new Moldovan wines, in order to be realized, must find an echo in a compatible 'imagined totality' (cf. Graeber 2013: 226), and this mechanism is not particular to wine marketing but applies to any commodity or exchange. What is particular here is to observe what kind of characteristics is imagined for a reinvented commodity: what is allowed or sensible to be advertised? Looking at Purcari's and Wine of Moldova practice, the underlying consensus is that small winemakers, careful harvesting, balanced processing and tastes are the characteristics of a universal quality wine. In the following two sections, I show how a variety of actors and materialities are brought together to prove or enhance 'quality'.

Soils

A terroir wine that is judged 'good' can come out of a vineyard without making very detailed claims to a priori knowledge of the soil composition and, likewise, without detailed research into which strains of yeasts would yield the most expressive varietal wine. However, capitalist market competition requires commodities to be subjected to quality standards that translate into generic features that enable comparison and value judgement (Harvey 2002; Karpik 2010) and soil mapping is the scientific way through which the soils or derived products can be commodified (Engel-Di Mauro and Van Sant 2020). At the same time, market competition makes brands ephemeral (Harvey 1989) – thus accelerating the need for differentiation strategies among producers, retailers and traders. It is in the above key that I read the complete soil mapping carried out on the Purcari estate in the late 2010s in the framework of two projects that had the common purpose of finding out which grapes grow best on Purcari soils and favouring those with the strongest 'typicity'.[2] One of the projects that required in-depth soil analysis was an application for a Purcari Protected Designation of Origin (PDO) label while the other was a project developed together with the ONVV called 'Best Grapes', which aimed to find out which grape varieties were most suitable for different soil plots in the vineyard through observations of yearly cycles of grapevine growth.

When compiling the information for the PDO label, Purcari Winery became involved in several projects concerning weather monitoring, grapes and viticulture styles, soil mapping and archival research. At the time of my fieldwork in Moldova, forty wines with Protected Geographic Indications (PGI) were being produced in the country but there were no PDO labels as yet. Under European legislation, PGI imposes a less strict control of origin than PDO: a PGI label requires only that at least one phase of the wine production takes place in the designated region. For the PDO label, the grapes and the processing must take place in the designated region,[3] and 'the link with the geographical area' – the influences of local geology, pedology, climate, hydrography, etc. on the product – must be documented and included in the file. In the case of wine, the oldest winemaking practices that can be traced in the designated perimeter must also be mentioned in the paperwork. These are the details that prove the uniqueness of a region and its product, but at the same time they serve as a standardizing practice. Indeed, Victor said that the more complex analyses carried out in the vineyards served to legitimate the Purcari (and Moldovan) wine area by emulating standards already recognized at international level:

> We want to make a PDO region that is truthful (Romanian, *pe adevărate*), that corresponds to the most rigorous international requirements – French standards – meaning somehow to copy those restrictions of the French: yield per hectare, taste, quality, international competitions, medals. Because we do not have this practice in Moldova, this was lacking too in the past. This is why we have to do it now, and I believe that the French practice is the best. It took them a few hundred years to create this system, and it works very well. (Chișinău, July 2017)

Exchanging technological knowledge between different regions and societies has been a constant process in human civilization, and the circulation and prioritization of knowledge and production organization is not devoid of power or outside politics. At the present day – when capitalism is the dominant, organizing, political and economic system globally – it is often the case that market logic and hegemonic projects influence the adoption of certain practices, which in the world of wine are highly visible (Jung 2016; Itçaina, Roger and Smith 2016). In other words, and going back to Victor's comments, the 'truth' in terroir needs to be proved not only through research but also through cultural and institutional allegiance with recognized actors. Providing evidence regarding Moldovan terroirs was one of the changes that local wine-industry decision makers saw as necessary in order to speak the language of the global wine market, given that terroir did not have much relevance in the socialist years. Certainly, there were programmes for the delimitation of production microzones in the Soviet Union in the 1930s, mimicking the French AOC (Walker and Manning 2013), but these mappings did not serve to develop systems of protection of origin. In the Eastern Bloc, grapes, often from different regions, were mixed in the production process and it was rarely possible to trace the resulting product back to a particular region regardless of its own 'uniqueness'. Now, the Purcari terroir only lacked the political and economic context to encourage this process, and quality-tracing systems such as PGI and PDO serve as policy tools that reify and commodify cultures (Gille 2010: 25).

The second project involving soil testing, 'Best Grapes', was developed by the ONVV together with the Soil Institute in Chișinău. In three sites in the country, evaluation of experimental plots planted with grapevines was carried out by a team of soil scientists. One of the three regions was Purcari, and in spring 2017 I came to learn more about it by meeting a television team in the Purcari Winery's vineyards. They were there to film a report about the project with experts in soil science and wine-marketing specialists from the ONVV. The lead soil scientist on the project explained how the data about the soil were gathered. In the first instance, geodesic research using GPS (the Global Positioning System) was carried out to demarcate the demonstration plots. Next, individual plots were mapped using GIS (Geographic Information System) and two-dimensional and three-dimensional maps were made. The final product of this analysis was a set of digital thematic maps of the vineyards showing digital models of the vineyard landscape with measurements of landform, slope, sun exposure and altitude; a pedological digital map was also generated. After all these data had been gathered from meteorological archives, current measurements and mapping, and satellite imaging, the scientists demarcated plots of soil and dug soil profiles.[4] On the Purcari estate, six plots of land measuring 4.25 hectares were demarcated and planted with three local grape varieties and three French ones. Over one year, the behaviour of the vines was observed in order to grasp which soil gave the best expression to the grapes.[5] The evaluation of the soils also allowed the size of the harvest to be estimated, so that production plans could be drawn up and the quantity of fertilizers needed assessed (Rozloga et al. 2017).

Through these processes, the wine world learned that the soils and bedrock in Purcari were particularly suitable for making red wines. Purcari would also remain in history as the first wine region in Moldova to be granted a PDO label, a detail that gives the winery a unique position in the country. But the process of acquiring a PDO label was a standardized one that asked for evidence of generic features in the vineyard and, later, in the wine. What is unique is relative to time and space because at the European or global level the same feature is a generic one, as the advertising texts explaining Purcari terroir also mention: 'While the whole region has favourable conditions for viniculture, specific areas are especially fertile for growing the most full-bodied grapes. The village ... lays at the heart of this special terroir. Recognizing similarities in the soil and climate with the Bordeaux region, French settlers entered into partnerships with the monastery and began cultivating Purcari's special vintages in the eighteenth century' (purcari.wine – accessed 27 June 2021). Frequently, in order to legitimize themselves, wineries outside France cite similarities with Bordeaux or Burgundy while simultaneously claiming their uniqueness. The world of wine marketing can thus have a circular logic and the description of certain works or products 'has no other function than to bring the work into an interminable circuit of inter-legitimation' (Bourdieu 1984: 53). Bourdieu used the example of luxury wines, in which the circularity makes it possible to entirely explain, present and qualify without any external inputs (cf. Guy 2003: 4).

Yeasts

The mutable definitions of 'terroir' can vary from the simplest version, which refers solely to the soil, to more complex ones that, besides soils, include 'the vine, subsoil, siting, drainage, and microclimate', but also 'an extreme position' (Unwin 2012: 40) that includes the indigenous or 'wild' yeasts and other microorganisms that evolve in a particular vineyard (Goode and Harrop 2011: 176). In the autumn of 2016, the Purcari Winery, together with the National Institute for Vine and Wine (INVV, the main wine-research unit in Moldova), started developing a local yeast-selection project in order to enhance the taste of the Purcari terroir. Scientists harvested local yeast cultures at Purcari so that in the future they could be used in winemaking in the factory.

In past few decades, until the mid-2000s, wineries in Moldova could use locally produced liquid yeasts from the Chișinău yeast factory, founded in 1964 as part of the bread-making plant in the capital. Since 1986, it functioned as a standalone enterprise, and in 1999 it was privatized. Sales decreased drastically after independence because of competition from imported products. The Chișinău factory only produced liquid yeasts for winemaking, and the active dry yeasts that became available as imports were easier to handle and more stable – so, finally, winemakers came to prefer them. Nevertheless, local yeasts in liquid form were available from this factory only until the early 2010s, after which time the factory went bankrupt due to low sales. At the time of my fieldwork, yeasts were mainly imported from Italy, Germany and France, and their price was higher than that for what used to come from the local yeast factory.

On the day that I visited one of the researchers in the indigenous-yeasts project, Lilia (32 years old), at the INVV in Chișinău, she explained to me the significance of the yeast selection and the multiplication process that could be carried out locally. Yeast cultures were isolated in order to be sent to a yeast factory in France to be processed.[6] To isolate wine-yeast cultures, Lilia took samples of fermenting must from a batch of grapes that had been fermented like homemade wine and placed them in nutritive environments in Petri dishes, where the yeasts started to grow and develop a day or two after seeding. They were selected from the wild yeast populations that appear on the plants and the soil surface in Purcari, which make grape fermentation in homemade wine possible. She explained that the important difference between homemade wines and those made by professionals was that while the former contained hundreds of cultures of yeasts (some of which were not suitable for fermenting grapes), the latter used a few cultures that 'were not wild' but selected yeast cultures that made a wine organoleptically optimal and could age well. Because of the presence of hundreds of yeast populations and other microorganisms in homemade wine, it spoils much more easily. The active dry yeasts contain cultures that take two to three weeks to consume all the sugar in the grape juice, whereas 'wild' mixes of yeasts and other microorganisms can take four to five weeks. I describe the selection process below.

On each Petri dish, a drop of growing yeasts contained large numbers of cultures, from which those that developed most uniformly were isolated because 'they have to be pure cultures'. The researcher showed me recent samples from Purcari that displayed a dotted pattern of beige drops that represented colonies of yeasts. Those that were growing in isolation from others like 'unique drops' were selected and then observed through a microscope to check the uniformity of their cells. Some of these were elongated, some round, some ovoid – but the aim was to select those colonies that had the most uniform cell shapes as that would mean a more stable fermentation process. After these uniform cells had been harvested, they were introduced into grape juice to be preserved for six months. After that, another round of yeast samples was harvested and the same process repeated, while the yeast's capacity to transform the sugars in the juice was monitored. Those cultures that fully fermented the juice and consumed all the sugar were selected. At the time of my visit, several yeast cultures from Purcari had already been isolated and the experiment was going beyond microvinification, now being extended to larger quantities of grape juice.

Lilia explained that the isolation of local yeasts became popular around the world and that 'this is the "terroir factor": this is where the grape was grown, where it was processed, this is also where it is fermented, with those yeasts, and this final product is original for that region'. She concluded that 'some winemakers are interested in using autochthonous yeast because it is something new and it will be like a brand ... when people hear that something is autochthonous it helps with trading [Romanian, *face bine la comercializare*]'. Branding ideally functions as a convergence of uniqueness and genericness in an object: it has an exchange value (a price), which, through branding, also acquires uniqueness (Foster 2005: 10). Victor also told me that this would 'allow us to have a better typicity and a more profound uniqueness to our wines. This is a very sought-after aspect for true consumers, which is why we started this long-term project, lasting two to three years'. This resonates with a more general strategy in advertising: that of seeking to cultivate an 'emotional connection and attachment to a brand that goes beyond reason' (Foster 2007: 708), for which higher prices can be charged. As Lilia suggested, terroir, although it is primarily associated with tradition and pre- or extra-capitalist interests, acts in the contemporary globalized wine market like a brand. Branding is a communication event, whereby producers and consumers are involved in a relationship in which products are linked to a source (Manning and Uplisashvili 2007; Manning 2012). Once a terroir has been presented to consumers and is recognized as valuable and respectable, it can become a brand.

Isolating microbial cultures that are indigenous to a specific place became popular in the niche-food sector for its marketing potential, as was the case with cheese as well (Paxson 2008), and the 'taste of place' has increasingly been seen as connected to microbes in the case of fermented foods, including wine (Trubek 2008). Notions such as 'microbial terroir' or 'signature flavours' (Paxson and Helmreich 2014: 177) are gaining in importance in these markets, where the microbiome of an environment is recognized as a crucial actor in influencing taste. Local yeasts are preferred for the claim that wines fermented only with local compounds are better from an organoleptic point of view and adapt better to fermentation. But there is a difference between using the entire population of yeasts and bacteria that occur in a vineyard and using selected populations that ensure a fermentation process that can be reproduced, thus giving a generic or standardized feature to wines.

Since the selected yeasts are in the first instance the wild yeasts that appear on the plants and the soil surface in Purcari, thus making possible grape fermentation in homemade wine, I initially misread the preference for them as an instance of 'rewilding' (Lorimer 2017) – as a return to a version of wine that is closer to 'natural' wine. Yet, the process of selection of the suitable yeast cultures from the wild yeasts, as well as the principles on which this selection is based, actually indicate very tight control of the winemaking process. Nevertheless, the concept of 'rewilding' – together with the 'probiotic turn' (Lorimer 2017) – are worth reflecting on in understanding how technology draws nature close to it in late capitalism, but in a highly controlled form. Yeast selection can ultimately be framed as a Pasteurian (i.e. technologically controlling) practice, although it has as its starting point the multitude of wild yeast strains. After several rounds of selection of yeast cultures that perform the optimal fermentation process, they can be considered to be domesticated yeasts – ensuring that the wild microbes that are selected are good for humans.[7]

In producing the active dry yeasts, a 'generic uniqueness' is achieved by, first, isolating what is unique and, second, by creating uniqueness around generic tropes. Through evidence of organoleptic characteristics; the typicity of certain grapes; and, ultimately, the claim to be a terroir, wines become subsumed into a globalized hegemonic discourse on taste and quality (Jung 2014). The standards for the selection of the yeast cultures come from the International Organisation of Vine and Wine (OIV 2012), which describes the characteristics in yeasts that influence vinification. Firstly, looking at soils draws attention to the extra profit that can come from land by claiming a monopoly rent for unique terroirs: I have shown how the evidence for a prestigious terroir is gathered by following the procedures for acquiring a PDO label. Secondly, by analysing the selection of the microscopic organisms that live and otherwise multiply spontaneously on the soil and on the grapes, one can gain a deeper understanding of the manner in which value is extracted from the environment. These two components, after classified as successful components of terroir, convey a sense of the uniqueness of the wine that is produced from them as much as they convey recognition of its generic features, which align the product with international expectations or standards and create material grounds for claims to a monopoly rent.

The Humans in Terroir

The third main aspect of terroir is a mix of local knowledge and technology, which is accumulated and harnessed to useful purposes by humans (Barham 2003). To various extents, I have already referred to the role of humans – winemakers, soil scientists, meteorologists and microbiologists, among others – in discovering and assembling terroir through measurements and selection. But in industrial winemaking, the division of labour further segments the production process by assigning manual workers the execution of different parts of the whole. The processes and implications for livelihoods and value production were analysed earlier in the book, and in this section I want to show further how at the exchange level the value of wine can be further enhanced through the use of rustic, manual-labour-infused imagery in viral advertising films.

One of these films was released by Purcari Winery in December 2016 and quickly gained a few tens of thousands of hits on YouTube. It paraphrased a Queen song, 'We Are the Champions',[8] and was meant to celebrate the success of the Purcari team – especially its manual workers. I observed part of the selection process for the manual workers who would appear in the video in the autumn of that year, when virtually every worker was asked to speak and sing for a few minutes in front of the camera. The video begins with a brief statement about how in 2015 and 2016 'Purcari has become the most awarded [sic] winery east of [the] Rhine.' It continues by saying 'This is a dedication to the people of Purcari village who made it happen', 'the real champions'. The video is a collage of 'villagers' singing the lyrics of the Queen song unplugged, set in different sites in the village: the village entrance, the Purcari Winery cellar, next to a blue limewashed house and then in the vineyard. When the final lyric of the song follows, a full, standing image of Victor appears and he utters, 'I thank you all' while holding a bottle of wine in his hand. The chorus, in which 'we are the champions' is repeated, is set in the winery's vineyard where a large group of workers are harvesting grapes. The final figure is of a man dressed in a suit holding a glass of Purcari wine in his hand, which he leaves on a barrel, the final caption being 'We are Purcari. Since 1827'. The figure of the man, thanking a group of workers dressed in overalls, suggests perhaps that he is the main character leading vineyards, grapes and executing manual workers into making the Purcari terroir wines.

Yet Purcari has used manual workers in vineyards as well as 'nature' and green hills in its advertising videos. Maxim revealed that the video was meant to show that Purcari had obtained numerous medals in wine contests, and they wanted to publicly thank 'the hands' that made this popular wine while also showing the environment with which winemakers and workers must collaborate, 'because the vineyard is a living organism and it is worked manually as much as possible, so that the wines have more personality'. In this part of the interview – when we were talking about terroir, market success and branding – Maxim went back and forth from assertions about how 'human warmth' makes terroir wines special to comparing his approach to well-known marketing strategies in winemaking, which employ similar methods of de-emphasizing the industrial component of winemaking and promoting the human one. Emphasizing the bond between the producer and the commodity is a method whereby the marketer denies the 'impersonality of the mass-produced, alienated objects' (Carrier 1990: 698), such objects being 'removed symbolically from the realm of commodities and put ... into the realm of possession'. The association of images of specific people or places in advertising commodities have the aim of invoking the right 'class and cultural loading' (Carrier 1990: 697). Indeed, the scripts in wine marketing follow similar structures, as schools of wine marketing are particularly transnational (Inglis 2019: 30; Itçaina, Roger and Smith 2016: 72).[9]

Apart from being a useful marketing move, Victor framed putting the image of the workers at the forefront as an acknowledgment of their importance – it was a testament to the management's appreciation of the manual workers – and that the video served as a token of respect and praise for those responsible for carrying out '80-90% of the work ... 300 days a year, which is not so simple work'; it is back-breaking, and it continues regardless of the weather. In discussions with both vineyard and factory workers, this interpretation was received with ambivalence. While being enthusiastic and flattered to be appearing in the media, on a more pragmatic level they felt unacknowledged. Their low salaries and long working hours were contrasted with the celebratory image on the screen, which for many remained on the symbolic level and prevented them from truly identifying with the image of the 'champion'.

For our discussion of value creation, the implication of the above is that value continues being enhanced after the commodity leaves the site of production. The calculations that the marketing department makes after the launch of every visible ad or controversial wine brand is that exposure to the story increase the company's sales as projected. Most value consists of the abstract social labour embodied in a commodity plus the unpaid energy that comes from the environment (Moore 2015: 62; Krzywoszynska 2020) and from household work, but it also includes the work of reattaching the products on to the consumers (Foster 2005) through branding and advertising.

Adjusting the Taste of Place

Thus as Robert Ulin (2007: 55) argued, 'whatever benefits come from climate and soil, it is surely the history of marketing and the investment of large [amounts of] capital that allows some wine-growing areas and wine estates to rise to a position of dominance'.[10] Purcari Winery, as a leading regional producer, has popularized its wine brands by emphasizing its distinctive terroir and through 'viral and digital marketing', which aims to 'keep up with the changing tastes' (Purcari Wineries Plc. 2018: 23). In order to capture terroir and convey it in the marketing discourse, the winery monitored, analysed, classified and selected parts of nature with the help of researchers. In both cases, some generic features were sought. For yeasts, homogeneous *Saccharomyces* yeast cultures were selected from the totality of wild yeasts that occur on the soils and plants of the estate. These selected yeasts ensured fermentation time and quality that followed the international standards set by the OIV – but in the end the selected cultures were local and specific, giving the wine its most typical (unique) expression. The case of the soils was similar; in a specific (unique) place, soil scientists analysed and classified soils first by ensuring that some collectively agreed standards were in place (proximity of bedrock to the roots, acidity of the soils, humidity) but at the same time looking for specific, local characteristics (e.g. the amount of rubidium in the soil, the combination of minerals). These characteristics were revealed and classified by scientists and engineers, this being another point at which the value of wine was created or enhanced, and the next step was to bring value closer to realization through marketing work.

The strategies of differentiation developed by Purcari Winery can be read as responses to globalization, which grew in importance after the first Russian embargo in 2006. The impact of globalization on winegrowers has been described as 'a synonym for acute competition, business failures, and anxiety' (Demossier 2011: 695), and it is also noticeable among Moldovan winemakers. Moreover, Moldova encountered a more complex set of challenges than already established actors in the global wine market did: as a post-Soviet wine-growing area, it is perceived by consumers and wine critics alike as a lower-quality producer (cf. Hann 2004 on Hungary; Jung 2016 on Bulgaria; and Itçaina, Roger and Smith 2016 on Romania). To oppose some of these preconceptions from both wine critics and consumers about wine produced in socialist countries, Purcari marketeers constructed a discourse of continuity that focuses intently on the presumed founding year of the winery, 1827.[11] It aimed to convey the idea of an 'ahistorical *terroir*' (Demossier 2011: 690) through its motto, 'Purcari remains Purcari, since 1827'. Maxim explained that this pointed to quality, the consistent attribute of Purcari wines:

> Purcari has had a very good *heritage* [sic] since 1827, and throughout this whole time period of 190 years we have been consistent in everything, meaning wines and quality ... Thus it results that we are consistent in [producing] very high quality, in making premium and super-premium wines, and that is what matters to the consumers. They are looking for a confirmation of that quality. ... We remain consistent in quality, but we are nonconformist in communication. We are trying to be trend-setters in certain matters, and from here follows [the fact] that the true values never change: Purcari remains Purcari, since 1827 ... For the clients, [Purcari] is a standard of quality wines. We are not leaders only in terms of numbers but also in terms of quality. (Chișinău, July 2017)

Heritage is a mental construct that endows places, things and actions with significance, connoting generational and historical depth (Weiss 2016: x), while heritage conservation is 'a form of cultural politics' (Logan, Kockel and Craith 2015: 1). In the field of heritage foods, it is quite common to claim unchanged ways of production – like Mediterranean olive-oil manufacturers claiming that their production method has remained unchanged since antiquity (Meneley 2007: 678) and also in the case of tea (Besky 2014) or of other wine-producing countries, where the qualities of wine are presented as eternal (Guy 2003; Monterescu and Handel 2019; Demossier 2018). Thus, the marketing mantra that Purcari remains the same and its strong focus on 'consistency' is commonplace, being a strategic convention for meaning- and value-making in the field of heritage foods. Yet the construction of this discourse of continuity based on terroir is apparently contradictory because it was brought about by change. Changes in the environment and in market dynamics are only two of the crucial factors that will not allow Purcari, or any other wine, to remain the same. Purcari wines need to be reassembled periodically to respond to market conditions and consumers, as classifying and providing the evidence for the characteristics of the soils and the selection of local yeasts also suggest. Additionally, a terroir wine is a wine that has been reinvented in order to compete on the market.

This is also noticeable in the strategies that the winery adopted following the successive geopolitical crises in the country. After the first Russian embargo, Purcari Winery began targeting markets for its wine to the west of the country – choosing not to wait too long for changes to occur in diplomatic relations with Russia. It invested massively in marketing campaigns and has been working with foreign consultants, or 'flying winemakers',[12] for more than a decade in order to adjust the taste of Purcari wine to the global trends. In this strategy of adjustment, flying winemakers are critical agents as they contribute to the globalization of certain tastes and of previously more localized technologies and practices. Through these itinerant consultants, different wines become 'subject to identical forms of control' (Inglis 2019: 33), and 'international varietals' become the grapes around which most knowledge is gathered. They help in making wines just generic enough to be compatible with contemporary trends, which in their turn are constructed through discourses and the marketing lobby. The consultant hired to advise the Purcari laboratory at the time of my fieldwork was Italian and – together with the laboratory chief, the head of production and the winery CEO – he tasted Purcari's wines on a monthly basis and decided the material alterations to the wine that would make it optimally fit for its target markets. Also, monthly visits were paid to the vineyards, and every plot of land planted with a different grape variety was checked so that the following actions would be decided together. These decisions were made with one eye on trends in the international wine market and the other 'the best local expression'. Vlad, the winery's head of production, explained how these flying winemakers acquire a 'global' sense of what wine should taste like and why they had become important for wine producers aiming to become global players:

> It's nothing bad, I mean frustrating, in having such a consultant. It is actually quite OK when you say, 'Look, we are consulted by Federico. It does not mean that you are a rookie [*boboc*] and Federico is writing down your steps. This means that the winery is OK, that we have a world-renowned consultant. … He has no function in the organization of the winery, he is rather adding some nuances. … All of us who studied know that a certain process needs to go like this or like that, but sometimes something intervenes, [I] call them production nuances. He intervenes because he has a larger amount of theoretical knowledge, perhaps even practical knowledge. He can gather that by being at this winery, at another one, by having his own laboratory, by researching. You don't have the time to do this, because the truck is waiting outside, and you quickly have to tell Dan to bring forty [bottle] containers to label them…you understand, this is your purpose. But his purpose is to gather this experience, to make it bigger and bigger, and he then sees from above… While you can see only your corner, he can see from above, so he can help you. (Purcari, April 2017)

What Vlad was hinting at was that winemakers who work as consultants can grasp the global trends and produce wine accordingly. In their activity, they help by capturing the terroir – that is, the local particularity of the wine – while reducing the risk of a winery coming up with a wine that is incompatible with international tastes. The expert needs to help the winery differentiate itself while also helping it to be generic enough so that it generates more value.

Providing the evidence for a specific Purcari terroir is necessary at this moment in time – one in which the wine market is being globalized and in which wine-marketing departments receive huge funding, whether from public subsidies or from the private funds of the wineries themselves (Itçaina, Roger and Smith 2016: 196). It is also a moment in which Moldova is emerging as a wine-producing country and meeting the generic rules of the global competition of wines. This means that, as my interlocutors showed, there was an acute awareness that their terroir and wine must also play the seemingly contradictory game discussed in the previous sections: Moldova and Purcari must demonstrate their viability by adhering to transnational standards, but at the same time by emphasizing the uniqueness of their places of origin. This results in the final and unique product that Purcari wine is, yet the backstage movements that led to the making of these commodities emphasized and captured successively something that is not a duality but a co-constitutive set of descriptors – the unique and the generic. The right balance between unique and generic features is what allows commodities to be sold in the market for an above-average price; or, in David Harvey's words (2002: 96), 'some way has to be found to keep some commodities or places unique and particular enough ... to maintain a monopolistic edge in an otherwise commodified and often fiercely competitive economy'.

Conclusion

By breaking down the processes of classification and selection that are carried out through measurements, laboratory analyses of soils and yeasts, and communication, I have aimed to show that the 'unique' and the 'generic' are codependent categories in relation to a commodity such as terroir wine and that it is through this relationship that surplus value is created. Control of the land that 'hosts' the elements that make terroir and the subsequent mobilization of a productive infrastructure make differentiation possible and enhance the wine's value in the wine market. A terroir must be unique: the climate, soil, microorganisms and local technology are what make the wine special by giving it a taste specific to its place of origin. At the same time, in a terroir certain generic features are necessary in order to make the product comparable with others and ensure its safety. But the distinction between these features is not a stable one: the characteristics that make a terroir singular in the south-east of Moldova are the same as those that make it generic at the European level – its soil composition is comparable with that of regions in Burgundy, its grapes ripen and yield Cabernets in the style of a Bordeaux, and its cooling systems delay the spontaneous fermentation of grapes just enough to reach the optimal point when it should start, as in New Zealand wineries. The unique/generic dualism seems to be a toolbox for strategies of differentiation used in emphasizing that a terroir or a wine are unique or standardized, respectively, in a relative manner – the ultimate aim being to release value in the market.

The work of marketing creates surplus value through this movement of meanings that are guided by trends, social debates, marketing research or itinerant consultants, among others. The importance of soil and climate are not undermined, yet they have to be seen in connection with political and economic contexts and histories. My contribution to a critical, materialist understanding of terroir has relied on tracing the ways in which it is articulated and disseminated in relevant environments in order to create value through claims of uniqueness and distinction. At the end, I added a discussion of the role of a flying winemaker in making Purcari terroir wines: acting as an expert in global wine trends, at the same time he is able to help individual wineries make their terroir speak through their wines as well as through their marketing campaigns and labels.

A final remark on the competitiveness of Purcari completes the context in which the winery makes its successful steps westwards: the adoption of standards that rely on advanced and often expensive technical infrastructure (such as coolers, presses, access to soil-analysis labs, yeast-processing plants or the unusual infrastructure of the flying winemakers) is not easily available to Moldovan wine producers in general. The primary impediment among other Moldovan winemakers was not related to knowledge or accepting rules per se, but to access to money for new infrastructure. As a Moldovan lawyer specialized in wine legislation told me when I explained to her my research topic, by focusing on Purcari 'you are looking at the wine industry through rose-tinted spectacles'. This does not mean that the process of implementing new standards in Purcari was easy, or that the research focus on the winery does not bring enough generalizable knowledge about wine in Moldova and in other post-Soviet countries. Purcari is indeed a privileged example – and specifically through this central position in the country, contrasting with it being located the peripheral position of Moldova in the transnational wine market, it offers a most complex vantage point for understanding how value is re-created and negotiated in societies dominated by market exchange.

Notes

1. Based on these elements, Romania is the most stable partner and Poland is the most promising given the rising level of wine consumption and its size. In Romania, although market share has been constantly growing in the last few years the competition is intensified by the continuity and popularity of domestic wine brands such as Cotnari, Jidvei or Recaș as Romanians are drinking almost 90% of their domestic wine production.
2. A term in wine-tasting from the French *typicité*, describing a varietal wine's 'signature' characteristics.
3. EU Council Regulation No. 479/2008 defines a PDO wine as follows: 'Its quality and characteristics are essentially or exclusively due to a particular geographical environment with its inherent natural and human factors' (here, referring to terroir). Furthermore, grape production and processing into wine need to take place in the designated geographical area.
4. A cross-section of the soil that reveals 'horizons', or layers of soil that are parallel and different from the layers above and underneath. This helps in classifying soils and in deciding on the optimal crops for those areas.
5. There are internationally agreed descriptions for each technical grape variety that prescribe what taste, smell and colour a balanced varietal wine should have.
6. Wine yeasts can be processed outside the PDO perimeter as the final product, the wine, does not contain yeasts, which are removed during the processes of decanting and filtration. Wine yeasts are oenological products, 'a specialized tool for wine production' (Wrobel and Lubasz 2015: 5).
7. Nevertheless – in addition to destruction caused by excessive pesticide use, or the reduction of vineyard biodiversity at microscopic levels or beyond – there is a protective potential in the terroir discourse in a world that is increasingly challenged by human-induced ecological disruptions. If the contemporary story of the appropriation of nature by capitalist relations of production includes destruction, the cheapening of ecological features and pollution, when it comes to value production from terroir the consequences are not as dramatic as the ecosystem that is framed, as terroir needs to be taken care of, analysed, 'listened to' and so on. Thus, terroir can be an ideal entry point into gaining a relational understanding on soils (cf. Krzywoszynska and Marchesi 2020).
8. www.youtube.com/watch?v=54liVNwwpS0 (accessed 27 June 2021).
9. Wine marketing became a structured field in the 1980s in Adelaide, where the *International Journal of Wine Marketing* was created in 1989. From here also came 'sensory descriptive analysis', which 'they claimed was scientific and that guaranteed them a monopoly over a segment of evaluation expertise' (Itçaina, Roger and Smith 2016: 72).
10. Terroir is usually seen by winemakers as a 'given' in the world, something bestowed upon a community of vintners by divinity (Demossier 2018: 5) or by natural order (Ulin 2013), and the politics and power relations behind the vineyard-features classification is seldom at the forefront, but these are not politically neutral processes (Engel-Di Mauro 2014: 31).

11. Insignia from Purcari Winery was a very common sight in Chișinău. Apart from Purcari wines being present on the menus of virtually all the bars and restaurants in the capital, the Purcari logo – which depicts the number '1827' beneath the name 'Purcari' – could be seen on terrace umbrellas, wine glasses, ashtrays and billboards, and at charity events, wine events, literature festivals and sports competitions.
12. 'Flying winemakers' are independent, expert oenologists who travel around the world advising local winemakers on production and marketing strategies (see also Lagendijk 2004).

 # Conclusion

Wine on the Periphery as an Illustration of the Transnational Dynamics of Value Creation

The foregoing chapters have followed the production of value in Moldovan winemaking principally through the case of Purcari Winery amid the reorganization of its export markets, its traditional Russian markets having been lost so that Moldovan wine started to be sold increasingly in countries outside the post-Soviet space. Looking at this process through the lens of labour and globalization is fruitful in understanding a wide range of dynamic transformations of the ways in which workers and winemakers live and conceptualize their lives in times of change and insecurity, and how value comes into being. The significance of the production of homemade wine for industrial labour relations and the domestic wine market has also been explored, along with the influence of the Soviet past in today's practices and discourses about Moldovan winemaking; for the changing Moldovan wine industry, these are uncomfortable realities that linger in society and need to be transformed or disposed of in order to cope with the intensified market competition of the twenty-first century.

An underlying theme in all chapters has been the materiality of changing politics of value seen through stories of labour, terroir and geopolitics. By drawing on a materialist approach (Ulin 1996; Harvey 2002; Moore 2015; Gille 2016; Itçaina, Roger and Smith 2016; Demossier 2018), the analysis has shown that prestige in winemaking is not merely a matter of culture or creativity but equally of historical, economic inequalities that are played out regionally and globally; it also showed that successful Moldovan wine takes its value from both production relations in the winery and the households of the workers, from marketing work as well as from monopoly claims on parts of nature. The insights that have surfaced from the ethnographic study of wine in this post-Soviet winemaking country that deserve further reflection here refer to matters of value; globalization and terroir; labour and social reproduction in a winemaking community; and, finally, to a set of remarks about wine as an object of ethnographic inquiry.

How Wines Become Transnational

The main challenge that globalization imposes on wines is that in order to be sold, they need to occupy a position in the global hierarchy of value (Jung 2016; Demossier 2018). The foregoing ethnography of the post-Soviet Republic of Moldova provided a complex example of this, showing the processes that wines need to go through in order to become transnational commodities. Before the global wine trade accelerated a few decades ago, even actors in advanced capitalist countries such as France (Demossier 2018) and Italy (Pratt 1994) could rely on stable markets and for a long time did not need periodic changes in identity or practices of the sort that the last couple of decades have required from virtually all wine regions around the globe. This serves to underline the similarity with the experiences of Moldovan winemakers; although the drive was different because Moldova could not choose its trade partners to the same extent as was possible for its Western counterparts, the geopolitical configuration within the Soviet Union maintained a form of constancy in production and consumption, and commodities were not subjected to such harsh competition as they are today.

Transnational standards are as much about prescriptions of the physical qualities of the products and the technologies and materials to be used as they are about politics (Gille 2016: 130). Politics – that is, discursive goals – are also included in regulations, but they are only one of the transformations that industries and countries need to go through in order to suit a specific community – here, primarily European Union countries. The present story has proved to be one of an ambivalent (and still ongoing) adaptation to globalized capitalism, in which what can be seen as an opportunity – namely, access to global markets – can at the same time mean a deepening of labour exploitation. I have shown how, by working extended hours, workers' daily time becomes stuck between the factory and reproductive domestic labour, and how the latter contributes to the creation of the value of Purcari terroir wines. Apart from the labour process in the vineyards and the winery, where the wage workers care for grapes and transform them into wine, scientific and marketing work is also necessary to capture and convey the distinction of the commodities being produced. The main criterion of differentiation, terroir, was not important or necessary in Moldova up until the mid-2000s, when a breakdown in trade between Moldova and its main trading partner Russia led many Moldovan winemakers to reorient themselves westwards.

I have therefore followed the dynamics of differentiation in the market through the terroir discourse by engaging with the concepts of uniqueness and genericness and showing how the branding strategy of the Purcari winery revolves around these two features that render wine marketable. The focus on indigenous grape varieties emerged from this need to find the 'uniqueness' of place for Moldovan wine, which acts as Moldova's passport in the global wine market. Although international grape varieties still predominate in Moldovan vineyards, much of the emphasis in marketing strategies has started to be placed on 'authentic' Moldovan places, grapes and wines. Replanting vines has also been accompanied by producing less sweet wine. Biodiversity in grape varieties is considered an advantage in wine markets, and Moldovan producers suffer from not being able to define the difference in their products. Purcari has made efforts to increase the areas of Rară Neagră, Fetească Albă and Fetească Neagră, some of the prominent indigenous varieties, yet any change in vineyard plantations takes at least five years before it can make a difference to gross wine production.

Although most Moldovan winemakers maintain a steadily West-oriented strategy of market enlargement through the USAID-backed National Office for Vine and Wine, the Russian market is still attractive for others. At the beginning of 2019, in January, Moldovan president Igor Dodon announced on his Facebook page that the 2013 sanctions on wine and fruit exports had been lifted by Russia for the following six months. The decision was announced in a few media outlets, but it had not yet been signed by the Russian prime minister Dmitry Medvedev. When Moldovan wineries started to ship wine towards the east, they were stopped at the Ukrainian border due to the new trade restrictions that had been imposed on the latter country by Russia. Once more, Moldovan winemakers found themselves in a stalemate over which they had little influence. The lifting of the ban was treated just like its imposition: as a political arrangement to encourage votes for pro-Russian candidates in the parliamentary elections held in Moldova from 24 February 2019.

If the ambiguous lifting of the embargo in January 2019 is seen as part of a political game, it would not be the first move of this kind since 2013. In the spring of 2017, six wineries approved unilaterally by Russia were allowed to export wine there. President Dodon announced on social media that achieving approval for these wineries' wines to be exported to Russia was the result of his personal ties with President Vladimir Putin. Despite this, many wineries from Moldova are no longer interested in investing in the Russian market – with several interlocutors uttering the same saying to me: 'One cannot keep stepping on the same rake' (Romanian, '*Să nu calci din nou pe aceeași greblă*'), a reference to the repeated sanctions that Russia had imposed on Moldovan exports, which had created major damage. I started this book by describing a wine event in Prague at which the Russian embargo was presented as 'a chance' for Moldovan winemakers, and most of the efforts made by the sector seemed to bypass Russia. Even so, some producers are still lured by memories of the easy-going and massive market that Russia had represented for Moldova in the past. In this state of oscillation, the fate of a considerable number of workers in the industry continues to rely on the will of politicians who are prepared to steer the wine sector to serve their own political agendas.

The Post-Soviet Place of Origin

The legacy of socialism in the Moldovan wine industry since the dissolution of the Soviet Union, as testified by both ethnographic and historical data, shows that the influence of the Soviet experience is still powerful on several levels. First, the growth of viticulture and wineries in Moldova has been closely tied to Soviet and, later, post-Soviet Russian market demand. Furthermore, in the Soviet era, as in the first two post-Soviet decades, socio-economic relations in the wine industry revolved around the existence of a large export market in Russia, in which Moldovan wine occupied predominantly the lower-quality segment. The transformation that the Moldovan wine industry is carrying out today in terms of production-quality standards and marketing discourses was often qualified by my interlocutors as changing the wine sector's old 'Soviet-style' organization so that it is compatible with the European market. This leads to a second, inter-related level – the discursive one – and the ambivalence with which Moldovans refer to the Soviet legacy in their wine industry. On the one hand, there is condemnation of practices under socialism – and expressions deriding Soviet winemaking are still prominent in the discourses of workers and wine experts alike, as they suggest rigidity, the prioritization of quantity over quantity, or arbitrariness in business and political relations. On the other hand, the Soviet experience is remembered for its steadiness, job security and equality, and the safety of a once-stable market. This East–West polarization has been maintained, as political relations between Russia and the Western powers still display Cold War dynamics. This is the political background against which negotiations on Moldovan wine's identity take place.

The long-term dependence on one main trading partner for exports had implications for the ways in which Moldova is currently perceived and recognized in the wine world – raising the question of what kind of claims to distinction the country can make as a wineproducer. Relations of power between Russia and Moldova have been asymmetrical throughout their shared history, and not only in the agricultural trade. The Republic of Moldova used to export a large share of its agricultural produce to

Russia, while its energy sector still relies almost exclusively on Russian gas. Unlike other Eastern countries, which began to specialize in specific products for the Eastern Bloc only in the 1960s, Moldova had a longer history of developing its wine industry to suit Russian demand – beginning in the early nineteenth century, when historical Bessarabia was part of the Tsarist Empire and when Bessarabia's vineyards were extended in order to supply the Russian market. The post-Soviet transformations of Moldovan winemaking, triggered by a deterioration in economic relations, have created a range of anxieties related to the image and identity of Moldova outside the country. Even if scientific and marketing work is able to carve out relevant and positive features, it still establishes a legacy that creates difficulties for many Moldovan winemakers. The emphasis on poverty is the main narrative of the foreign observer when reporting about Moldova, regardless of the topic being addressed, and this acts as an obstacle to the country's wineries and the ONVV, who are spending large amounts of money on marketing in order to promote their wines (close to 70% of the ONVV's 2017 budget went to marketing) and trying to counter the country image dominated by lack. Having read news articles in English, Romanian and German reporting on Moldova for the last several years, I found that virtually none failed to mention at some point that the Republic of Moldova was 'the poorest country in Europe'. I do not mean to encourage glossy depictions of a country that is certainly troubled, yet there is a sense in which poverty is being exoticized – in which journalists search for defunct industrial sites and dramatic mixtures of poverty and affluence. Looking at Moldova, it is also obvious that the country's media 'persona' is incompatible with the initiatives that the wine sector is taking to support their main export product. Certain statuses, symbols and imageries are compatible with promoting (quality) wine, while others equally certainly are not. Although claiming to look for diversity, the field of wine operates within a rather exclusionary aesthetic framework.

Furthermore, in researching in detail the challenges and local relations in Moldovan winemaking, the risk of creating on my own part a 'Moldovan exceptionalism' has been present throughout the pages of this book. I have attempted to make the best use of ethnographic theory, analysing the particularities of the Moldovan winemaking place in a continuous comparison with wine places and with global processes elsewhere. There is, however, an exceptional dimension to how the entry on globalized wine markets unsettles winemaking Moldova. In the ongoing processes of the institutionalization of the Wine of Moldova brand, the marketing specialists and policy makers involved were conditioned and advised to formulate specific representations of Moldovan wine. Moreover, wine is a commodity whose value on the market often depends less on its production costs than on the historically accumulated prestige that translates into a basis for monopoly rent. However, the task of the Moldovan marketing specialists (or those employed by the ONVV) is hardly comparable with that faced in other nations which have had to undertake market research and figure out what imaginary consumers in target markets associate their country with – Portuguese wine, for instance, was associated with reds, so in its reinvention the country produced more whites (Domingos 2016: 35), it was a rather uncomplicated shift. In the case of Moldova, for some target markets they had to explain that the country's wine even existed, that it had a long history and was keen on exporting. My own experience living in Germany as an anthropologist focusing on Moldovan wine production was marked by basic discussions about firstly, the existence of Moldova as a country and secondly, by surprised reactions about its winemaking history and ambitions. Very few of its potential future buyers have Moldova as a wine producer on their mental map. There is marketing potential in this radical novelty, but wine functions socially rather differently: its value grows with accumulated prestige and with the strong work of popularization backed by significant financial support –neither of which is in plentiful supply in Moldova.

The Local Winemaking Community and SRT

The present work is the first detailed study of industrial labour and winemaking in Moldova, and it shows the changes that have taken place in the political economy of Moldovan wine through the case of a winery that reoriented its markets from East to West amidst geopolitical tensions. Winemaking in this ethnography also serves to expose broader social processes that accelerated in the aftermath of the first Russian embargo on the country. The Soviet past informs the present-day views of the workers and their evaluations of the current system of social organization as well. I have attempted to trace the politics of work in winemaking from the reorganization of the winery during Soviet times up until the present day. While bearing in mind that the distinction between socialism and capitalism is not straightforward, I have followed an emic conceptualization of the present – frequently contrasted with the experience of socialism, which is seen as more positive. The dissolution of the Soviet Union was followed by multiple waves of out-migration that have affected the organization of the wine industry, especially through shortages of both highly specialized staff and manual workers. With reference to the past, the villagers of Purcari conceptualized fairness and the 'good life' as connected to the meaning and recognition of work, continual access to holiday packages and better rural infrastructure.

I have described the economic coping strategies that are required to supplement the low incomes of the post-Soviet years from the perspective of social reproduction (Meillassoux 1972; Edholm, Harris and Young 1978; Harris and Young 1981; Harvey 2006; Bhattacharya 2017), arguing that agricultural communities contribute part of their subsistence work to capitalist production and this unacknowledged contribution is normalized. The theoretical aim of employing social reproduction theory (SRT) in the analysis of this ethnography is twofold: firstly, the research into Moldovan winemaking makes a contribution to SRT by showing how late, flexible, capitalist production in a postsocialist rural area depends on domestic labour in order to be competitive on transnational markets. It also shows that gender can be as relevant as class in the exploitation of labour, given that in the Purcari households it is common that women workers earn at least as much as men do. But class creates in every wage workers' household similar kinds of dependencies: unless they have access to remittances or they own a small business, manual workers rarely have access to a living wage. Their household production is thus a crucial aspect in the reproduction of the labour force, and also in making Purcari wines as competitive as they are. Secondly, the employment of SRT helps us to better understand the nature of wine production in peripheral regions: the situation in countries with low GDP, where poverty is widespread, is that manual work in winemaking is lowly paid. In more affluent, less peripheral countries, manual work is also lowly paid in comparison with the profits that wineries make but the inequality does not mean that workers remain breadline-poor. In Moldova, in order to be competitive, a winery has several hindrances that are far less present in central regions: labour costs need to stay as low as possible and subsidies from the state that make wines competitive at an entry level (similar to those in Australia, New Zealand or Chile starting in the 1970s, and later the EU countries that received CAP subsidies to compete starting in the 1980s) are much lower. The 'cultural', or marketing, component is a challenge because in a market in which elitism and prestige are decisive, a poor country has to struggle disproportionately. Part of this struggle is then transferred to the household – and it is not merely a problematized aspect of winemaking, because domestic work in capitalism is disguised as not producing real value (Graeber 2013: 224); it is a given. One of the aims of this ethnography has been to understand and explain the multiple levels – including the greyed-out ones – on which the commercial value of wines is produced.

A further reflection on value comes from the coexistence and vehement competition in Moldova of commercial and household forms of wine, which can be seen as material avatars or embodiments of the limits and overlapping of the two broad meanings of value – with homemade wine starring as 'values' and commercial wine as 'value' (see Graeber 2013: 224). Homemade wine is predominantly conceived as a symbol and material representation of community values, a way of living, and its consumption as an event in which market competition is dissolved or irrelevant. But this is not all, because homemade wine is used as a means of payment and is sold among villagers, and because some peasants aim to become capable of making their peasant wine a viable commodity, not only a petty commodity in the village market. From here, one can make a transition to commercial wine: producers and consumers of commercial wine alike do see non-commercial meanings in this product. It can be gifted, it can be part of rituals and it does represent for many wine aficionados the richest in meanings among alcoholic beverages. But its conception, production and circulation depend on its being competitive and profitable; when this component fails, this kind of production will no longer be possible.

This ties into the distrust of commercially produced food and the perceived changes of taste in industrially produced fruit and vegetables that are present in the Purcari community. While in Western countries this reaction takes the form of organic-food movements organized by conscious consumers, in poorer countries it is a mixture of a taste for necessity, made possible by subsistence agriculture, and the desire to avoid unhealthy foods. In the specific case of wine, there are the so-called 'natural wine' movements. In Moldova, although not subsumed into the natural-wine movement, the majority of people are enthusiastic consumers of natural or homemade wine. In the earlier chapters, I discussed homemade-wine production and consumption in Moldova as a prominent instance of tradition and ritual, as an act of resistance to the industrialization and anonymisation of wine and as a coping strategy of rural proletarian Moldovans. Homemade wine also has a major influence on the wine industry since virtually every industrial manual worker in the winery is an 'artisan' winemaker at home, and 72% of Moldovans cited homemade wine as their favourite in a 2016 study (Magenta Consulting 2016).

Homemade wine was therefore placed in opposition to industrial wine, creating a polarity that affects the structure of both the domestic and export markets. At the time of my fieldwork, the unwritten rule was that homemade wine was for Moldovans and industrial wine for export, as only a maximum of 10% of Moldova's industrial-wine production was consumed in the country. In order to reduce consumption of homemade wine and create a market for a product that had previously been made at home, Moldovan wine-sector experts are in essence promoting the following principle: good wine is made by professional winemakers. Peasants, however, view industrial wine with scepticism, and the majority prefer the consumption of homemade wine above any other type of alcohol. In household production, as they see it, the winemaker can fully trace the process of winemaking, from the work in the vineyard over the year that culminates in the harvest to the processing and storage of the grapes. This ensures that household viticulture is ecological, because almost no chemical inputs are used in home vineyards. Although secondary in villagers' discourses, the economic aspect of wine consumption is also important – homemade wine being more affordable than bottled wine, which makes the latter prohibitive for many villagers. On the other hand, in the factory a more detailed type of control is emphasized concerning quality standards in the vineyard, the processing section, the cellar and on the bottling line. Altogether, the book addresses the tensions that arise at the village level when the production of an industrial global commodity is still strongly embedded in local social relations.

In explaining how domestic wine production is partly responsible for the dependence of commercial wineries upon export, I have focused on issues of hierarchization and differentiation in the field of winemaking, as they are key to understanding the political economy of wine at large. To show this, I have relied not only on participant observation in the village but also on interviews with wine experts in the capital, Chișinău. The latter group added a new layer to the hierarchy between house and commercial wine. Efforts to look different and to embrace the terroir discourse are the market's way of forcing on Moldova the notion of a 'blank slate' (Gille 2016: 12–13). The idea of the tabula rasa is discussed in the literature on postsocialist transitions, as these were desirable stages in which to implement market policies. But every 'transiting' society in the Eastern Bloc had its own legacy, which meant that the new policies had to grapple with local 'obstacles'. Or, as Gille (2016: 13) puts it, 'people of the future were people of the past', which here I interpret as meaning that in the new political regimes there would be considerable continuity.

Wine as Ethnographic Object

Here, I wish to add a few reflections on wine as an object of ethnographic inquiry and why it forms a particularly rich nexus of the meanings and values of human communities. In the volume *Wine and Culture: Vineyard to Glass*, edited by Rachel Black and Robert Ulin (2013), several authors adopt a critical position to wine writing and to the political economy of wine in different regions of the globe. They depict wine as a sociocultural and historical commodity by bringing 'anthropology's unique emphasis on culture, social relations, representation, and power to a critical understanding of wine' (Black and Ulin 2013: 7). The authors thereby offer accounts of the social relations behind winemaking, involving power structures, the construction of place, the politics of wine and its commodification, relationships with technology and nature, and globalization. The present work has aimed to continue in a similar key by contributing to the critical anthropology of wine. Wine is of enormous cultural, ecological and economic complexity, and anthropological research in the field of wine, when combined with a critical political-economy lens that places history and material inequality at the forefront, brings us closest to a full understanding of this often over-fetishized commodity. There are a few aspects in this context that I consider to be of the utmost relevance for future anthropological research.

The first point is related to the conceptualization of terroir. Winemakers frequently see terroir as a 'given' in the world. Anthropologists have pointed to two important dimensions that deconstruct this image of a terroir unchanged since time immemorial (Demossier 2011). First, coming from a new materialist perspective, Teil (2012) shows that terroir does not exist in a discrete, positivist sense and that vintners need to 'collect as many traces of terroir as possible' (Teil 2012: 482) in order to 'implement' proof of it. It therefore does not have an a priori existence, and it cannot be separated from the winegrowing production process. It is for this reason that terroir needs to be provided with evidence and classified through scientific work. However, new materialist approaches stop before they can explain why certain networks are created to start with. This is the point at which a historical, materialist approach is useful. Political-economy approaches to the anthropology of wine (Ulin 1996, 2007, 2013; Demossier 2018; Harvey 2002) criticize the emphasis on natural conditions as being responsible for the value and distinctiveness of wine. While not denying the importance of geological and climatic conditions, Ulin (2013: 72) draws attention to the socially produced quality of terroir. This approach acknowledges the processual, social and historical facets of terroir, and it also supports the view put forward in the present chapter that additional work in providing evidence and communicating terroir is paramount in creating prestige. A viable 'terroir' is rarely self-evident, and only exists through the good wines that come out of that territory – but in the competition on the globalized wine market, each winery needs to have technical proof that the natural endowments of its vineyards are genuinely distinct. The materialist approach to terroir shows that value is produced through the human labour of selecting, classifying and differentiating 'nature'. Historical materialism includes a dimension of political economy in its analysis, which has a structuring effect (Howard 2018: 71).

On a related note, relevant moreover in the COVID-19 crisis that is ongoing as I wrap up this conclusion, are matters of labour and migration in winemaking. Wine provides a peculiar example of the mobility of labour power and production facilities. Wine production differs from other commodities in capitalism essentially through its material immobility. While service offices or car and food factories can be relocated more or less easily, wine production is dependent on specific localities. This dynamic is characteristic of any commodity of protected origin, yet wine differs in that although it is one of the most globalized food industries in terms of trade, knowledge and production practices, its production cannot be moved around. And if in the Western wine-producing countries the workforce can be imported, in Purcari – as in Moldova in general – that is not the case; its wineries therefore provide important provisioning hubs for local workforces. Employing only a local workforce for manual labour is actually a tricky situation for winemaking countries in Western Europe, as in the US. The documentation of dynamics of manual-labour mobility in winemaking thus remains virtually unexplored.

It is inevitable that the majority of anthropologists will study their ethnographic sites through the lens of COVID-19 in the near future. As it brought the world to a state of emergency, the pandemic rapidly and deeply affected multiple aspects of the lives of humans and nonhumans alike. The localizing effects of the pandemic are also noticeable in my field in Moldova, where the ONVV, the agriculture ministry and the wine producers have been urging Moldovans to buy local and to buy wines with the awareness that wineries and all the connected industries that are based locally need them now in order to survive as businesses and to keep their workers employed. The shrinking of the hospitality industry has already started to affect wine production but also, more deeply, the manner in which wine is consumed: wine sales in supermarkets have grown since the onset of the pandemic, while those in hotels, restaurants and bars have decreased. How will an industry so dependent on exports and circulation at the global level on the one hand, and on sociality and conviviality on the other cope with the effects of the economic and social crisis that COVID-19 has provoked?

Anthropologists have already started to observe and infer theoretical insights following the few months of the global crisis that started in early 2020, pointing to matters of experience of time and space (Bermant and Ssorin-Chaikov 2020) or to the effects of a slowdown of an already overheated world (Eriksen 2020), among other themes. Eriksen (2020: 286) asked whether the present cooling down could be a gateway to an intentionally more 'sustainable, less overheated and less unequal postpandemic world'. As the ethnography in this book has showed, matters of sustainability and inequality are a prominent part of wine industries around the globe and in Moldova alike. On 24 March 2020, the Purcari Winery web page published a 'call for solidarity' in which it announced that one million MDL coming from the Purcari Group and another million from the winery's founding director, Victor Bostan (the total sum equals around 100,000 euros) would be donated to campaigns working against the spread of the coronavirus, to purchase ventilators, and to support medical and care personnel. Regarding employees of the Purcari Winery, there was a two-week break in April 2020, during which hygiene rules were established and all the equipment sanitized. The company management announced that the current crisis could not be compared with any other crises in the wine sector's recent past, that no clear plans could be made, but that the company would strive to keep all its employees for the upcoming year as the management was aware that agricultural and factory workers were the most vulnerable during the pandemic. The additional money necessary to keep the current number of employees afloat comes primarily through voluntary reductions in salaries of the management team, with the CEO ceding 50% of his salary for six months and the rest of the top-management team ceding 25% of theirs for three months, while the employees outside management will have their salaries maintained throughout the year. This was a sign of good will in a class society in which inequality is normalized and redistribution comes not through the socialization of the means of production and of resources but through benevolent, philanthropic individuals. If the COVID-19 pandemic indeed enables humans to see more clearly the strong interdependence among themselves and with the environment, and also to acknowledge the lethal effects of exploitation, one can only hope that building truly more egalitarian and solidary societies becomes increasingly a priority in Moldova and elsewhere.

Glossary of Terms

Divin—the name designating Moldovan wine distillate since 1993 when the country signed up to the 1958 Lisbon Treaty, which regulates protected-origin products in signatory countries; before that year, it was called 'cognac' but this conflicted with the French Cognac PDO.

Embargo—(used interchangeably with the term 'ban') denotes an order issued by a government to prohibit some or all trade with a foreign nation. In the book, I use 'embargoes' and 'bans' to refer to the prohibitions that Russia imposed on Moldovan wine imports in 2006 and 2013 (and for shorter periods in 2008 and 2010).

Factory—(used interchangeably with 'winery') refers here to the grape-processing unit and the cellars, or to the wine company. My Moldovan interlocutors used the Romanian *fabrică de vin* and the Russian *vinzavod* to refer to wineries more often than the standard Romanian term *vinărie*. As the Purcari vineyards are close to the processing facilities and the cellars, the word 'factory' helps to differentiate the two main areas of production where the grapes are grown and where they are processed.

Flying winemakers—(used interchangeably with 'itinerant consultants') independent, expert oenologists who travel around the world advising local winemakers on production and marketing strategies.

Homemade wine—(similar to 'house wine' and 'natural wine') 'house wine' (Romanian, *vin de casă*) is more frequently used by my interlocutors, though in English the translation can lead to confusion as 'house wine' refers more frequently to the bulk-wine option in restaurants. For this reason, I have settled on using 'homemade wine' throughout the book.

Hybrid direct-producers—(shortened as 'hybrid grapes') are crossings between *Vitis* varieties, frequently a *V. Vinifera* variety, the common grapevine, and other species of vine, which are usually more resistant to disease but produce less aromatic grapes. Criticism of the quality of hybrid-grape wine has lasted until the present day, and most hybrids were outlawed by the European Commission in 1979 because of the 'gustatory defects' of the wine produced from these grapes.

Indigenous grapes—(or 'local'/ 'autochthonous' grapes) are grapes that have originated and/or adapted and evolved in a certain place or region as a result of natural processes, with minimal human intervention.

Microzone—a 'microzone' in the Soviet Union designated a restriction production zone for a branded wine, the closest concept to the French terroir in Soviet winemaking practices.

Organoleptic properties—the characteristics of a food or drink as experienced through senses: taste, smell, touch and sight.

Phylloxera—an aphid-like insect that feeds on the roots of grapevines, causing them severe damage. Starting in the second half of the nineteenth century, the phylloxera blight destroyed most European vineyards after the insect was unwittingly introduced along with rootstocks from North America.

Premium and super-premium—price categories in the wine industry, with premium referring to prices per 0.75 liter bottle between 12 and 18 euros and super-premium 18–28 euros.

Purcari—the name of the village housing my main research site, and also of the winery where I carried out most of my fieldwork. A third meaning for Purcari is Purcari terroir, which includes the village itself and a few other neighbouring villages. Mostly in the book, I use 'the village of Purcari' or 'Purcari village' when I refer to the administrative unit, to 'Purcari Winery' or the 'Purcari company' when referring to the second meaning and 'Purcari terroir' in the case of the third.

Terroir—the characteristics of the environment in which a food or wine is produced, including local climate, soil and topography, and the human technology used to harness the 'local taste'.

Winemaker—the terms used by my interlocutors were the Romanian *vinificator* and the Russian *vinodel*. They can refer both to the person who coordinates the vinification of grapes (professional winemakers) or the person who grows grapes and vinifies them (peasant winemakers).

Wine of Moldova—the name of the wine country brand created in 2014 by the Office for Vine and Wine, with the aim of promoting individual Moldovan wineries as a group in exhibitions or contests in both the country itself and abroad.

References

Aistara, Guntra Anda. 2015. 'Good, Clean, Fair… and Illegal: Paradoxes of Food Ethics in Post-socialist Latvia', *Journal of Baltic Studies* 46(3): 283–98.
———. 2018. *Organic Sovereignties: Struggles over Farming in an Age of Free Trade*. Seattle, WA: University of Washington Press.
Annist, Aet. 2016. 'Losing the Enterprising Self in Post-Soviet Estonian Villages', in Nicolette Makovicky (ed.), *Neoliberalism, Personhood, and Postsocialism*. Farnham: Ashgate, pp. 103–22.
Artiukh, Volodymyr. 2013. 'Coping Strategies and Working Class Formation in Post-Soviet Ukraine: A Case of Bila Tserkva Tire Factory', Master's thesis. Budapest: Central European University.
Bacalov, S. 2013. 'Diversitatea etnosocială a elitei basarabene. Studii de caz: Boierii moldoveni Bostan' [The Ethnosocial Diversity of the Bessarabian Elite. Case Studies: The Bostan Moldovan Boyars], *Studii de Arhondologie și Genealogie* (1): 253–337.
Banks, Glenn, and John Overton. 2010. 'Old World, New World, Third World? Reconceptualising the Worlds of Wine', *Journal of Wine Research* 21(1): 57–75.
Barham, Elizabeth. 2003. 'Translating Terroir: The Global Challenge of French AOC Labeling', *Journal of Rural Studies* 19(1): 127–38.
Benzing, Brigitta, and Bernd Herrmann (eds). 2003. *Exploitation and Overexploitation in Societies Past and Present* (Vol. 4). Münster: LIT Verlag.
Berdahl, Daphne. 1999. '"(N)ostalgie" for the Present: Memory, Longing, and East German Things', *Ethnos* 64(2): 192–211.
Bermant, Laia Soto, and Nikolai Ssorin-Chaikov. 2020. 'Introduction: Urgent Anthropological COVID-19 Forum', *Social Anthropology* 28(2): 218–20.
Besky, Sarah. 2014. 'The Labor of Terroir and the Terroir of Labor: Geographical Indication and Darjeeling Tea Plantations', *Agriculture and Human Values* 31(1): 83–96.
Besky, Sarah, and Alex Blanchette (eds). 2019. *How Nature Works: Rethinking Labor on a Troubled Planet*. Albuquerque, NM: University of New Mexico Press.
Bhattacharya, Tithi. 2017. 'Introduction: Mapping Social Reproduction Theory', in Tithi Bhattacharya (ed.), *Social Reproduction Theory: Remapping Class, Recentering Oppression*. London: Pluto Press, pp. 1–21.
Bhattacharya, Tithi. (ed.). 2017. *Social Reproduction Theory: Remapping Class, Recentering Oppression*. London: Pluto Press.
Bhattacharya, Jay, Christina Gathmann, and Grant Miller. 2013. 'The Gorbachev Anti-Alcohol Campaign and Russia's Mortality Crisis', *American Economic Journal: Applied Economics* 5(2): 232–60.

Bîrlădeanu, Virgil. 2013. 'Wine and Speed: The Post-Soviet Holidays in the Republic of Moldova (2001–2009)', *History and Anthropology* 24(1): 36–55.
Bittner, Stephen V. 2015. 'American Roots, French Varietals, Russian Science: A Transnational History of the Great Wine Blight in Late-Tsarist Bessarabia', *Past & Present* 227(1): 151–77.
Black, Rachel. 2013. 'Vino Naturale: Tensions Between Nature and Technology in the Glass', in Rachel Black and Robert Ulin (eds), *Wine and Culture: Vineyard to Glass*. New York and London: Bloomsbury, pp. 279–94.
Black, Rachel E., and Robert C. Ulin (eds). 2013. *Wine and Culture: Vineyard to Glass*. New York and London: Bloomsbury.
Bourdieu, Pierre. 1984. *Distinction: A Social Critique of the Judgement of Taste*. Cambridge, MA: Harvard University Press.
Bowen, Sarah, and Kathryn De Master. 2011. 'New Rural Livelihoods or Museums of Production? Quality Food Initiatives in Practice', *Journal of Rural Studies* 27(1): 73–82.
Brockhaus, Friedrich Arnold, and I.A. Efron. 1891. 'Vinurile Basarabene' [Bessarabian Wines], Encyclopedic Dictionary Volume 6, St Petersburg: Publishing House Brockhaus & Efron.
Buchowski, Michał. 2012. 'Intricate Relations Between Western Anthropologists and Eastern Ethnologists', *Focaal* 2012(63): 20–38.
Burawoy, Michael. 1982. *Manufacturing Consent: Changes in the Labor Process Under Monopoly Capitalism*. Chicago: University of Chicago Press.
Burawoy, Michael, and Katherine Verdery. 1999. 'Introduction', in Michel Burawoy and Katherine Verdery (eds), *Uncertain Transition: Ethnographies of Change in the Postsocialist World*, Oxford: Rowman and Littlefield, pp. 1–17.
Burawoy, Michael, and Katherine Verdery (eds). 1999. *Uncertain Transition: Ethnographies of Change in the Postsocialist World*. Oxford: Rowman and Littlefield.
Caldwell, Melissa L. 2009. 'Introduction: Food and Everyday Life After State Socialism', in Melissa L. Caldwell (ed.), *Food & Everyday Life in the Postsocialist World*. Bloomington, IN: Indiana University Press, pp. 1–28.
Caldwell, Melissa. (ed.). 2009. *Food & Everyday Life in the Postsocialist World*. Bloomington: Indiana University Press.
Campbell, Gwyn, and Nicole Guibert (eds). 2007. *Wine, Society, and Globalization: Multidisciplinary Perspectives on the Wine Industry*. New York: Palgrave Macmillan.
Candea, Matei. 2007. 'Arbitrary Locations: In Defence of the Bounded Field-Site', *Journal of the Royal Anthropological Institute* 13(1): 167–84.
Cantarji, Vasile, and Georgeta Mincu. 2013. 'Country Report: Moldova', part of the project 'Costs and Benefits of Labour Mobility Between the EU and the Eastern Partner Partnership Countries', Chișinău.
Cantemir, Dimitrie. 2016 [1716]. *Descrierea Moldovei* [The description of Moldova]. Bucharest: Litera.
Carrier, James G. 1990. 'The Symbolism of Possession in Commodity Advertising', *Man* 25(4): 693–706.
Carrier, James G., and Peter G. Luetchford (eds). 2012. *Ethical Consumption: Social Value and Economic Practice*. New York: Berghahn Books.
Cash, Jennifer R. 2011. *Villages on Stage: Folklore and Nationalism in the Republic of Moldova* (Vol. 26). Münster: LIT Verlag.

———. 2013. 'Charity or Remembrance? Practices of Pomană in Rural Moldova', Working Paper 144. Halle/Saale: Max Planck Institute for Social Anthropology.
———. 2014. 'What Do Peasants Want? Equality and Differentiation in Post-Socialist Moldova', *The Museum of the Romanian Peasant Anthropology Review* 19: 163–74.
———. 2015a. 'Economy as Ritual: The Problems of Paying in Wine', in Stephen Gudeman and Chris M. Hann (eds), *Economy and Ritual: Studies of Postsocialist Transformations* (Vol. 1). New York: Berghahn Books, pp. 31–50.
———. 2015b. 'How Much is Enough? Household Provisioning, Self-Sufficiency, and Social Status in Rural Moldova', in Stephen Gudeman and Chris M. Hann (eds), *Oikos and Market: Explorations in Self-sufficiency after Socialism* (Vol. 2). New York: Berghahn Books, pp. 47–76.
———. 2015c. 'Between Starvation and Security: Poverty and Food in Rural Moldova', in Ida H. Knudsen and Martin D. Frederiksen (eds), *Ethnographies of Grey Zones in Eastern Europe: Relations, Borders and Invisibilities*. London and New York: Anthem Press, pp. 41–57.
———. 2019. 'The Changing Value of Food: Calculating Moldova's Poverty', in Valeria Siniscalchi and Krista Harper (eds), *Food Values in Europe*. London and New York: Bloomsbury, pp. 178–93.
Catalogul Soiurilor de Plante al Republicii Moldova [The Republic of Moldova's Plant Varieties Catalogue]. 2017. Chișinău.
Certomà, Chiara. 2011. 'Standing-up Vineyards: The Political Relevance of Tuscan Wine Production', *Environment and Planning D: Society and Space* 29(6): 1010–29.
Chamberlain-Creangă, Rebecca A. 2011. 'Cementing Modernisation: Transnational Markets, Language and Labour Tension in a Post-Soviet Factory in Moldova', Ph.D. dissertation. London: London School of Economics.
Chelcea, Liviu, and Oana Druță. 2016. 'Zombie Socialism and the Rise of Neoliberalism in Post-Socialist Central and Eastern Europe', *Eurasian Geography and Economics* 57(4–5): 521–44.
Ciocanu, Maria. 2015. 'Contribuții Etnografice la Cunoașterea Viticulturii Țărănești din Basarabia' [Ethnographic Contributions to the Knowledge of Peasant Viticulture in Bessarabia], *Anuarul Muzeului Etnografic al Moldovei*, no. XV: 247–87.
Cohen, Paul. 2013. 'The Artifice of Natural Wine: Jules Chauvet and the Reinvention of Vinification in Postwar France', in Rachel Black and Robert Ulin (eds), *Wine and Culture: Vineyard to Glass*. New York and London: Bloomsbury, pp. 261–78.
Conquest, Robert. 1986. *The Harvest of Sorrow: Soviet Collectivization and the Terror-Famine*. Oxford: Oxford University Press.
Corrado, Alessandra, Carlos de Castro, and Domenico Perrotta (eds). 2016. *Migration and Agriculture: Mobility and Change in the Mediterranean Area*. London: Routledge.
Counihan, Carole, and Penny Van Esterik (eds). 2012. *Food and Culture: A Reader*. London: Routledge.
Creed, W. Gerald. 1998. *Domesticating Revolution: From Socialist Reform to Ambivalent Transition in a Bulgarian Village*. University Park, PA: Penn State Press.
———. 2011. *Masquerade and Postsocialism: Ritual and Cultural Dispossession in Bulgaria*. Bloomington, IN: Indiana University Press.

Crenn, Chantal. 2016. 'Wine Heritage and the Ethnicization of Labour: Arab Workers in the Bordeaux Vineyards', in Alessanda Corrado, Carlos de Castro, and Domenico Perrotta (eds), *Migration and Agriculture: Mobility and Change in the Mediterranean Area*. London: Routledge, pp. 66–81.

Demirdirek, Hülya. 2006. 'Step Across the Border: Transnational Encounters and Nation-Making', *Anthropology of East Europe Review* 24(1): 44–50.

———. 2007. 'New Modes of Capitalist Domination: Transnational Space Between Turkey and Moldova', *Anthropology of East Europe Review* 25(1): 15–20.

Demossier, Marion. 2010. *Wine Drinking Culture in France: A National Myth or a Modern Passion?* Cardiff: University of Wales Press.

———. 2011. 'Beyond Terroir: Territorial Construction, Hegemonic Discourses, and French Wine Culture', *Journal of the Royal Anthropological Institute* 17(4): 685–705.

———. 2018. *Burgundy: A Global Anthropology of Place and Taste* (43). New York: Berghahn Books.

Dempsey, Jessica. 2016. *Enterprising Nature: Economics, Markets, and Finance in Global Biodiversity Politics*. Hoboken, NJ: John Wiley & Sons.

Dölkers, Johannes. 1974. *125 Jahre Landwirtschaft in Bessarabien* [125 Years of Agriculture in Bessarabia]. Oldentrup: Eigenverlag des Verfassers.

Domingos, Nuno. 2016. 'The Market as Mediator: The Corporate Creation of Portuguese Wine', *Gastronomica*, 16(3): 31–43.

Dorondel, Ștefan. 2016. *Disrupted Landscapes: State, Peasants and the Politics of Land in Postsocialist Romania* (Vol. 8). New York: Berghahn Books.

Dougherty, Percy H. (ed.). 2012. *The Geography of Wine: Regions, Terroir and Techniques*. Berlin and Heidelberg: Springer Science+Business Media.

Douglas, Mary. 1972. 'Deciphering a Meal', *Daedalus* 101(1): 61–81.

Dunn, Elizabeth C. 2004. *Privatizing Poland: Baby Food, Big Business, and the Remaking of Labor*. Ithaca, NY: Cornell University Press.

———. 2009. 'Standards Without Infrastructure', in Martha Lampland and Susan L. Star (eds), *Standards and Their Stories: How Quantifying, Classifying, and Formalizing Practices Shape Everyday Life*. Ithaca, NY: Cornell University Press, pp. 118–21.

Dunn, Elizabeth C., and Michael S. Bobick. 2014. 'The Empire Strikes Back: War Without War and Occupation Without Occupation in the Russian Sphere of Influence', *American Ethnologist* 41(3): 405–13.

Durst, Judith. 2018. 'Out of the Frying Pan into the Fire? From Municipal Lords to the Global Assembly Lines–Roma Experiences of Social Im/Mobility Through Migration from North Hungary', *Intersections. East European Journal of Society and Politics* 4(3): 4–28.

Dzenovska, Dace. 2018. 'Emptiness and its Futures: Staying and Leaving as Tactics of Life in Latvia', *Focaal* 2018(80): 16–29.

Edholm, Felicity, Olivia Harris, and Kate Young. 1978. 'Conceptualising Women', *Critique of Anthropology* 3(9–10): 101–30.

Eiss, Paul K., and David Pedersen. 2002. 'Introduction: Values of Value', *Cultural Anthropology* 17(3): 283–90.

Engel-Di Mauro, Salvatore. 2014. *Ecology, Soils, and the Left: An Ecosocial Approach*. New York: Palgrave Macmillan.
Engel-Di Mauro, Salvatore, and Levi Van Sant. 2020. 'Soils and Commodification', in Juan Francisco Salazar et al. (eds), *Thinking with Soils: Material Politics and Social Theory*. New York and London: Bloomsbury, pp. 55–69.
Eriksen, Thomas H. 2020. 'The Enforced Cooling Down of an Overheated World', *Social Anthropology* 28(2): 285–6.
Ernu, Vasile, Ovidiu Țichindeleanu and Vitalie Sprînceană. 2017. 'Moldova's Movement from below'. Jacobin. Retrieved 17 March 2016 from https://www.jacobinmag.com/2016/03/moldova-chisinau-protests-russia-eu-ukraine.
Ferguson, James. 2013. 'Declarations of Dependence: Labour, Personhood, and Welfare in Southern Africa', *Journal of the Royal Anthropological Institute* 19(2): 223–42.
Foster, Robert J. 2005. 'Commodity Futures: Labour, Love and Value', *Anthropology Today* 21(4): 8–12.
———. 2007. 'The Work of the New Economy: Consumers, Brands, and Value Creation', *Cultural Anthropology* 22(4): 707–31.
Garcia-Parpet, Marie-France. 2008. 'Markets, Prices and Symbolic Value: Grands Crus and the Challenges of Global Markets', *International Review of Sociology–Revue Internationale de Sociologie* 18(2): 237–52.
Gagyi, Ágnes, and Mariya Ivancheva. 2017. 'The Rise and Fall of Civil Society in East-Central Europe.' In Marcin Moskalewicz and Wojciech Przybylski (eds), *Understanding Central Europe*. London: Routledge, pp. 281–89.
Gille, Zsuzsa. 2010. 'Is There a Global Postsocialist Condition?', *Global Society* 24(1): 9–30.
———. 2016. *Paprika, Foie Gras, and Red Mud: The Politics of Materiality in the European Union*. Bloomington, IN: Indiana University Press.
Goode, Jamie, and Sam Harrop. 2011. *Authentic Wine: Toward Natural and Sustainable Winemaking*. Berkeley, CA: University of California Press.
Goody, Jack. 2012 [1982]. 'Industrial Food: Towards the Development of a World Cuisine', in Carole Counihan and Penny Van Esterik (eds), *Food and Culture: A Reader*. London: Routledge, pp. 86–104.
Gouez, Aziliz, and Boris Pétric. 2007. 'Wine and Europe: The Metamorphoses of a Land of Choice', *Volume 56 of Studies & Research / Notre Europe*. Paris: Institut Jacques Delors.
Graeber, David. 2013. 'It is Value That Brings Universes into Being', *HAU: Journal of Ethnographic Theory* 3(2): 219–43.
Grdešić, Marko. 2015. 'Workers and Unions after Yugoslavia', in Srećko Horvat and Igor Štiks (eds), *Welcome to the Desert of Post-Socialism: Radical Politics After Yugoslavia*. London: Verso Books, pp. 65–81.
Gudeman, Stephen, and Chris M. Hann (eds). 2015a. *Economy and Ritual: Studies of Postsocialist Transformations* (Vol. 1). New York: Berghahn Books.
———. 2015b. *Oikos and Market: Explorations in Self-Sufficiency After Socialism* (Vol. 2). New York: Berghahn Books.
Gunyon, Reginald E.W. 1971. *Wines of Central and South Eastern Europe*. Golden Court, Richmond: Gerald Duckworth & Co. Ltd.

Gusti, Dimitrie, Constantin Orghidan, Mircea Vulcănescu, and Virgil Leonte. 1940. *Enciclopedia României* [The Encyclopaedia of Romania]. Bucharest: Monitorul Oficial și Imprimeriile Statului, Imprimeria Națională.

Guthman, Julie. 2007. 'The Polanyian Way? Voluntary Food Labels as Neoliberal Governance', *Antipode* 39(3): 456–78.

Guy, Kolleen M. 2003. *When Champagne Became French: Wine and the Making of a National Identity* (Vol. 121). Baltimore, MD: JHU Press.

Hamvas, Béla. 2003 [1989]. Filosofia vinului [*The Philosophy of Wine*]. Transl. Laszlo Attila Hubbe. Bucharest: Curtea Veche.

Hann, Chris M. 1980. *Tazlar, a Village in Hungary*. Cambridge: Cambridge University Press.

———. 1993. 'From Production to Property: Decollectivization and the Family-Land Relationship in Contemporary Hungary' *Man* 28(2): 299–320.

——— (ed.). 2002. *Postsocialism: Ideals, Ideologies, and Practices in Eurasia*. London: Routledge.

———. 2003a. 'Introduction: Decollectivisation and the Moral Economy', in Chris M. Hann (ed.), *The Postsocialist Agrarian Question: Property Relations and the Rural Condition*. Münster: LIT Verlag, pp. 1–46.

——— (ed.), 2003b. *The Postsocialist Agrarian Question: Property Relations and the Rural Condition* (Vol. 1). Münster: LIT Verlag.

———. 2004. 'Wine, Sand and Socialism: Some Enduring Effects of Hungary's "Flexible" Model of Collectivisation', in Martin Petrick and Peter Weingarten (eds), *The Role of Agriculture in Central and Eastern European Rural Development: Engine of Change or Social Buffer?* Leipzig: IAMO, pp. 192–208.

———. 2011. 'Moral Dispossession', *InterDisciplines. Journal of History and Sociology* 2(2001): 11–37.

Hann, Chris M., and Keith Hart (eds). 2009. *Market and Society: The Great Transformation Today*. Cambridge: Cambridge University Press.

Hann, Chris M., and Jonathan Parry (eds). 2018. *Industrial Labor on the Margins of Capitalism: Precarity, Class, and the Neoliberal Subject* (Vol. 4). New York: Berghahn Books.

Harris, Olivia, and Kate Young. 1981. 'Engendered Structures: Some Problems in the Analysis of Reproduction', in Joel S. Kahn and Josep R. Llobera (eds), *The Anthropology of Pre-Capitalist Societies*. New York: Palgrave Macmillan, pp. 109–47.

Harvey, David. 1989. *The Condition of Postmodernity* (Vol. 14). Hoboken, NJ: Blackwell.

———. 2002. 'The Art of Rent: Globalisation, Monopoly and the Commodification of Culture', *Socialist Register* 38:93–110.

———. 2006. *The Limits to Capital*. London: Verso Books.

Heintz, Monica. 2005. 'Time and the Work Ethic in Post-Socialist Romania', in Wendy James and David Mills (eds), *The Qualities of Time Anthropological Approaches*. London: Routledge, pp. 171–83.

———. 2006. *'Be European, Recycle Yourself!' The Changing Work Ethic in Romania* (Vol. 12). Münster: LIT Verlag.

———. 2008. *Weak State, Uncertain Citizenship: Moldova*. Bern: Peter Lang, Internationaler Verlag der Wissenschaften.

Horvat, Srećko, and Igor Štiks (eds). 2015. *Welcome to the Desert of Post-Socialism: Radical Politics After Yugoslavia*. London: Verso Books.

Howard, Penny M. 2018. 'The Anthropology of Human-Environment Relations: Materialism with and without Marxism', *Focaal* 2018(82): 64–79.

Humphrey, Caroline. 1983. *Karl Marx Collective: Economy, Society and Religion in a Siberian Collective Farm*. Cambridge: Cambridge University Press.

Iarovoi, Valentina. 2007. 'Vița-de-vie în Cultura Moldovenilor' [Grapevine in the Culture of Moldovans], *Revista de Etnografie, Științele Naturii și Muzeologie (Serie Nouă)* 7(20): 208–17.

Inglis, David. 2019. 'Wine Globalization: Longer-Term Dynamics and Contemporary Patterns', in David Inglis and Anna-Mari Almila (eds), *The Globalization of Wine*. New York and London: Bloomsbury, pp. 21–47.

Inglis, David, and Anna-Mari Almila (eds). 2019. *The Globalization of Wine*. New York and London: Bloomsbury.

Itçaina, Xabier, Antoine Roger, and Andy Smith. 2016. *Varietals of Capitalism: A Political Economy of the Changing Wine Industry*. Ithaca, NY: Cornell University Press.

James, Wendy, and David Mills (eds). 2005. *The Qualities of Time: Anthropological Approaches*. London: Routledge.

Jansen, Stef. 2015. *Yearnings in the Meantime: 'Normal Lives' and the State in a Sarajevo Apartment Complex* (Vol. 15). New York: Berghahn Books.

Jung, Yuson. 2011. 'Parting the "Wine Lake": The Revival of the Bulgarian Wine Industry in the Age of CAP Reform', *Anthropological Journal of European Cultures* 20(1): 10–28.

———. 2013. 'Cultural Patrimony and the Bureaucratization of Wine: The Bulgarian Case', in Rachel Black and Robert Ulin (eds), *Wine and Culture: Vineyard to Glass*. New York and London: Bloomsbury, pp. 161–78.

———. 2014. 'Tasting and Judging the Unknown Terroir of the Bulgarian Wine: The Political Economy of Sensory Experience', *Food and Foodways* 22(1–2): 24–47.

———. 2016. 'Re-creating Economic and Cultural Values in Bulgaria's Wine Industry: From an Economy of Quantity to an Economy of Quality?', *Economic Anthropology* 3(2): 280–92.

———. 2019. *Balkan Blues: Consumer Politics After State Socialism*. Bloomington, IN: Indiana University Press.

Kahn, Joel S., and Josep R. Llobera (eds). 1981. *Anthropology of Pre-Capitalist Societies*. London: Macmillan International Higher Education.

Kalb, Don. 2014. 'Elias Talks to Hayek (and Learns from Marx and Foucault): Reflections on Neoliberalism, Postsocialism and Personhood', in Nicolette Makovicky (ed.), *Neoliberalism, Personhood and Postsocialism: Enterprising Selves in Changing Economies*. Farnham: Ashgate, pp. 187–201.

Kaneff, Deema, and Monica Heintz. 2006. 'Bessarabian Borderlands: One Region, Two States, Multiple Ethnicities', *Anthropology of East Europe Review* 24(1): 6–16.

Karpik, Lucien. 2010. *The Economics of Singularities*. Princeton, NJ: Princeton University Press.

Kasmir, Sharryn, and August Carbonella (eds). 2014. *Blood and Fire: Toward a Global Anthropology of Labor* (Vol. 13). New York: Berghahn Books.

Keough, Leyla J. 2016. *Worker-Mothers on the Margins of Europe: Gender and Migration Between Moldova and Istanbul*. Bloomington, IN: Indiana University Press.

Kesküla, Eeva. 2016. 'Temporalities, Time and the Everyday: New Technology as a Marker of Change in an Estonian Mine', *History and Anthropology* 27(5): 521–35.

Kideckel, David A. 2002. 'The Unmaking of an East-Central European Working Class', in Chris M. Hann (ed.), *Postsocialism: Ideals, Ideologies and Practices in Eurasia*. London: Routledge, pp. 126–44.

Kim, Eleana. 2019. 'Metabolic Relations: Korean Red Ginseng and the Ecologies of Modern Life', in Sarah Besky and Alex Blanchette (eds), *How Nature Works: Rethinking Labor on a Troubled Planet*. Albuquerque, NM: University of New Mexico Press, pp. 115–30.

King, Charles. 2000. *The Moldovans: Romania, Russia, and the Politics of Culture*. New York: Hoover Press.

King, Juliette Kon Kam, and Céline Granjou. 2020. 'Mapping Soil, Losing Ground? Politics of Soil Mapping', in Juan Francisco Salazar et al. (eds), *Thinking with Soils: Material Politics and Social Theory*. New York and London: Bloomsbury, pp. 39–53.

Kjaerulff, Jens. (ed.). 2015. *Flexible Capitalism: Exchange and Ambiguity at Work* (Vol. 25). New York: Berghahn Books.

Kjellgren, Björn. 2004. 'Drunken Modernity: Wine in China', *Anthropology of Food* [Online] (3). Retrieved 28 June 2021 from journals.openedition.org/aof/249.

Knudsen, Ida H., and Martin D. Frederiksen (eds). 2015. *Ethnographies of Grey Zones in Eastern Europe: Relations, Borders and Invisibilities*. London and New York: Anthem Press.

Kofti, Dimitra. 2016. '"Communists" on the Shop Floor: Anticommunism, Crisis, and the Transformation of Labor in Bulgaria', *Focaal* 2016(74): 69–82.

———. 2018. 'Regular Work in Decline, Precarious Households, and Changing Solidarities in Bulgaria', in Chris M. Hann and Jonathan Parry (eds), *Industrial Labor on the Margins of Capitalism: Precarity, Class, and the Neoliberal Subject*. New York: Berghahn Books, pp. 111–34.

Kopczyńska, Ewa. 2013. 'Wine Histories, Wine Memories and Local Identities in Western Poland', in Rachel Black and Robert Ulin (eds), *Wine and Culture: Vineyard to Glass*. New York and London: Bloomsbury, pp. 109–25.

Krzywoszynska, Anna. 2020. 'Nonhuman Labor and the Making of Resources: Making Soils a Resource Through Microbial Labor', *Environmental Humanities* 12(1): 227–49.

Krzywoszynska, Anna, and Greta Marchesi. 2020. 'Toward a Relational Materiality of Soils: Introduction', *Environmental Humanities* 12(1): 190–204.

Kubicek, Paul. 2002. 'Civil Society, Trade Unions and Post-Soviet Democratisation: Evidence from Russia and Ukraine', *Europe-Asia Studies* 54(4): 603–24.

Lagendijk, Arnoud. 2004. 'Global "Lifeworlds" Versus Local "System Worlds": How Flying Winemakers Produce Global Wines in Interconnected Locales', *Tijdschrift voor Economischeen Sociale Geografie* 95(5): 511–26.

Lampland, Martha, and Susan L. Star (eds). 2009. *Standards and Their Stories: How Quantifying, Classifying, and Formalizing Practices Shape Everyday Life*. Ithaca, NY: Cornell University Press.

Lazăr, Diana. 2010. *Re-Think Wine Sector – Relansăm Sectorul Vitivinicol.* Chișinău: Asociația Patronală a Viței de Vie și Vinului din Republica Moldova și Uniunea Oenologilor din Republica Moldova.

Leașco, Ion, Andrei Smolin, and Marina Smolina. 2009. *Raionul Ștefan Vodă: Schiță Istorică* [The Ștefan Vodă Raion: Historical Sketch]. Chișinău: Pontos.

Ledeneva, Alena. 2009. 'From Russia with Blat: Can Informal Networks Help Modernize Russia?', *Social Research: An International Quarterly* 76(1): 257–88.

Lem, Winnie. 1999. *Cultivating Dissent: Work, Identity, and Praxis in Rural Languedoc.* New York: SUNY Press.

———. 2002. 'Articulating Class in Post-Fordist France', *American Ethnologist* 29(2): 287–306.

———. 2013. 'Regimes of Regulation, Gender, and Divisions of Labor in Languedoc Viticulture', in Rachel Black and Robert Ulin (eds), *Wine and Culture: Vineyard to Glass.* New York and London: Bloomsbury, pp. 221–41.

Lewontin, Richard C. 1998. 'The Maturing of Capitalist Agriculture: Farmer as Proletarian', *Monthly Review* 50(3): 72–85.

Liddell, Alex. 2003. *The Wines of Hungary.* London: Mitchell Beazley.

Logan, William, Ullrich Kockel, and M. Nic Craith. 2015. 'The New Heritage Studies: Origins and Evolution, Problems and Prospects', in William Logan, Máiréad Nic Craith, and Ullrich Kockel (eds), *A Companion to Heritage Studies.* Hoboken, NJ: John Wiley & Sons, pp. 1–25.

Logan, William, Máiréad Nic Craith, and Ullrich Kockel (eds). 2015. *A Companion to Heritage Studies.* Hoboken, NJ: John Wiley & Sons.

Lorimer, Jamie. 2017. 'Probiotic Environmentalities: Rewilding with Wolves and Worms', *Theory, Culture & Society* 34(4): 27–48.

Madan, Stas, and Vlad Furdui. 2015. *Studiu: Trendurile Industriei Vinicole din Republica Moldova* [Study: Trends in the Wine Industry in the Republic of Moldova]. Chișinău: Ministerul Agriculturii si Industriei Alimentare a Republicii Moldova, IP Oficiul National al Viei si Vinului, Vinul Moldovei, USAID CEED II.

Magenta Consulting. 2016. *Studiu: Piața Vinurilor din Republica Moldova* [Study: Wine Market in the Republic of Moldova]. Chișinău.

Makovicky, Nicolette. 2014a. 'Me, Inc.? Untangling Neoliberalism, Personhood, and Postsocialism', in Nicolette Makovicky (ed.), *Neoliberalism, Personhood, and Post-socialism: Enterprising Selves in Changing Economies.* Farnham: Ashgate, pp. 1–16.

——— (ed.). 2014b. *Neoliberalism, Personhood, and Postsocialism: Enterprising Selves in Changing Economies.* Farnham: Ashgate.

———. 2020. 'The Seduction of Craft: Making and Value in Artisanal Labour', *Journal of Material Culture* 25(3): 209–323.

Manning, Paul. 2012. *Semiotics of Drink and Drinking.* London: A&C Black.

Manning, Paul, and Ann Uplisashvili. 2007. '"Our Beer": Ethnographic Brands in Postsocialist Georgia', *American Anthropologist* 109(4): 626–41.

Marandici, Ion. 2016. 'Statul Fără Autonomie: O Istorie de Succes la Periferia Uniunii Europene?' [The State Without Autonomy: A Tale of Success at the Periphery of the European Union?], in Petru Negură, Vitalie Sprînceană, and Vasile Ernu (eds),

Republica Moldova la 25 de ani: O încercare de bilanț [Republic of Moldova at 25: an attempt towards a balance sheet]. Chișinău: Cartier, pp. 53–79.
Meillassoux, Claude. 1972. 'From Reproduction to Production: A Marxist Approach to Economic Anthropology', *Economy and Society* 1(1): 93–105.
Meloni, Giulia, and Johan Swinnen. 2013. 'The Political Economy of European Wine Regulations', *Journal of Wine Economics* 8(3): 244–84.
Meneley, Anne. 2007. 'Like an extra virgin', *American Anthropologist* 109(4): 678–87.
Mezzadri, Alessandra. 2019. 'On the Value of Social Reproduction: Informal Labour, the Majority World and the Need for Inclusive Theories and Politics', *Radical Philosophy* 2(4): 33–41.
Mikuš, Marek. 2018. *Frontiers of Civil Society: Government and Hegemony in Serbia*. New York: Berghahn Books.
Mincyte, Diana. 2009. 'Everyday Environmentalism: The Practice, Politics, and Nature of Subsidiary Farming in Stalin's Lithuania', *Slavic Review* 68(1): 31–49.
——. 2011. 'Subsistence and Sustainability in Post-Industrial Europe: The Politics of Small-Scale Farming in Europeanising Lithuania', *Sociologia Ruralis* 51(2): 101–18.
——. 2012. 'How Milk Does the World Good: Vernacular Sustainability and Alternative Food Systems in Post-Socialist Europe', *Agriculture and Human Values* 29(1): 41–52.
Ministry of Heath, Labour and Social Protection in the Republic of Moldova, 2017. *Notă Informativă Privind Progresul Implementării Programului Național Privind Controlul Alcoolului pe Anii 2012–2020, pentru Anul 2017* [Informative Note Regarding the Progress of the Implementation of the National Program for Alcohol Consumption Between 2012 and 2020, for the Year 2017]. Chișinău.
Mintz, Sidney W. 1974. 'The Rural Proletariat and the Problem of Rural Proletarian Consciousness', *Journal of Peasant Studies* 1(3): 291–325.
Mollona, Massimilano. 2009. *Made in Sheffield: An Ethnography of Industrial Work and Politics* (Vol. 5). New York: Berghahn Books.
Monterescu, Daniel. 2017. 'Border Wines: Terroir Across Contested Territory', *Gastronomica: The Journal of Critical Food Studies* 17(4): 127–140.
Monterescu, Daniel, and Ariel Handel. 2019. 'Liquid Indigeneity: Wine, Science, and Colonial Politics in Israel/Palestine', *American Ethnologist* 46(3): 313–27.
Moore, Jason W. 2015. *Capitalism in the Web of Life: Ecology and the Accumulation of Capital*. London: Verso Books.
Moskalewicz, Marcin, and Wojciech Przybylski (eds). 2017. *Understanding Central Europe*. London: Routledge.
Müller, Birgit. 2007. *Disenchantment with Market Economics: East Germans and Western Capitalism* (Vol. 1). New York: Berghahn Books.
Narotzky, Susana. 2015. 'The Payoff of Love and the Traffic of Favours', in Jens Kjaerulff (ed.), *Flexible Capitalism: Exchange and Ambiguity at Work*. New York: Berghahn Books, pp. 173–206.
——. 2018. 'Rethinking the Concept of Labour', *Journal of the Royal Anthropological Institute* 24(S1): 29–43.
Negură, Petru. 2016. 'Republica Moldova la un Sfert de Veac de Tranziție: Intre un Communism Ratat și un Capitalism Neînceput? [The Republic of Moldova After

a Quarter of a Century of Transition: Between a Failed Communism and an Uncommenced Capitalism?] in Petru Negură, Vitalie Sprînceană, and Vasile Ernu (eds), *Republica Moldova la 25 de ani: O încercare de bilanț* [Republic of Moldova at 25: an attempt towards a balance sheet]. Chișinău: Cartier, pp. 19–53.

Negură, Petru, Vitalie Sprînceană, and Vasile Ernu (eds). 2016. *Republica Moldova la 25 de ani: O încercare de bilanț* [Republic of Moldova at 25: an attempt towards a balance sheet]. Chișinău: Cartier.

Nemtsov, Alexander V. 1998. 'Alcohol-Related Harm and Alcohol Consumption in Moscow Before, During and After a Major Anti-Alcohol Campaign', *Addiction* 93(10): 1501–10.

Nenescu, Lilia, and Vitalie Sprînceană. 2018. 'Salariul de Trai Minim în Republica Moldova. Studiu de Caz: Industria Textilă' [The Minumum Living Age in the Republic of Moldova. Case Study: The Textile Industry], *Platzforma*. Retrieved 2 May 2020 from https://www.platzforma.md/arhive/386466.

OIV. 2012. *Guidelines for the Characterization of Wine Yeasts of the Genus Saccharomyces Isolated from Vitivinicultural Environments*. Izmir: Resolution OIV-OENO 370-2012.

Organizația Națională a Viei și Vinului (ONVV). 2017. 'Moldovan Winemaking Sector: Pathways to Qualitative Restructuring'. Prague.

Paris Exposition Universelle. 1900. *Exposition Universelle Internationale De 1900. Classes 36 et 60 : Viticulture, Vins et Eaux-De-Vie: Rapports* [International Universal Exhibition of 1900. Classes 36 and 60: Viticulture, Wines and Brandy: Reports]. Paris: Conservatoire Numérique des Arts et Métiers.

Paxson, Heather. 2008. 'Post-Pasteurian Cultures: The Microbiopolitics of Raw-Milk Cheese in the United States', *Cultural Anthropology* 23(1): 15–47.

Paxson, Heather, and Stefan Helmreich. 2014. 'The Perils and Promises of Microbial Abundance: Novel Natures and Model Ecosystems, From Artisanal Cheese to Alien Seas', *Social Studies of Science* 44(2): 165–93.

Pelivan, Ion G. 1920. *L'état Économique de la Bessarabie* [The Economic State of Bessarabia]. Paris: J. Charpentier.

Petrick, Martin, and Peter Weingarten. 2004. 'The Role of Agriculture in Central and Eastern European Rural Development: Engine of Change or Social Buffer?' (No. 25). *Studies on the Agricultural and Food Sector in Central and Eastern Europe*. Halle/Saale: IAMO.

Petrovici, Norbert. 2015. 'Framing Criticism and Knowledge Production in Semi-Peripheries–Post-Socialism Unpacked', *Intersections: East European Journal of Society and Politics* 1(2): 80–102.

———. 2017. *Zona Urbană: O Economie Politică a Socialismului Românesc* [The Urban Zone: A Political Economy of Romanian Socialism]. Cluj-Napoca: Tact.

Pine, Frances. 2007. 'Dangerous Modernities? Innovative Technologies and the Unsettling of Agriculture in Rural Poland', *Critique of Anthropology* 27(2): 183–201.

Poenaru, Florin. 2016. 'România – Pământ Basarabean' [Romania – Besarabian Land], in Petru Negură, Vitalie Sprînceană, and Vasile Ernu (eds), *Republica Moldova la 25 de ani: O încercare de bilanț* [Republic of Moldova at 25: an attempt towards a balance sheet]. Chișinău: Cartier, pp. 79–95.

Pratt, Jeff C. 1994. *The Rationality of Rural Life: Economic and Cultural Change in Tuscany* (Vol. 17). London: Psychology Press.

———. 2007. 'Food Values: The Local and the Authentic', *Critique of Anthropology* 27(3): 285–300.
Pratt, Jeff C., and Peter Luetchford. 2014. *Food for Change: The Politics and Values of Social Movements*. London: Pluto Press.
Purcari Wineries Plc. 2018. 'Corporate Presentation'. Chișinău. Accessed 11 May 2018.
Rajković, Ivan. 2018. 'For an Anthropology of the Demoralized: State Pay, Mock-Labour, and Unfreedom in a Serbian Firm', *Journal of the Royal Anthropological Institute* 24(1): 47–70.
———. 2019. 'Yugoslav Peasants Land Apollo 8', *Anthropology News* 60: e99–e102.
Ringel, Felix. 2016. 'Beyond Temporality: Notes on the Anthropology of Time from a Shrinking Fieldsite', *Anthropological Theory* 16(4): 390–412.
Roșca, Dorina. 2017. *Antropologia Schimburilor în Cadrul Migrației Moldovenești. Practici Comunitare și Rețele de Solidaritate Printre Moldovenii din Regiunea Pariziană* [The Anthropology of Exchanges in the Framework of Moldovan Migration. Community Practices and Solidarity Networks Among Moldovans in the Parisian Region], *Plazforma*. Accessed 4 January 2021.
Rozloga, Iurie, et al. 2017. 'Etapa Intermediară I: Evaluarea Geomorfologică și Pedologică a Lotului Experimental-Demonstrativ pentru Viticultori din S. Purcari, Raionul ȘtefanVodă' [Geomorphological and Pedological Evaluation of the Viticultural Experimental-Demonstrative Plot in Purcari Village, Ștefan Vodă Raion], in *Evaluarea Geomorfologică și Pedologică a Trei Loturi Experimental-Demonstrative Pentru Viticultori, în Cadrul Proiectului ONVV "Lot-Ex"*, Cod CPV – 79311200-9, Chișinău.
Rusu, Emil. 2011. *Vinificația Primară* [Primary Vinification]. Chișinău: Continental Group.
Salazar, Juan Francisco, et al. (eds). 2020. *Thinking with Soils: Material Politics and Social Theory*. New York and London: Bloomsbury.
Schmidt, Ute. 2012. *Basarabia: Coloniștii Germani de la Marea Neagră* [Bessarabia: The German Colonists at the Black Sea]. Chișinău: Cartier.
Simpson, James. 2011. *Creating Wine: The Emergence of a World Industry, 1840–1914* (Vol. 36). Princeton, NJ: Princeton University Press.
Siniscalchi, Valeria, and Krista Harper (eds). 2019. *Food Values in Europe*. New York and London: Bloomsbury.
Smith, Robin, and Cristina Grasseni. 2020. 'Ambivalent Solidarities: Food Governance Reconfigurations in Croatia and Italy', *Anthropology Today* 36(1): 12–16.
Spittler, Gerd. 2003. 'Work–Transformation of Objects or Interaction Between Subjects', in Brigitta Benzing and Bernd Herrmann (eds), *Exploitation and Overexploitation in Societies Past and Present* (Vol. 4). Münster: LIT Verlag, pp. 327–38.
———. 2008. *Founders of the Anthropology of Work: German Social Scientists of the 19th and Early 20th Centuries and the First Ethnographers* (Vol. 14). Münster: Lit Verlag.
———. 2009. 'Contesting the Great Transformation: Work in Comparative Perspective', in Chris M. Hann and Keith Hart (eds), *Market and Society: The Great Transformation Today*. Cambridge: Cambridge University Press, pp. 160–74.
Spoor, Max (ed.). 2009. *The Political Economy of Rural Livelihoods in Transition Economies: Land, Peasants and Rural Poverty in Transition*. London: Routledge.

———. 2012. 'Agrarian Reform and Transition: What Can We Learn from "the East"?', *Journal of Peasant Studies* 39(1): 175–94.

Spoor, Max, and Felicia Izman. 2009. 'Land Reform and Interlocking Agricultural Market in Moldova', in Max Spoor (ed.), *The Political Economy of Rural Livelihoods in Transition Economies: Land, Peasants and Rural Poverty in Transition*. London: Routledge, pp. 99–122.

Swinburn, Robert. 2013. 'The Things that Count: Rethinking Terroir in Australia', in Rachel Black and Robert Ulin (eds), *Wine and Culture: Vineyard to Glass*. New York and London: Bloomsbury, pp. 33–50.

Teil, Geneviève. 2012. 'No Such Thing as Terroir? Objectivities and the Regimes of Existence of Objects', *Science, Technology, & Human Values* 37(5): 478–505.

———. 2017. 'The Microbes, Stowaways of the Milk', in *Acts of the 12th Mountain Cheese Network*, conference paperpresented at Padua University: RMT Fromages au lait cru.

Thelen, Tatiana. 2011. 'Shortage, Fuzzy Property and Other Dead Ends in the Anthropological Analysis of (Post) Socialism', *Critique of Anthropology* 31(1): 43–61.

———. 2012. 'Economic Concepts, Common Grounds and "New" Diversity in the Anthropology of Post-Socialism: Reply to Dunn and Verdery', *Critique of Anthropology* 32(1): 87–90.

Thompson, Edward P. 1967. 'Time, Work-Discipline, and Industrial Capitalism', *Past & Present* (38): 56–97.

Tlostanova, Madina. 2015. 'Can the Post-Soviet Think? On Coloniality of Knowledge, External Imperial and Double Colonial Difference', *Intersections. East European Journal of Society and Politics* 1(2): 38–58.

Trubek, Amy B. 2008. *The Taste of Place: A Cultural Journey into Terroir* (Vol. 20). Berkeley, CA: University of California Press.

Turner, Terence. 2008. 'Marxian Value Theory: An Anthropological Perspective', *Anthropological Theory* 8(1): 43–56.

Ulin, Robert C. 1996. *Vintages and Traditions: An Ethnohistory of Southwest French Wine Cooperatives*. New York: Smithsonian Series in Ethnographic Inquiry.

———. 2002. 'Work as Cultural Production: Labour and Self–Identity Among Southwest French Wine-Growers', *Journal of the Royal Anthropological Institute* 8(4): 691–712.

———. 2007. 'Writing about Wine', in Gwyn Campbell and Nicole Guibert (eds), *Wine, Society, and Globalization: Multidisciplinary Perspectives on the Wine Industry*. New York: Palgrave Macmillan, pp. 43–62.

———. 2013. 'Terroir and Locality: An Anthropological Perspective', in Rachel Black and Robert C. Ulin (eds), *Wine and Culture: Vineyard to Glass*. New York and London: Bloomsbury, pp. 67–85.

Unwin, Tim. 2012. 'Terroir: At the Heart of Geography', in Percy H. Dougherty (ed.), *The Geography of Wine: Regions, Terroir and Techniques*. Berlin and Heidelberg: Springer Science+Business Media, pp. 37–48.

Vankeerberghen, Audrey. 2012. 'Today, One Can Farm Organic without Living Organic: Belgian Farmers and Recent Changes in Organic Farming', in James G.

Carrier and Peter G. Luetchford (eds), *Ethical Consumption: Social Value and Economic Practice*. New York: Berghahn Books, pp. 146–72.

Verdery, Katherine. 1996. *What Was Socialism, and What Comes Next?* Princeton, NJ: Princeton University Press.

———. 2001. 'Inequality as Temporal Process: Property and Time in Transylvania's Land Restitution', *Anthropological Theory* 1(3): 373–92.

———. 2003. *The Vanishing Hectare: Property and Value in Postsocialist Transylvania*. Ithaca, NY: Cornell University Press.

Visser, Oane, and Don Kalb. 2010. 'Financialised Capitalism Soviet Style? Varieties of State Capture and Crisis', *European Journal of Sociology/Archives Européennes de Sociologie* 51(2): 171–94.

Visser, Oane, Natalia Mamonova, Max Spoor, and Alexander Nikulin. 2015. '"Quiet Food Sovereignty" as Food Sovereignty Without a Movement? Insights from Post-Socialist Russia', *Globalizations* 12(4): 513–28.

Vodopivec, Nina. 2010. 'Textile Workers in Slovenia: From Nimble Fingers to Tired Bodies', *Anthropology of East Europe Review* 28(1): 165–83.

Walker, Adam, and Paul Manning. 2013. 'Georgian Wine: The Transformation of Socialist Quantity into Postsocialist Quality', in Rachel Black and Robert C. Ulin (eds), *Wine and Culture: Vineyard to Glass*. New York and London: Bloomsbury, pp. 201–20.

Weiss, Brad. 2016. *Real Pigs: Shifting Values in the Field of Local Pork*. Durham, NC: Duke University Press.

Wrobel, Agata and Dominik Lubasz. 2015. 'PDO's and PGI's Scope of Protection – The Polish Case of Wine Yeast', *145th EAAE Seminar, Parma 14–15 April 2015*. Retrieved 1 May 2019 from ageconsearch.umn.edu/handle/199830.

Index

advertising, 131, 136, 140–45
accumulation
  capital, 84
  flexible, 7, 107–8
agriculture, 32, 38, 60, 73, 79, 92, 103n10, 109, 120, 132, 163
  biodynamic, 13
  ecological, 61
  industrial, 17
  organic, 13, 28n3, 61
  subsistence, 39, 48–51, 88, 160
alcohol, 29, 37–38, 49, 65–66, 71–72, 79, 81n1, 90, 136
  content, 60
alcoholism, 37, 72
alienation, 26, 95, 107, 116
anhydride, 13, 68, 71, 81n1. *See also* SO2
Antonești, 84
Appellation, 10, 43, 133

ban. *See* embargo
bio, food, 61
  wine, 67, 81
biodiversity, 73, 75, 151n7, 155
blog. *See* wine blog
bottling, 22, 49, 94, 128
  section, 96, 105–9, 112–15, 118–21, 123–25
brand, 26, 106–8, 136, 138, 142, 145–6
  country, 2, 76, 157
Bulgaria, 8, 17, 31, 35–36, 71, 86, 126, 146
Bordeaux, 14–15, 140, 150
border, 29, 97, 155
brandy, counterfeit, 99, 115
Burgundy, 11, 76, 137, 140, 149

canning factory, 83, 94, 114, 118
capitalism, 5, 7, 9, 16, 18, 25, 84–85, 87–88, 98, 101–2, 139
  flexible, 107
  late, 11, 26, 96, 128, 143
  postmodern, 107
cellar, 13, 22, 33, 63, 70, 79, 144, 161
  Cricova, 35
  Industrial, 21, 86, 94, 96, 113, 129n4
charmat, 78
Chauvet, Jules, 13, 27n2
circulation, of wine, 12, 14, 80, 86, 107, 135, 139, 160, 163
civilization, 125–26, 130n8, 139
class, 7, 18, 78, 80, 85, 145, 159, 164
  working, 17, 100
collectivization, 34, 116
colonists, 47
  French, 32
  German, 32, 46, 70
  Swiss, 70
commensality, 107, 109, 122–23, 129
commodity, 80, 84, 132, 135, 137, 157, 160–61, 163
Communist Party of Moldova, 20, 39
comparison, 10, 27, 84, 86–87, 99, 157
competition (wine)
  global, 149
  market, 17, 26, 108, 132, 138
  transnational, 2
consumption, 20, 73, 80, 82n11, 87–88, 91, 96, 136
  alcohol, 37, 71–72
  domestic, 23
  household, 34–35, 51, 59, 66

wine, 2, 3, 21–25, 49, 65–67, 70, 78, 135, 137, 154, 160–61
continuity, 8, 20, 111, 122, 125, 136, 146–47
cooperative, 14, 100
conservation, and heritage, 76, 147
control, and alcohol production, 37
  and the production process, 13, 59, 67, 69, 146
  and quality, 34, 43, 138, 161
cota, 51, 57
COVID-19, 162–64
craft, 32, 54, 69
craftsmanship, 63, 65, 67
crisis
  economic, 20, 39
  in the wine sector, 2–3, 19, 100, 125

decollectivization, 8, 38–39, 51–52, 84, 89, 100
dependence,
  and export markets, 20, 24–25, 30, 37
  in/with the Soviet Union, 34
divin, 90, 137
dry law, 37, 60. *See also* ucaz

East, -west polarization, 156, 158
  Germany, 17
Eastern Bloc, 7–8, 18–19, 87–88, 108, 139
Eastern Europe, 7, 38, 88, 136
ecology, 28n4, 48, 60
economy, 28, 51, 56n20, 65, 70–71, 92, 142
  command, 36
  informal, 61
  market, 19, 38, 41, 92, 101
  planned, 41, 87
  political, 10, 23, 25, 132, 135, 158, 161–62
  of quality, 8, 42
  of quantity, 8, 42
  shadow, 126
  subsistence, 3, 18
  virtual, 55
embargo, 1, 4, 19, 24, 26, 30, 40, 42, 100, 106, 108, 115, 128, 129n3, 134, 146–47, 155, 158

European Union, 2, 10–11, 19–21, 55n8, 61, 75, 154
exchange, 22–23, 51, 54, 95, 99, 106, 136–37

feast, 122
fermentation, 72, 105, 109, 113, 141–43, 146, 150
fetishism (commodity), 14, 162
flexibility, 16
flying winemaker. *See* winemaker
France, 5, 6, 10, 15, 23, 31–32, 63, 70, 73, 77–78, 137, 140–41
French AOC, 12, 34, 133, 139
  countryside, 15
  standards, 138
  terroir, 27n1
  varieties, 33, 43, 63, 140
  wine region, 27

Gamza, 47
garden, 34, 46, 51, 56n18, 63, 65, 76, 97, 116–17
gardening, 22, 25, 84, 86, 89–91, 129
Găgăuzia, 19
gender, 22, 85, 112, 115, 159
  and division of labour, 18
genericness, 132, 142, 154
geography, 6, 15
Georgia, 8, 29, 31, 35, 43, 45, 63, 74, 82n12, 96
Germany, 11, 31, 99, 37, 141, 158
globalization, 5–6, 10–11, 15, 45, 80, 105, 132, 135, 146, 148, 153–54, 162
gospodar, 64–67, 70. *See also* craftsmanship
grape, 12, 32, 33, 36–38, 43–45, 49–50, 58–60, 62–70, 74–76, 108–9, 131–2, 138–44, 148–50
  clone, 82n15
  cultivation, 13
  indigenous, 33, 44, 74
  storing, 13, 161
  table, 40, 81n4
  varieties, 8, 11, 32, 40, 44–45, 54, 62, 69, 74–78, 133, 137, 148, 155
grapevine, 32–34, 38–39, 40, 47, 51,

63–64, 67, 73–75, 82–83, 105, 125, 138–39

harvest, 21–22, 50, 52, 57n40, 58, 66, 69, 91, 93, 105, 109, 119, 140, 161
hegemonic discourse, 15, 143
heritage, 58, 71, 73, 75, 136–37, 147
holiday, 95, 127–8, 158. *See also* leisure
home, 51, 58–58, 62–63, 71–79, 89–94, 96–97, 105–6, 112, 115–18
homemade wine. *See* wine
household, 12–13, 28n5, 34, 37, 39, 48, 51, 57n28, n37, n38, 58–59, 61–66, 70–74, 84–85, 88–91, 103n11, 111, 114, 116–17
  state-, 49
hram, 123–24, 130n13
humans, in terroir, 144–45, 151n3, 162
hybrid grape, 33, 55n8, 55n10, 63, 70, 74–76

identity
  local, 11, 132, 135
  national, 3, 40, 157
indication, geographical, 2, 43, 77, 138
industrialization, 13, 35, 60–61, 133
inequality, 5, 87, 159, 162–64
infrastructure, 84–86, 96–98, 101, 149–50
investment, 96, 146
Italy, 5–6, 10–11, 31, 45, 78, 141, 154

kinship, 88, 111–12

labelling, 110–5
laboratory, 21, 68, 148.9
labour, 2–3, 14–18, 107–9
  division of, 34, 88, 113
  domestic, 18
  wage, 51, 92–95
labour force reproduction, 83–85, 102, 158–61
land reform, 39
legislation
  European, 43, 61, 138
  wine, 2, 133
leisure, 86, 89, 95–99
lider de pământ, 51, 89, 102n2

livelihoods, 16–17, 20, 101, 144
locality, 132

mapping, 74, 138
market, 2, 4–6
  competition, 2, 11–12, 17, 108–9
  domestic (for wine), 25, 59–60, 70–73, 76–78
  export, 9, 12, 19–20, 31–33, 40–45, 75, 153–56
  globalized, 2, 8–9, 25, 115–16, 132–35, 147–49
  transnational, 3, 106, 132, 150, 159
marketing,
  campaign, 106, 147
  wine, 129n3, 131–37, 140, 145–46, 149–50, 151n9, 152n12
maternity leave (and workplace), 90, 115
memory, of socialism, 86, 95
microbes, 142–43
microzone, 12, 15, 27n1, 139
migration, 32, 72, 92–93, 103n7, 103n8, 108
modernization, 33, 35, 55n9, 87, 96, 101, 103–4n14
money, dependence on, 38, 40, 72, 87, 91, 116, 123
monopoly rent, 131–32, 135, 143, 158

nature, 66, 75–76, 109, 132, 151n7
  cheap, 85
  and food production, 13, 67
  metabolic exchange with, 16
nostalgia, 90, 96–98, 100

Odessa, 37, 90–91, 115, 117
OIV, 41, 143, 146
Olănești, 46, 51, 73, 75, 83, 90–91, 94, 100, 118
ONVV, 42–44, 73–74, 76, 138–9

pandemic, 163–64
peasants, 32–33, 39, 47–49, 61–63, 71–75, 160
periphery, 153
phylloxera, 5, 8, 32–33, 57n30, 78
place

of origin, 6, 8, 10–11, 133
  taste of, 73, 142
Poland, 32, 89, 109, 151n1
postsocialism, 3–10, 87
postmodernity, 108
post-Soviet period, 8–9
poverty, 33, 35, 39, 70, 99–101, 118, 157
  line, 89–90
power, 108, 116, 126, 132–35, 139
  relations of, 5, 11, 54, 151n10
prestige, 8–9, 54, 126, 132, 143
privatization, 23, 39, 49–51, 84, 92–93, 98
producer, local, 43
  wine, 5, 10, 14, 62, 76, 134, 146–48
  small wine, 73, 75, 137
production
  process, 12, 23, 52, 59, 67, 69, 85, 102, 114, 123
  technology, 2, 79
  of value, 2, 153
proletariat, 17
  rural, 17, 26, 87, 98
provisioning, 26, 86–90
pruning, winter, 52, 62
Pryvoz, 90
Purcari
  terroir, 11, 78, 102, 131–32
  village, 21–24, 45–53, 63–66, 83–89
  wine, 48, 78–79
  winery, 2, 10, 15–17, 45–53, 68–69, 101, 108, 136–40

quality, 5–8, 10–11, 15, 33, 36, 40–43, 69–70, 77
quantity, 8–9, 36, 156
quota, 28n6, 51, 89

Răscăieți, 47, 49, 75–76, 81n9
refrigeration, 129n4
religion, 94
reproduction, (of the labour force), 18, 85, 102, 159
rhythm (at work), 22, 26, 105–6, 113, 120, 128
ritual, 26, 40, 65, 73, 78, 106–7, 123, 126
Romania, 10, 21, 35, 45, 60, 78, 92. 97
  union with, 33–34, 48, 27, 29

Russia, 2, 7, 19, 91, 95, 99–101, 108, 119, 136, 155–56

Saturday, 89, 105, 117–8, 121–22
science, 135, 139
shift
  day, 114–18, 129
  long, 110, 115–19
  night, 106, 114–18, 125, 121–22, 125
  Saturday, 106, 123–24
singing, 110, 123, 144
sleep, 116–17, 122
SO_2, 13, 67–68, 79
social reproduction theory, 18, 84, 102, 159
sociality, 5–60, 66, 74, 86, 106, 109, 118, 128
soil, 10–12, 77–78, 132, 146
  mapping, 137–41
  scientist, 144
solidarity, 29, 121, 129, 164
sommelier, 24, 77–79, 134
sota, 57n38
Soviet Union, 5, 7, 12, 20, 27, 30, 34–37, 79, 84, 99, 102, 139, 154–56
space programme, 35
standard (quality), 9, 11, 13, 43, 59, 69, 77, 121, 138, 147
state, 33, 37, 60–61, 72, 75, 98
  capitalist, 80
  captured, 98
  postsocialist, 3
  socialist, 3
  weak, 98
  welfare, 18
strategies
  coping, 61, 72, 86, 88, 90, 93, 128, 160
  economic, 83, 88
sustainability, 66, 163
system, capitalist, 88, 102, 107
  socialist, 17, 88

Talmaza, 37, 49, 97
tank, steel, 78, 103
taste, 9, 25, 36, 45, 59–60, 63–66, 69, 71, 73, 77–79, 132–33, 135, 142–43, 146–49, 160

technology, 10, 43, 77, 107, 132, 143, 149
terroir, 8–11, 13, 15, 77–78, 131–33, 135–37, 139, 140, 142–49, 151n7, 151n10, 161–62
theft, 20, 92
time (perception of), 14, 40–41, 83, 85, 88–89, 105–9, 116–19, 121–25, 129, 163
tour, winery, 79
tourism, 73–74, 127
tourist, 21, 51n20, 121
trade, 38, 88, 91, 107, 163
  petty, 12, 79, 90
  wine, 2, 5–6, 40–41, 54n5, 154–55
trader, 7, 138
tradition, 6, 11, 14–15, 68, 71, 75, 77, 79, 125, 137, 142, 160
Transnistria, 19, 34, 41, 83, 97, 99, 104n14
trellising, 62
Tsar, 31, 137
Tsarist, Empire, 31–32, 54, 157

ucaz, 37. *See* dry law
uniqueness, 45, 77, 80–81, 132, 138–39, 142–43, 150, 154–55
union, trade, 29, 127–28

value, 2–3, 5, 8–11, 15–16, 58–59, 61, 73–75, 101, 123, 128, 132, 137, 143–44, 146–48, 153, 159–60
  creation of, 2, 108, 132, 145
  exchange-, 142
  hierarchy of, 5, 11, 131
  local, 45
  production, 84, 151n7
  social, 62, 73
  surplus, 17–18, 107, 131
  use-, 72, 135
video, 144–5
village
  neighboring, 37, 45, 52, 65, 73, 97–98, 100, 115, 118
  Purcari (*see* Purcari)
  winemaking, 16, 20–21, 25, 45
Viișoara, 45, 52, 97, 114
*vin de cas*ă, 59. *See* homemade wine
viticulture, 22, 34, 36, 43, 51, 62, 67, 69, 70,
81n3, 109, 126, 138
  Bessarabian, 33
  School of, 8
Vitis vinifera, 55n8

wage, 6, 28n5, 60–61, 64, 77, 84–85, 88, 91–96, 98–99, 114, 117–18
  living, 89, 158
war
  cold, 156
  First World, 48
  Russo-Turkish, 30
  Second World, 30, 34, 47–49
  Transnistria, 97
West, 3, 47, 108, 158
whiteness, 15
wine, 14–15, 77–79, 162–63
  adulterated, 41–42, 56n24
  biodynamic, 28n3
  Bessarabian, 47
  bottled, 1, 2, 28n6, 70–71, 76, 80
  bulk, 28n6, 34
  cheap, 70
  commercial, 4, 12, 59–60, 67, 160–61
  dry, 64
  fortified, 36, 49
  factory, 58, 62, 79
  homemade, 12–14, 58–64, 66–67, 70–73, 79–80, 81n10, 106, 115, 141, 143, 159–61
  house, 12, 59
  ice, 108
  industrial, 13–14, 59, 70, 79–80, 81n10, 160
  Moldovan, 1, 2, 3, 8, 12, 20, 23, 29–30, 35, 40, 73, 128, 131, 134, 153, 156
  natural, 12–13, 27n2, 6, 81n1, 143, 160
  organic, 28n3, 61
  peasant, 33, 70, 74
  postsocialist, 6, 8
  Purcari, 2, 21, 50, 64, 69, 120, 131–32, 135–36, 144, 147–48, 152n11, 159
  red, 36, 67, 79, 140
  sparkling, 76, 78, 108
  terroir, 114, 131–33, 135, 137–38, 144–45, 147
  white, 62

winemaker, 9–11, 32–34, 36–37, 40, 42, 45, 66, 68, 70, 78, 111, 114, 144–46, 154–57
　commercial, 12, 74
　flying, 69, 147–50, 152n12
　peasant, 13, 47, 60–63, 68–69, 73–75, 77–78, 81n2, 81n4
　professional, 68, 81n2, 160
winemaking, 2–3, 14–16, 21, 42–43, 54n5, 55n9, 67–69, 105, 109, 125–26, 134, 137–38, 143, 145, 161–63
　Bessarabian, 32, 47
　domestic, 75
　ecological, 13
　household, 59–63, 69, 70
　industrial, 8, 23, 113, 144
　Moldovan, 2, 5, 9–10, 23–24, 31, 33–36, 70, 153, 157
women, 25, 62, 84–85, 109, 113, 122–23, 129, 159
work, 14–17, 22, 48–49, 94–95, 106–9, 115–16, 126–28
　domestic, 18, 86, 106, 159
　household, 22, 84, 117, 145
　factory, 22, 118–19, 122
　marketing, 131–32, 146, 153–54
　night, 119–22
　political, 135
　reproductive, 88, 101
　scientific, 131–32, 162
　wage, 16, 28n5, 84–84, 92–93, 114
workers, 17–18, 51–52, 85–86, 92–95, 106–7, 110–15, 123, 127–28, 144–45, 158–59
　reproduction of, 84–85
World, New, 6, 132–34
　Old, 6, 44, 132–34
Württemberg, Kingdom of, 32

yeasts, 11, 13, 132, 134, 151n6
　active dried, 141, 143
　indigenous, 141–43
　liquid, 141

www.ingramcontent.com/pod-product-compliance
Lightning Source LLC
Chambersburg PA
CBHW051546020426
42333CB00016B/2126